S. M. Dolores

W9-CLG-154

# THE LIFE AND TIMES OF
# CATHERINE DE' MEDICI

*Photograph: "The Yorkshire Post"*

## CATHERINE DE' MEDICI AND HER CHILDREN
### BY FRANÇOIS CLOUET

(In the possession of the Hon. Geoffrey Howard at Castle Howard)
In 1561, the probable date of this picture, six of the children of Catherine
and Henry were alive. The four shown here are, from left to right, Hercule
(Duke of Alençon and later of Anjou), Charles IX, Marguerite ("Margot,"
later Queen of Navarre), and Henry (later Henry III)

Mount Mary College
LIBRARY
3168

# THE LIFE AND TIMES
## OF
# CATHERINE de' MEDICI

### BY FRANCIS WATSON

## WITH SIXTEEN ILLUSTRATIONS

D. APPLETON-CENTURY COMPANY
INCORPORATED
NEW YORK        1935        LONDON

COPYRIGHT, 1935, BY

D. APPLETON-CENTURY COMPANY, INC.

All rights reserved. This book, or parts
thereof, must not be reproduced in any
form without permission of the publisher.

PRINTED IN THE UNITED STATES OF AMERICA

921
C 288 Wa

*To*

MY MOTHER

## PREFATORY NOTE

THE modern fashion of removing the scaffolding after a book has been finished has obvious advantages, but it is not a very polite practice. There is no need to mention here the original sources for a biography of Catherine de' Medici, since they are sufficiently familiar to students of the period and of no interest to others. It would be discourteous, however, to make no reference to the work of later historians and commentators of which I have made use. All who know the three fascinating volumes by Edith Sichel which cover the ground I have chosen will recognize my great debt to that unrivalled interpreter of the more intimate side of sixteenth-century French history. H. Noel Williams on Henry II, A. W. Whitehead on Gaspard de Coligny, Martin Hume on Mary Stuart, Edward Armstrong on Charles V, Maurice Wilkinson on the League and G. F. Young on the House of Medici, have all been at my elbow for the elucidation of difficulties and the reconciliation of conflicting contemporary accounts; while Plattard, Bouchot, Bourilly, Clouzot, and other modern French investigators of their country's Renaissance in many aspects have for long provided companionable reading. Nor have I scrupled to refer to Jehanne d'Orlac's "Diane de Poitiers," a work of obvious bias which is nevertheless exceedingly well documented.

His Majesty the King has graciously permitted the reproduction of a painting in the royal collection at Hampton Court Palace, and to Sir Herbert Cook and the late Hon. Geoffrey Howard I am grateful for similar favours in respect of three other pictures. By the kindness of Dr. John Rothenstein, Director of Art Galleries at Sheffield, I am able to reproduce, for the first time, the portrait of Diane de Poitiers which hangs in the Graves Gallery. Ready and valuable assistance has been given by Mr. Richard Bedford, Mr. Bernard Rackham and others at the Victoria and Albert Museum, by the Curator of the Hampton Court Collection and by the photographic staff of *The Yorkshire Post*. To the co-operation of the Editor of *The Studio* is due the inclusion of Pourbos' interesting painting of a Harlequinade at the Court of Charles IX. This picture appears as an illustration in the *Studio* Spring Number, "Elizabethan Pageantry," which has been of help to me in several ways and may be warmly recommended to any who find the age of Elizabeth and Catherine sufficiently exciting to excuse the pages which here follow.

F. W.

# CONTENTS

| CHAPTER | | PAGE |
|---|---|---|
| I. | DUCHESSINA | 1 |
| | Amboise | 3 |
| | Italy | 14 |
| | Marseilles | 43 |
| II. | DAUPHINESS | 55 |
| | Fontainebleau | 57 |
| | Paris | 79 |
| | Rambouillet | 84 |
| III. | QUEEN-CONSORT | 95 |
| | Saint-Germain-en-Laye | 97 |
| | Lyons | 114 |
| | Paris | 129 |
| | Anet | 139 |
| | Vaucelles | 149 |
| | Paris | 155 |
| IV. | QUEEN-REGENT | 175 |
| | Amboise | 177 |
| | Chenonceaux | 191 |
| | Poissy | 201 |
| | Dreux | 214 |
| | Orleans | 224 |
| V. | QUEEN-MOTHER | 229 |
| | Rouen | 231 |
| | Saintes | 235 |
| | Bayonne | 241 |
| | Montaigne | 247 |

ix

CHAPTER                                                   PAGE

Blois . . . . . . . . . . . . 258

Paris . . . . . . . . . . . . 271

Lusignan . . . . . . . . . . . 290

Chenonceaux . . . . . . . . . . 299

Paris . . . . . . . . . . . . 307

Blois . . . . . . . . . . . . 312

INDEX . . . . . . . . . . . 317

# ILLUSTRATIONS

CATHERINE DE' MEDICI AND HER CHILDREN . . . *frontispiece*

FACING PAGE

FRANCIS I AND HIS SISTER MARGARET OF NAVARRE . . . 6

THE BATTLE OF PAVIA . . . . . . . . . . . 22

CATHERINE DE' MEDICI IN HER YOUTH . . . . . . 46

VENUS, CUPID, FOLLY AND TIME . . . . . . . 68

HENRY II . . . . . . . . . . . . . . . 100

DIANE DE POITIERS IN HER BATH . . . . . . . 122

DIANE DE POITIERS . . . . . . . . . . . 142

MARY STUART AS QUEEN OF FRANCE . . . . . . 156

CHARLES DE GUISE, CARDINAL OF LORRAINE . . . . 184

ANTOINE DE BOURBON, KING OF NAVARRE . . . . . 204

COLIGNY . . . . . . . . . . . . . . 226

HARLEQUINADE AT THE COURT OF CHARLES IX (1572) . . 262

CHARLES IX . . . . . . . . . . . . . 282

CATHERINE DE' MEDICI . . . . . . . . . . 296

HENRY III . . . . . . . . . . . . . . 308

# I
## DUCHESSINA

# AMBOISE

LEONARDO DA VINCI had one more year to live. Beyond the age of seventy even a body trained perfectly to serve the greatest mind of the Renaissance must be nearing the term of its office, and he knew that the end could not long be delayed. His mind sought still by habit to resolve problems whose very postulation was beyond the reach of lesser men, and with his left hand he could still draw, translating in the margins of his note-books, into flowers and knots of hair and cascades of water and astronomical diagrams, the lovely and ultimate rhythms by which man lives and dies, and perhaps survives. But the right hand which had laid so much beauty before the world was paralyzed, and the picture which stood unfinished in his room near Amboise, beside the *Virgin and Child with Saint Anne* and the portrait of a Florentine lady, would remain forever unfinished. Unfinished, yet all the more potent for that, Leonardo's hermaphrodite *Saint John the Baptist* confronts us today, disturbing the intellect, troubling the senses, lifting the soul to a region where Christ and Dionysos, Venus and the Virgin are symbols of the same surging emotion, promising the impossible and so nearly fulfilling it that the mind reels beneath the magic of the questing line.

Leonardo would die in exile, here in this French valley where he planned castles and gardens, engines and waterways for the splendid young monarch who chose from France and Italy the fairest women and the cleverest men to be the jewels of his crown. "I am able to make a prince," said King Francis, "but only God can make an artist"; and God just then had made plenty for his choice. Flushed with the spectacular victory of Marignano, eager to transfuse into the veins

3

of France the rich blood of the Italian Renaissance, the King had summoned the old painter across the Alps, had given him a pleasant manor-house near the castle of Amboise, and had bought *Mona Lisa* for his own collection. And now, when spring was spreading lilies and violets and wood-sorrel through the hunting-forests on the banks of the Loire, as if to compliment the new architects who scattered their stone flowers among the mediaeval fortresses, Leonardo knew that he would not again see spring in Italy. Yet this valley, that was one great pleasure-garden for the King and his resplendent Court, had something of a Tuscan suavity about it. Lilies were lilies, whether of France or Florence, and he was tolerably content to die here among so many things that his own mind had conceived and his own hands fashioned. *The Last Supper* might moulder slowly on the refectory wall in distant Milan, but across the Loire, a few miles above Amboise, the new white stairway of Blois twisted upwards like the cross-section of a *turritella* in his manuscript notes on conchology.

In this month of April, 1518, Leonardo watched before he died a festival that was partly of his own designing, one of the most sumptuous displays of the pageant-loving monarch who two years later was to astonish even Henry of England with the Field of the Cloth of Gold. The occasion was a double one, the baptismal fête of the Dauphin Francis—already a year old—and a near-royal union with the house of Medici; and the Court was at Amboise for the celebrations. In Italy the Renaissance diffused itself through the cities, where each overlord strove to outdo his neighbor by the number and genius of the artists and men-of-letters whom he gathered round him. The artists worked for their patrons, but they worked also for the glory of adorning their native city. In France it was otherwise. The new learning and the new artistic impulse were fostered by the Court, and the Court moved from castle to castle as it pleased the King, restlessly seeking fresh diversions and never content to remain long enough in a city to leave upon it the impress of the revival. The cultural centres were the mediæval ones—Paris Poitiers, Montpellier and so on. There were no Renaissance cities save perhaps Lyons, proudly planted on the cross-roads of Europe, the house of change for money and goods and new ideas.

Amboise at this time shared with Blois the greatest favor as a royal residence. Chambord, Fontainebleau, Anet, Azay-le-Rideau were not yet built. Loches, the grim stronghold of Louis XI, where Lodovico Sforza had died of joy when word was brought him that his twenty years' captivity was at an end; where the historian de Commynes had lain shackled and the Cardinal la Balue had languished, so legend runs, in the hideous cage which he had designed for others—Loches, even with the gracious memory of Agnes Sorel about it, was too gloomy to house Francis I and his gay companions. Amboise seemed built for gallant spectacle. The great round tower, the dancing outlines of the new Italianate wing, the slender spire of St. Hubert's chapel and the cool, lime-shaded gardens hung dizzily above the town, all would come upon the traveller from the south so suddenly as he reached the brow of the hill that they seemed to have risen magically in an instant out of the clear waters of the Loire which held their image. Inside the round tower a broad carriage-way climbed spirally to the summit, and four horsemen could ride abreast from the town to the castle within its massive walls.

The tower was hung with tapestries and precious stuffs that swayed and lifted in the spring breeze to show their various colours subtly shot. The courtyard became a huge tent within which elaborate banquets were held, and a peal of trumpets drowned the merry conversation to announce the serving of each new course. The flower of French chivalry was in attendance, arrogant, superbly dressed, willing actors in the gorgeous masque of the Renaissance. Their easy familiarity with the Most Christian King astonished foreign envoys. They acknowledged him by virtue of his wealth and military power, but yielded little or nothing to him in hereditary rank. With hawk on fist and hound at leash they followed him to the chase as they followed him to war. They followed the fashion of his beard, his perfumed gloves, his taste in epigrams and women. They entertained him and were entertained by him, and they remained his peers.

The pivot of this small and powerful and brilliant world was not so handsome as his royal contemporary of England, the young Henry VIII, for whose favour he was shortly to contend with the swarthy, scheming Charles V of Spain. All three monarchs were to be candidates for the vacancy of Holy Roman Emperor, and the history of Europe hung on the decision of the Electors. Francis poured wealth from his coffers, the envoys of Henry hurried back and forth on delicate errands. But Charles had the Fuggers of Augsburg behind him and his ascent of the Imperial throne in the following year was the first great victory of the credit system. If Henry had become Emperor, would Wolsey have reached the papacy, and England have remained Catholic? At every turn history prompts these tremendous, unanswerable questions. But to speculate thus vainly is at all events to realise what manner of gilded plaything these three young men tossed between them—Henry, Defender of the Faith, Charles, Most Catholic King, and Francis, Most Christian King.

Francis was twenty-four years old, and this was the fourth year of his reign. The painter Clouet gives him at this brightest period of his life the face of a pleasantly sensual, brown-bearded youth, eyes narrow and sparkling, with a trace of irony peeping at their corners; a long, irregular nose, a smile that shows a full lower lip. He may be little more than the equal of the high-born lords who stroll beside him through the trim gardens, but he has a royal manner; for he is fully conscious of his ability to win a dashing victory, to coin a graceful classical witticism, to ride like a centaur, to recog-

FRANCIS I AND HIS SISTER MARGARET OF NAVARRE
BY R. P. BONINGTON (1802-1828)
(Wallace Collection)

nise at a glance the beauty of a Leonardo drawing or a well-bred hound, and to attract women by something more than royalty.

In the King's company at Amboise moved the Duc de Bourbon, Constable of France, the blood of his Italian mother visible in his dark eyes and hair, his high French breeding apparent in the delicate pallor of his face. The Bourbon had wide and ancient properties which Francis would one day be tempted to seize, and that act was to make a rebel of the mighty Constable. But as yet there was no breach, nor cause of breach between them. Bourbon, de Montmorency, de Lautrec, Rohan, de Chabot, Bonnivet, la Trémouille, de Foix—the heads of the greatest families in France were all at Amboise with the King. And from one of them, the fair-haired Sieur de Fleuranges, we have a first-hand account of the junketing and jousting that accompanied the baptism and marriage for which they were met.

But before we watch the Court at revel we must take note of the women at Amboise, for this is the great age of women. Through them, in France at all events, flows the true current of the Renaissance. Soon, when it comes to a battle for the new opinions, the men will take up arms, but at present, as in Rabelais' Thélème, "all was done for the pleasure of the ladies." Without them there would be no stately châteaux, no encouragement of artists and learned men, no tolerance for the dangerous habits of free-thinking, nor even, perhaps, any Italian wars. Louise of Savoy, mother of the King, is one type of the Renaissance woman—the ambitious politician. Francis she has called her Cæsar, and she watches with un-wearying eyes the development of his power, ready at the moment of crisis to step in and guide matters with her own strong hand. The King's sister, Margaret of Angoulême, Pearl of the Valois, *Marguerite des Marguerites,* is another type, perhaps the most perfect that France produced. Her emancipation is intellectual. Scholar, poetess, Platonist, beloved protectress of artists and men of letters, she moves in disturbing beauty among the courtiers, never far from the royal brother whom she is to save repeatedly by her gentle influence from the excesses to which love of power and pleasure will urge him. The gallants who are captivated by her long-lashed violet eyes and her fair abundant hair find her strangely different from the easy partners of their other amours. She reads the ancient pagans with avidity, yet guards an unorthodox piety of her own. She can turn Boccaccian jests as none other, yet the most entrancing thing about her is her *"doux Nenny"*—the soft denial with which she meets advances. The fortunate may find the type of Margaret, though scarcely her equal, in the twentieth century, and indeed there are lesser Margarets in every generation. She is the woman with complete liberty of mind whom a certain fastidiousness preserves from physical excess.

Like the Queen, Margaret has her train of attendant ladies of noble birth, and one of them is called Anne Boleyn. Two years later she will follow her to the meeting with Henry VIII at the Field of the Cloth of Gold.

His mother, his sister, and his mistress of the moment—the passionate, olive-skinned Françoise de Foix—hold close beside the King. In the background, remote and pale and dignified, his wife keeps quiet converse with her ladies. The salamander, glorious in the flames which cannot consume it, is the symbol of Francis, and Italian sculptors carve it over against the porcupine of Louis XII on every balustrade. But for Queen Claude the ermine serves, or the swan, white devices of purity. The pale lilies of her cheeks were the legacy of a lame mother and an exhausted father, Anne of Brittany and Louis XII. Yet she had brought Francis his throne and she was the mother of his children. Already, before this baptismal fête of the year-old Dauphin Francis, she had been delivered of a second son, the future Henry II of France and husband of Catherine de' Medici.

The fates were spinning strange threads at Amboise in this sixteenth-century April. The sponsor who held the Dauphin at the font in the chapel of St. Hubert the Hunter was Lorenzo de' Medici, usurping Duke of Urbino, and three days later the festivities were renewed in more lavish form for the marriage of this young Italian to Madeleine de la Tour d'Auvergne, princess of the Bourbon blood. Lorenzo was a grandson of his namesake the Magnificent, and a nephew of the reigning Pope Leo X. King Francis, his eyes always on Italy, welcomed the Medici bridegroom with such pomp as had never before been seen in France, and Pope Leo, menaced by Charles of Spain, saw to it that rich gifts should cement the bond with France. There had been a time, not so long ago, when the marriage of a Medici to an exalted foreigner had been accompanied by no presents from the Florentine family. For the Medici, vast as was their wealth, were bourgeois in origin, and kings did not accept favours from tradespeople in public. But Lorenzo the Magnificent had changed all that. A family that could buy the papacy must be allowed to give wedding presents, and moreover diligent scholars had invented a Medici ancestry worthy of acceptance by the highest standards of chivalry. It had been a simple matter to derive the family name from a mythical hero who had won great victories over the Medes.

So thirty-six pack-animals had left Florence, laden with the testimonies of Pope Leo's goodwill for the coming bridal. Three hundred thousand ducats was the value of the burdens that the mules bore slowly up the Alpine passes and across France, and even in those days of princely bounty that was an almost fantastic sum.

The Sieur de Fleuranges watched the rich baggage train wind down the hill to Amboise and the Loire, and a sardonic smile played about his hard and handsome face. He knew that Lorenzo, an experienced profligate at the age of twenty-six, brought another and a less pleasant gift to his young bride. "When she married the Duke of Urbino," he wrote, "she did not marry him alone, for the pox also was her bridegroom. And on this very day the King made him a Knight of his Order."

As we read these words the grinning skull detaches itself from the gaudy Renaissance trappings. It is no Galahad whom the French King knights with all the ceremony of a vanished chivalry. The lilies of Florence gleam on his embroidered surcoat, but poison riots in his veins, the poison that darted its serpentine colours of death through the shining marble edifice of the New Age. The disease that was to carry off Francis I, Henry VIII and Charles V, had many lowlier victims marked for destruction. Spreading in Europe with mysterious suddenness towards the close of the fifteenth century, its responsibility was handed from nation to nation, —in England "the French disease," in France "la maladie Anglaise." For moralists (who were apparently never called upon to explain theologically why the Romans of the decadence were immune), it was a heaven-sent weapon so efficiently wielded that for centuries little progress could be made in combating its ravages. It was destined to perform many outlandish pranks, to amuse Restoration playgoers, to blind Milton and to deafen Beethoven.

But the revellers did not heed it. The fountains of Amboise ran wine and hippocras, and the pageant went from one splendour to another. Lorenzo de' Medici was married to Madeleine de la Tour d'Auvergne, and a beauty chorus of seventy-two damsels, garbed in the costumes of divers nations, danced before the bridal pair to the sound of flutes and tambours. Night fell, and was cheated of its dominion by the flare of a thousand torches. The company sat down to banquet, King and Queen, princes and ambassadors and ladies of honour according to their rank. The feasting and dancing lasted till two o'clock in the morning, "and then," says the frank Fleuranges, "they escorted to bed the young

bride, who was far more handsome than the bridegroom."
The sacrificial couch to which her husband followed her had
come from Florence among the sanctified gifts of His Holiness. It was of tortoise-shell, encrusted in the cunning Florentine manner with pearls and precious stones. "The most
dreadful wedding in Renaissance history," as one historian
has called it, was consummated in the luxurious fashion of
the period.

On the next day the gladiatorial games began, and nearly
six weeks went by in jousts and tourneys before it was decided that justice had been done to the occasion, or that the
excuse had been exhausted. Besides the traditional combats
on foot and horse there was a gigantic pitched battle for
which a wooden citadel had been erected, and siege engines
of the great Leonardo's devising were brought to the assault.
King Francis enjoyed himself hugely at his tournament, and
the keen-eyed Fleuranges, after bearing his part with distinction in this elaborate mimic warfare, sat down to record
naïvely that "the newly-married Duke of Urbino did as well
as he could in the presence of his lady," and that the affair
was "the finest engagement that ever was seen, and the closest
to actual war; but the pastime did not please everybody, for
there were many killed and wounded; when all was over,
they separated; which was by no means an easy thing to do,
and would have been still more difficult if horses and men
had not been out of breath; for as long as breath remained
to them they continued to fight."

Among the ladies of honour to Queen Claude at this time
was an eighteen-year-old girl whom we may not pass over
in silence. Diane de Poitiers, Grande Seneschale, married to
the ageing Louis de Brézé, was here at Amboise with the
Queen. She had been born to nobility and great wealth, and
her husband had served four kings faithfully and well. A
succession of calumniators, doubtful of the possibility of
fidelity between a girl of eighteen and a man of fifty-eight,

have conspired to suggest that King Francis received from Diane more intimate services than those her husband paid him. There is no evidence for this view, and much that is against it. Receiving by chance the name of the Dorian goddess, and by another resembling her in her narrow hips, her tall and boyish figure, her agility and even some inborn traits of her character, Diane must even at this time have been beginning to model herself after her chaste prototype Diana. One view of her wonderful career, indeed, points at the very least to a genius for publicity. The new delight in ancient learning and the courtly devotion to the royal sport of hunting combined to make Diana a name to conjure with, and Diane de Poitiers saw to it that the conjuring was kept up. The multitude of representations of Diana in the castles and parks of Renaissance France, the sculptures of Jean Goujon, the metal-work of Cellini and the paintings of the school of Fontainebleau, did honour to the cult and to its living embodiment, and only rarely can we be certain that we have before us the actual features of Diane herself. But there is one portrait of her in her first beauty, and perhaps it is from the hand of Leonardo. Her almond eyes have that enigmatic wistfulness which none could seize so well as he. Her hair is of a chestnut brown, her skin of that porcelain purity which never, even in old age, was to leave it. There is a little tilt to her nose, and her chin, like all the features of the body that is to be praised in such a torrent of verse, is well defined. There is a lithe vigour about her, but a delicate breeding as well. She is the divine huntress condescending to the courts of men.

As the moon-goddess stooped but once to earth to love the sleeping Endymion, so Diane, whom her detractors called a common trull, loved but one man in all her life, and him she subjected completely to her spell. He was not her husband, though she remained faithful to Louis de Brézé while he lived. He was a king of France, eighteen years younger than herself, and throughout the protracted pageant of Amboise he lay in his cradle. Could Diane, drawing back the silken coverings for Queen Claude to see her son, guess what she was to mean to this infant who was not even the Dauphin, and through him to France?

And that is but one of the threads which the fates were spinning at Amboise. The other must take us to Florence with the Duke of Urbino and his young wife.

# ITALY

IT was an uneasy city to which Lorenzo returned with Madeleine in the late summer of that year 1518. The splendid days of Florence were over. Of her artists, Botticelli, the Pollaiuoli, Ghirlandaio, Fra Bartolommeo, Verrocchio, Settignano, Donatello, Filippino Lippi, Luca della Robbia were all dead. Andrea del Sarto had followed Leonardo to France. Michelangelo was at present working in Rome. Lorenzo di Credi still painted in his *bottega* beside the Arno, and the younger Della Robbias carried on Luca's wondrous craft. But the artist who opened the most brilliantly creative epoch in European history had given place to the historians who were to close it—chief among them the grim Macchiavelli, whose supple prose armed Italy's invaders with the moral satisfaction of the supreme virtue of expediency.

The tale that the historians would have to record was a calamitous one. The Eastern Empire, shaken by the infidel, had spilled its blossom westwards upon soil that was urgent for the Renaissance. But now the axe was laid to the roots of Rome itself, and the wood-cutters were Christian monarchs. The rape of Milan was already a thing of the past, and that proud city was decking herself in fresh loveliness to delight her French ravisher and draw again the covetous eyes of violent princes. But the clouds were gathering on the horizon for the greatest tragedy of the Renaissance, the tragedy that Florence escaped only to meet her own bitter fate, the terrible sack of Rome.

"There is not now a nation left," wrote Castiglione, "that hath not made us their prey, so that there remaineth little behind to prey upon, and yet for all that cease they not to prey still." Assuredly the Niobe of nations had the fatal gift of beauty, and her conquerors, half-loving what they destroyed or carried off but never wholly understanding it, were glutting with fire and sword a monstrous and perverted passion. And Florence, within the sculptured garland of her gates and towers, knew the poison that shatters the fine-blown glass, the dreaming love that wakes on a sudden to reeking sadism. The flames of two sinister bonfires had licked upwards towards Brunelleschi's dome and Giotto's campanile. For the first the pyre was built of Botticelli's exquisite nudities, of Pico's love-poems, of illuminated books and chased perfume-boxes, of every precious vanity that Florentine artistry could conceive and Florentine craftsmanship execute. From the shadows of his cowl the fierce, hypnotic eyes of Savonarola roused the people to something of his own consuming fury, the Puritan fury that must exhaust its desires in the destruction of the terrestrial beauty that coils about the soul of man and will not let it go. The children who were the monk's favourite converts helped mightily with that bonfire, gleefully hurling to the flames the treasures at which we can only guess from the things that remain—and it is a guess that might drive a man mad. The fuel for the second bonfire was Savonarola himself. For the final vanity that the reformer attacked was the Pope, and Popes have swift weapons of redress.

The Medici Palace in the Via Larga was an enormous building, erected some ninety years earlier by the elder Cosimo as the luxurious headquarters of the rising household. But Piero de' Medici had died in it with the wistful whisper that his palace was all too big for his shrunken family; and here was Piero's sickly descendant returning to it with his pale northern bride. It could scarcely be hoped that the luckless Madeleine would escape the taint of her husband's malady, nor did she. But before she died she brought to birth a girl-child, lively and healthy, who was given the names of Catarina Maria Romola de' Medici.

The Medici stock had about it a capricious strength which must have been doubly baffling in the centuries which had made no guess at Mendelian principles. Its greatest products have by common consent remained mysteries. Lorenzo the Magnificent is a prodigy raising Florence in his short life to its cultural apotheosis, slandered only by those who cannot believe in the perfect union of strength and sensibility. Leo X is the epicurean Pope whose atheism can be glimpsed but never quite proven; Clement VII the brilliant schemer who bent his power to narrow or even ignoble ends, whose greatest failure is so much more spectacular then his successes; and Catherine is the proverbial monster of iniquity who yet was spoken of in terms of praise and affection by witnesses who must be trusted. Most extraordinary of all is the swift alternation between magnificence and power on the one hand, and degradation and disease on the other, that is the tale of a century of Medici blood. At the fith generation the stock of Cosimo became extinct, yet that stock produced Lorenzo the Magnificent, Leo, Clement, the great captain Giovanni delle Bande Nere, and Catherine. It produced the infamous Alessandro also, and Lorenzo of Urbino, struck down by his own excesses at the age of twenty-seven.

The usurping Duke of Urbino was somewhat coldly received on his return to his native city. The Florentines could could stand a dictator if he were a Lorenzo the Magnificent, but it is an ancient law that dictators leave no succession, and republicans had a worthy target in the decadent Duke, held in his place by the machinations of Medici churchmen. There were many things about young Lorenzo which gave cause for dissatisfaction, and in a city of shaven chins his new French beard was one of them. Cardinal Giulio de Medici himself (who was later to become Pope Clement) was outraged by the insolence of his depraved cousin when he arrived from Rome to greet him and his bride. Here, as the

Cardinal saw, was one who was bringing at the best dis-
credit, at the worst ruin upon the family.

But Lorenzo did not live long to stain the Medici name.
Death by death the palace in the Via Larga grew emptier.
Catherine was born on April 13, 1519. On the 28th of the
same month her poor young mother died, and on May 4 her
father followed her to the grave, to lie at length, the most
worthless of the Medici, beneath Michelangelo's masterpiece,
the noblest funeral monument in Europe. It seemed that
the entire population of Florence turned out to watch the
passing of the Duke's *cortège,* and the power of the Medici
was still sufficient to clothe all the citizens in deepest black—
all, that is, save one. It is related that in the sombre procession that escorted Lorenzo to his tomb beside his illustrious
ancestors one vivid note of scarlet astonished all eyes. The
young and handsome Francesco Villani, president for that
year of the guild of apothecaries, strode boldly at the head
of his company in cap, doublet and hose of brilliant red,
and with flowers in his hand. The chronicler tells us that his
temerity had a sorry ending, and that hint of Medici reprisal
is all that we know of the fate of the daring Francesco.

Cardinal Giulio was in Florence again for the funeral.
Hearing of Lorenzo's illness he had hurried north over
difficult roads, but he had not been at his cousin's deathbed. Never, he said, while Lorenzo breathed and owned
it, would he set foot inside the Medici Palace. He stayed
close by at the Convent of St. Mark, whence, some twenty
years earlier, Savonarola had been led to the stake. The
Cardinal was needed in Florence, for the Medici prestige
had suffered sad reverses, and the Republicans were active.
And now the elder branch had dwindled to one little orphan
girl. The hope of the Medici was centred on this tiny bundle
of unsuspicious humanity who had so surprisingly escaped
the physical weakness of her father and was destined to

demonstrate to all the world that she had escaped also his weakness of character. For the first fourteen years of her life Catherine was to be moved hither and thither on the chessboard of diplomacy in a game on which supreme issues were staked.

And while she lay quietly in her cradle the flower of the Renaissance withered on its stem. Far away in Amboise, with one weeping pupil stooping to catch his last whisper, Leonardo da Vinci leaned back in his chair and died.

Cardinal Giulio did his work well. "It was the universal opinion," says the historian Nardi, "that never since the city had been founded had it been governed with greater appearance of civil liberty and more skilful concealment of despotism." But trouble was never far below the surface, and when the important little baby was six months old it was deemed prudent to remove her to Rome. Her grandmother, Alfonsa Orsini, to whose care the orphan had at first been confided, did not long survive the Duke and his wife, and the dead Duke's aunt, Maddalena Cibo, died at the same time in the Villa of Careggi. Death was pruning the Medici tree with no light hand.

There remained only Clarice Strozzi, an aunt of the newborn child. She was married to the celebrated banker, and lived in Rome, where Leo found much use for the Strozzi credit. It is said, indeed, that the demands on the luxurious and uxorious papacy at this time were such that Leo was borrowing money at forty per cent.

Clarice Strozzi had high notions of the proper education of a Medici, and six months seemed a good age at which to begin it. When the infant was carried into the presence of the Pope, that learned voluptuary greeted her with a sonorous line from the Æneid, and as soon as she could walk and talk a sense of her high position and its responsibilities was sternly imposed on her. The square stone palace of the Strozzi stamped the rigid perfection of its proportions upon all who

Mount Mary College
LIBRARY
31687

lived within it. It cannot have been a very cheerful place for
the first six years of a girl's life.

But it is not possible to discover the details of those early
years of Catherine's short girlhood. In 1525 she was sent back
to Florence to live in the great Medici Palace, now emptier
than ever, under the charge of Cardinal Passerini.

In Europe meanwhile, events had moved swiftly, events
that were to shape the destinies of Catherine and of many
other high-born children whose portraits the artists have
left to us—pathetic little figures in jewelled bodices and great
hooped skirts; or else in slashed breeches and plumed hats,
standing with a tiny hand upon a tiny sword-hilt beside some
huge hunting-dog.

First let us look at Rome, "the world's capital," as all
true men of learning still regarded it. On the first day of
December, 1521, shortly after the infant Catherine had been
presented to him, Pope Leo died very suddenly at the age
of forty-five. Castiglione and others said that he had been
poisoned, and the pamphleteer Pasquino put it this way:
"Leo X came to power like a fox, reigned like a lion and died
like a dog." However he died, he left enormous debts with
his friends, and the papal treasury in pawn. Renaissance
pomp in Rome, elegant villas in the hills, beautiful gardens
kept cool by cunning waterways, lavish patronage of painters,
sculptors, musicians and scholars, political bribes and the
expensive maintenance of "mistresses with great smooth
marbly limbs," had played havoc with an income substantially diminished since the sale of indulgences had dropped
off in Germany and elsewhere. The Conclave of Cardinals
met at the end of the month to elect a successor to Leo, but
they found it a difficult matter, partly because each of them
had his own ambitions and partly because the one with most
influence was Giulio de Medici, and the pontificate of Leo,
marvellous Roman holiday as it had been, had left things
in such a state that there was natural diffidence about choos-

ing another Medici to succeed him. But nobody could have foreseen the decision which, almost as much to their own amazement as to that of the selected man, they reached after a fortnight's deliberation.

Adrian of Utrecht was to be the new Pope. He was a Fleming who had been Charles V's tutor at the University of Louvain and to whom his illustrious pupil, now Emperor, had presented a Spanish archbishopric. Nobody in Italy knew anything about him except that he was a foreigner and a man of exemplary character, both highly suspicious circumstances. To appoint another Medici might have appeared rash, but to appoint this Flemish saint was simply flying in the face of providence.

Poor Adrian himself, we are told, received the call with groans, and for many months he delayed his coming, so that it was thought that he intended to exercise his high office from Spain. While he hesitated a new wound appeared in the side of Italy, for Genoa, once one of the great free cities and now in French possession, fell in fire and carnage to the army of the Italian League. Its ruins, says a contemporary, "shook the fortune of every merchant in Europe."

Then came the saintly foreigner as Pope Adrian VI. He made heroic efforts, but the Vatican was no place for an idealist, or at all events for a Christian one. He spent long hours at his devotions, and endeavoured to live like a hermit in the very midst of the splendour created by his predecessors. Where Leo had thrown a hundred ducats to a singer who pleased him, a thousand to an artist who fashioned some intoxicating vision of pagan loveliness, Adrian lived with a couple of servants and an aged Flemish housekeeper on a ducat a day. He checked Medici influence in Florence by restoring the rightful Duke of Urbino. In home affairs he introduced the revolutionary principle of "presenting good men to benefices rather than men to good benefices." In foreign affairs he struggled to find a way of peace amongst the tortuous coils of diplomacy—as sinuous as the snakes of the *Laocoön* which he stigmatised as a heathen idol. The end- was inevitable. After little more than a year of office, de- feated and exhausted, he died. He had seen the failure of his hopes of reform, there had been a terrible plague in Rome, and a French army was again pouring into Italy over the Alpine passes.

And this time the Medici Cardinal reached the goal of his ambitions. At the end of 1523, after the Conclave had sat for fifty days, Giulio de Medici became Pope Clement VII.

Clement might have taken a lesson from the unhappy fate of Lodovico Sforza, once the leader in quattrocento Milan of the most brilliant court of Renaissance Europe. Lodovico and Clement, gifted members of different despotic houses, both lacked nerve—the despot's essential. Lodovico's hesitation and double-dealing led him at last to moulder in the dark prison of Loches. Clement's restless shifting from one alliance to another was crowned with the sack of Rome. Six-year-old Catherine, wandering through the vast rooms of her Florentine palace while the storm gathered over the Vatican, was one day to prove that the Medici talent for temporising, with the addition of courage, could become in- vincible. If she had shared the failing of her exalted relative, history would have been different. It might, of course, have made pleasanter reading, but one cannot be sure of that.

Charles V held Naples and was threatening Rome. Ac- cordingly, in the year following his election, Clement strove to adjust the balance by an alliance with Francis I. These two superb princes, lusting for the fair body of Italy, were to be cajoled in turn with tempting glimpses of her favours until at last her limbs were torn by pent-up passion. But French affairs had recently taken a turn which should have shown the volatile Clement that his policy was fatal.

Francis was indeed in Lombardy again at the head of his army, while at home his Queen lay dying as she had lived, neglected and unregarded. But Francis was in difficulties. The Field of the Cloth of Gold, a masque within a masque, had made its glittering mark upon the annals of Renaissance pageantry. Diplomatically it had accomplished nothing. The trees of silver with silken leaves, the glass pavilion for Henry VIII, the golden tissue spread beneath illustrious feet, had made a carnival setting for feminine beauty and masculine chivalry. But Henry, excellent athlete in many respects, was somewhat heavy upon a horse and had sustained in the cere-monial exercises an inglorious fall. He went home in a tem-per—smoothed over with elaborate surface courtesies, but a temper none the less. And Katherine of Aragon, Henry's Queen (he had just met Anne Boleyn for the first time) was an aunt of Charles V and an unofficial representative of Im-perial interests at the English Court. The way of Francis was not an easy one.

It was made very much more difficult by a bad mistake, for which his mother Louise of Savoy was mainly responsible. Money had been spent like water and now there was a drought. A silver trellis taken from Tours Cathedral, a few golden apostles here and a few silver saints there, several new taxes and further mortgages by princely landowners, were not sufficient to set the river in spate again for the new Italian war. Louise of Savoy had her eagle's eye upon the vast properties of the Bourbon Constable, who had been im-prudent enough to make some show of his power. A lawsuit was the first step, direct action the second. The Bourbon lands were seized for the Crown, and the dark-eyed Con-stable, crying "Victory or death!" went over to the service of the Emperor, who had been quietly waiting for this to happen.

Francis met the Imperial force under Bourbon at Pavia, in northern Italy, on February 24, 1525. The French army was utterly and disastrously routed, Bonnivet, de Foix, la Trémouille, and many another great lord killed. The King

*Reproduced by gracious permission of H. M. the King*

## THE BATTLE OF PAVIA
### GERMAN SCHOOL, C. 1530
(Hampton Court Palace)

himself was captured, and Bourbon, concealing his triumph beneath a mask of chivalry, received in his tent the sword of the sovereign who had so rashly wronged him. The disaster made Charles V for the time being master of Europe. It rang through France to the tune of chivalric laments and scurrilous ditties that are remembered to this day. "All is lost but honour," wrote Francis, but he was to show that honour is a slippery commodity.

The Most Christian King, the personal embodiment of the efforts of France to take her place as a great Renaissance power, was carried to captivity in Madrid, a step at which the victorious Bourbon had probably not connived. In the Spanish, capital the King's handsome looks and proud bearing created such an effect that the people cheered him in the streets and noble ladies sickened for love of him. But he was a prisoner, and the Emperor was free to make his own conditions. They were crippling ones: the restoration of the hardly-won Duchy of Burgundy to its former Hapsburg possessors, the establishment of a feudal state in central France for the Constable, the relinquishment of all Italian claims. It looked indeed like the utter extinction of France.

But in France there was a strong hand at the helm. Her son a captive, the masterful Louise was Regent. Aided by the sly Chancellor Du Prat, who had already shown himself expert in extorting fresh taxes from an impoverished people, she played a truly astonishing card. From the people of Burgundy themselves, as represented in the Estates, she obtained a vigorous protest against surrender to the Hapsburgs and thus to Charles himself. This early political resort to the weapon of self-determination was followed by the employment of another modern device, that of propaganda. The Pope, the King of England, the Venetians, the remaining Italian Princes and some of the seceding Princes of Germany were won over to the view that the Emperor had become unhealthily powerful in Europe. The personal magnetism of the name of Francis was exploited to the full. Among the learned men who appealed to the Emperor on behalf of the patron of letters and leaders of chivalry was the great Erasmus himself. Meanwhile Margaret of Angoulême galloped to Spain with the speed of an express courier to aid the release of her beloved brother. In the dust and heat she rode to Madrid, to Toledo, to Alcala, to Madrid again. Wherever she went, a little Court gathered about her. She brought Spaniards to her feet as she had brought Frenchmen to them. She had long interviews with the Emperor, pitted her wits against his, while the metallic gaze of Charles searched her half-closed eyes for their secrets and his jutting lower lip kept its sinister determination. When Margaret came to Madrid the Sacrament was being administered to Francis, for despair had brought him to the verge of death. When her horse thundered north again, halving the accepted time for the journey to defeat the crafty Emperor's device of putting a time-limit to her safe conduct so as to gain another hostage, her brother's case was won. He was conducted over the border on the conclusion of certain pledges for which his two elder sons were to be sent back as sureties. Pausing for a while to celebrate his escape with feasting and love-making, he then set about the re-establishment of the balance of power.

From the Vatican Clement watched these stirring events uneasily. His Medici guile sought first one ruse and then another. The calamity of Pavia frightened him out of his league with Francis into a new pact with the ascendant Emperor, so close upon his gates and now so immeasurably powerful, the master as it seemed of the Two Worlds. But a few months later he was conspiring once more against his Imperial ally, this time by secret and dangerous ways. Charles's general in Lombardy was the Marquis of Pescara, now encamped before Milan, and the same who had pillaged Genoa for the League of Princes. Pescara is to-day remembered less as a military leader than as the husband of the learned and lovely Vittoria Colonna, whose sweet Roman name fell in limpid cadence from the lips of scholars and lovers, equal flamens at her shrine. But now he had his part to play in European history. Clement tried the ancient game of bribery. In return for aid against the Emperor, Pescara was to have the crown of Naples—if he could get it. The Marquis listened courteously to the Pope's advances and then laid the whole of the evidence before the Emperor.

The discovery of the plot set the pendulum of Clement's policy swinging once more with the violence of alarm, and he hastened to regain the favour of Francis. The French King, restored to his kingdom, required a service of the Pope, and the Pope immediately conceded it. By virtue of his tenure of the Keys of St. Peter he absolved Francis from the undertakings he had made to the Emperor in Spain. Clement was now floundering hopelessly. A desperate appeal for the concord of Christendom in face of the menace of the Turks, who had just won a victory in which the chivalry of Hungary had perished almost to a man, failed of its purpose; for Francis was already turning over in his mind the revolutionary step of allying himself with the infidel to check the power of the Emperor. The fiery sunset of Rome was reddening in the sky.

That great gentleman Baldassare Castiglione was at this time Papal Nuncio at the Spanish Court, but he seems to have been deliberately kept in ignorance of the march of affairs in Italy. For the sack of Rome the Emperor cannot be held entirely responsible. Charles was in truth the Most Catholic King, though none the better for that, and the outrages wrought upon the Holy City must have grieved and shocked him. But the Bourbon was a difficult ally, and Clement's vacillation and bad faith made Rome's fate inevitable. At the head of thirty thousand mercenaries the Constable was moving south through Italy, his banner with the flaming sword and the legend *Espérance* mocking the wreckage of his life. He had defeated and captured the powerful king who had dared to lay hands on the Bourbon estates. But the high politics of Europe had turned the tables against him once more. He was alone, absolutely alone in the midst of his foreign army, his dark eyes burning tragically in his white face. Of every house in which he had lived in France the door was now painted yellow, the colour of the traitor, and the Spanish hidalgos whose battles he had won for them turned from him in scorn. After the brilliant victory of Pavia the Emperor had requested one of his noblest knights to entertain the victor in his castle. "I will obey you, Sire," was the proud answer, "and afterwards I will burn my castle to the ground." And as if this were not enough, there was another wound to sear the Constable's desperate soul. More passionately, more hopelessly even than his rivals who lay dead at Pavia, he had loved the inviolable Margaret of Angoulême, adoring sister of the King against whom he had turned.

His men were Germans, Spaniards, Italians, Flemings, a few Frenchmen. Nominally serving the Emperor they paid allegiance to nobody. Even had his own fierce destiny not driven him relentlessly towards this crowning calamity he would have been helpless among these men. They lived for pillage, each nation according to its instincts, the Lutheran *Landsknechte* to overthrow the idols of Catholicism, the Spaniards to glut their passion for cruelty, the French renegades to be in at the last glorious riot of the freebooting age that was passing. The Constable knew himself their servant, not their master. Frequently unpaid or underpaid, they pressed ever southwards, their eyes filled, as those of their barbarian forefathers had been, with visions of the splendours of the world's capital, theirs for the taking. The Pope sent envoys, money, proposals for fresh pacts. But nothing could save Rome.

Florence was in a panic, and took desperate measures for

defence. But the invaders turned aside, making for the passes
of the Apennines. No lesser prize than the western Babylon
would suffice them. On May 4th, within six miles of Rome,
the Constable sent a last message to the Pope inviting terms
of peace. But he knew that he could not hold back his men.
No reply was received.

Two days later, at dawn, the assault began. The besiegers,
after the outworn manner which they represented, took ladders from a vineyard and brought them to the low walls
on the Vatican hill. There were forty thousand men in Rome
who might have repulsed the attack, but no attempt was made
to organise them. The Pope and some of his cardinals took
refuge in the Castle of St. Angelo on the Tiber.

The Constable, with nothing more to live for, determined
to die in the glory of battle, before the inevitable massacre
should begin. In shining silver armour and with an orange
plume in his helmet, he was an easy and willing target. It
was a misty morning but he was seen plainly by the defenders
as he advanced at the head of his soldiers with a scaling-
ladder. An arquebus-shot took him in the heart, and he fell
mortally wounded. That wonderful goldsmith and braggart,
Benvenuto Cellini, tells us that it was he who fired the fatal
shot. And perhaps it was.

When Bayard, the knight without fear and without reproach, leaned against a tree to die, his lips on the cross of
his sword-hilt, there were some who said that the chivalry of
the former age died with him. That was just before Pavia.
But the shot that slew the Constable de Bourbon three years
later slew a strange remnant of mediævalism. Of all the lords
and captains, emerging with a sort of amazement from feudalism, who thronged the terraces of Amboise in that April of
a new age when Catherine de' Medici's parents were married,
none was so handsome, none so noble nor so magnanimous
as the Constable. But the delicately perfumed Renaissance
glove could not hide from him the grasping Macchiavellian

fingers beneath it. He had the feudal conception of property and he was prepared to lose everything in defence of his rights—not only life, which was an easy sacrifice, but honour, love and the esteem of his peers, which were hard ones. He fought like a paladin of that chivalry which was now little more than the breath of sumptuous pageants and the stuff of popular romances. He died like a robber-baron, without country, friend, or hope, leading his mercenaries to plunder.

A breach was made, and like wolves the army poured into Rome over the dying body of their captain. For eight days slaughter, rape, looting and every bestial outrage continued uncontrolled. The Pope remained a prisoner in his fortress while within his sight the soldiers defiled the sanctuaries and did violence to the inhabitants whom he had done so little to protect. For nine months Rome remained in the hands of her invaders and Clement powerless. And meanwhile, in the wake of rapine, the plague returned.

The plague was creeping, too, into Florence. Catherine de' Medici was eight years old, learning Latin and Greek, music and dancing and every accomplishment of a great Renaissance lady within the high walls of the Medici Palace. Two relatives, her companions in Rome, had returned with her to Florence under the charge of Cardinal Passerini. Ippolito, the illegitimate son of her father's cousin, was now eighteen, and Catherine was very fond of him. Handsome, romantic, with a healthy distrust of clerical intrigue and a fondness for the company of soldiers and scholars, Ippolito seemed to her the pattern of what a Medici should be, and she learned much from him. Even at this early age she grew to share his suspicions of the twisting schemes of Clement, and Clement knew well enough that Ippolito was likely to prove awkward. It was a recognition that spelt doom to the unfortunate young man, who had too much of Lorenzo the Magnificent in him to be tolerated in these days of Medici decadence.

Catherine's other youthful companion was Alessandro, and him she detested. Alessandro, nicknamed "the Moor" from the cast of features derived from his unknown mother, was fourteen years old. He was certainly a bastard, but it has never been satisfactorily settled whether he was the son of Catherine's father by a Barbary concubine or the son of Pope Clement by a maidservant. The abominable preference which Clement showed for him over Ippolito induces one to think that some paternal instinct must have animated the Pope, who was himself illegitimate. Nothing could make Catherine tolerate the repulsive little mulatto, and Alessandro's subsequent career abundantly justified her hatred.

In the company of this strange pair of playmates, Hyperion and the satyr, and forced to breathe from her earliest years the very atmosphere of intrigue and chicanery, Catherine had ample opportunity of learning two things which would be necessary to her survival in the maelstrom of sixteenth-century politics into which she was shortly to be plunged—the talent for dissimulation and the attitude of cynicism. But her loathing of Alessandro she never attempted to dissemble, and their quarrels became so violent that at last they had to be separated. Alessandro was sent to the beautiful villa of Poggio a Caiano, half a day's ride from Florence and to-day one of the royal residences. Catherine, moved from one refuge to another in the city at the bidding of political expedience, returned at length with Ippolito to the Via Larga.

And here, on May 19, 1527, Clarice Strozzi arrived in high indignation. News of the sack of Rome had reached Florence, and while the tale of the horrors perpetrated by the Imperial army appalled every hearer, Clement's imprisonment in St. Angelo roused the spirits of the Republicans. The time had come for the Medici to be expelled from Florence for the third time in the history of the house. And it was Clarice Strozzi, herself a member of the family, who had determined upon it. The ruthless plotting of the Pope had outraged her Medici pride. The family was born to rule, but not to be tyrants, and those who lived in the Palace in the Via Larga seemed to her unworthy to bear the name handed down by the magnificent Lorenzo. Lorenzo had reigned with the consent of the Republic, and Clarice too was a Republican. The Signoria—the city fathers—were conferring in their palace, uncertain as yet of the advisability of action.

Cardinal Passerini and the three young people—for Alessandro had come to join them—were assembled that day in the Medici Palace. The Via Larga was filled with a closely packed throng of citizens, ready if need be to take matters into their own hands. The angry voice of Clarice Strozzi floated out to them from the high windows on the still air of early summer.

She lost no time in assailing the Cardinal in round terms. "It is you," she cried, "who are responsible, you and your master Clement! The Medici have fallen on misfortunes before to-day, but never yet has the name been brought so low as this. The Florentines are at your very door, waiting not to bless you as they blessed Lorenzo, but to demand the liberties which you use as playthings. How different were matters when my ancestors ruled, my ancestors who were true Medici, gaining the loyalty of their fellow-citizens by wisdom and benevolence, and finding them steadfast in adversity. When Pope Sixtus called for the surrender of Lorenzo, the Florentines would not yield him up. But they would yield you, and rightly, to the first enemy that came for you. As for you, Ippolito and Alessandro, who by your actions have betrayed your birth, and convinced the world that you have no Medici blood in you—and not only you, but Clement also, unjustly and unworthily made Pope, and now most deservedly a prisoner in St. Angelo—can any of you be surprised that all men hate you? Therefore go now, leave this house to which you have forfeited your claim, and this city which bears you no love. For at this evil pass the honour of the family rests with me alone. The palace of the Medici was built to be the home of glory and fair dealing, not to be a stable for mules. It must be cleansed, and you may believe that I will do the cleansing more mercifully than others that have a mind to it!"

The trembling Cardinal had no reply to this onslaught. He dared not meet Clarice's eyes, and he dared not look down from the window at the restless Florentines. Ippolito, too proud to refute accusations which he at all events had not deserved, stifled his indignation at being coupled thus with Alessandro and held his tongue. Alessandro's petulant chatter died away to a grumble. Eight-year-old Catherine stared wide-eyed at her towering aunt, once regarded as a prim pedagogue but now suddenly beautiful in her passion. Clarice turned on her heel and left them.

So the haphazard remnants of the Medici were driven from Florence, and Clement, thus openly flouted by his own relative, became the grim and implacable enemy of the city. He intended the Medici to rule in Florence, and he now intended it to be done in the person of the despicable Alessandro. To this one fierce ambition he bent all the resources of his guile. The whole of European diplomacy, centring still on Rome, was to be cunningly spun into a thread which should strangle the Florentine Republic.

But Catherine did not leave Florence. The "Duchessina" —the little Duchess—as everyone called her (though only Clement still regarded her dead father as the Duke of Urbino), was kept in the city as a hostage. With the exception of Clarice, married into another family, she was the last legitimate scion of the Medici house. She would be a useful commodity in political bargaining.

For six months she lived in the Convent of All Saints,

and thence, in December, she was carried by night through the plague-stricken city to the Nunnery of Le Murate. Built against the wall on the other side of Florence, the Murate had a beautiful walled garden from which one looked across the winding Arno to the mountains. Years later Catherine remembered this view so vividly as to describe it in verse. The nunnery had received its name—which means "the walled-up ones"—from an ancient ceremony of breaking down a piece of the wall for each novitiate, and rebuilding it again after she had passed in. The building survives as a prison, aptly retaining its name.

The nuns of the Murate were expert in education, and Catherine was a clever pupil. They grew to love their Duchessina, sheltered by their walls from the storms outside. And Catherine, though she must have known of the dangers that threatened her, was happy and diligent and amiable. Indeed, she became so popular that the Republican Government, fearing the possibility of political intrigue among the nuns, decided that she must be removed elsewhere.

That was during the ten months' siege of Florence by Pope and Emperor. The story of the events leading up to this siege is one of almost unbelievably sinister diplomacy. Pope Clement had escaped from St. Angelo—after having his tiara melted down for him by Benvenuto Cellini—to Orvieto, where he sat like a fat spider in its web. Florence was to be crushed under the Medici heel and the way to that end was intricate and treacherous. In December, 1527, while the Republic was deliberating where best to bestow its eight-year-old hostage, Francis I reopened the war with the Emperor Charles. Henry VIII was now angling for a papal divorce from Katherine of Aragon so that he could marry Anne Boleyn, and by promising to use his influence with the Pope, Francis won the English king's support. Florence was closely affected by this new development. She lay temptingly between Francis and the Emperor, and she had to choose for

her life. As the crafty Clement hoped, she chose the side of
the French king. It was a tragic and fatal choice.

In October of the following year the plague had driven
from Rome the last remnants of the soldiery that had despoiled the city, and Clement was able to return to his pillaged Vatican. Here his designs were carried a step further.

In August, 1529, was signed the Peace of Cambrai, the
famous "Ladies' Peace" of which Louise of Savoy and Margaret of Angoulême, who could give points in diplomacy to
many of their male contemporaries, were the chief negotia-
tors. Francis was to pay the Emperor an agreed ransom for
his sons, to abandon his allies England, Venice, Ferrara and
Florence, and once more to renounce his ambitions in Italy.
Henry VIII was skilfully pacified by the watchful Clement,
who gave him just sufficient encouragement, and no more,
in his hopes of a divorce. It was not a bad arrangement for
France, for a rest from the Italian wars was needed. It was
not a bad arrangement for England, except that Clement's
promises meant very little. It was an excellent arrangement
for the Emperor.

And for Clement it was superb. Charles was now once
more master in Italy, and able to attack the northern cities
without fear of interference from France. Venice and Ferrara were swiftly brought to terms flattering to themselves.
Florence, to whom no terms were offered, was now isolated.

The Pope loved nothing so much as a secret compact, and
the agreement which he now made with his old enemy, the
Emperor, was concluded in strict privacy at Barcelona. The
terms are staggering even to those who feel that they have
got the measure of the Medici Pope. One clause provided
for the marriage of the decadent Alessandro to the Emperor's
natural daughter; by another the Emperor consented to recognise Alessandro as absolute ruler, under himself, of
Florence; by a third the Pope agreed to crown Charles with
the Imperial diadem in Rome.

And the manner in which Florence was to be subjected to the illegitimate mulatto formed the ugliest clause of all. The Pope was to borrow the Imperial army—the very mercenaries who had put Rome to fire and sword and polluted her holy places—in order to bring the same fate upon Florence, his native city.

When at last the Florentines saw the terrible jaws of the trap which had been set for them they recovered in adversity something of the noble spirit of the former age. They set themselves with the utmost determination to defend their city. Michelangelo, the great artist whose tragedy was to see Florence lose her glory and her liberty, was among them, and he left his studio to devise new methods of repulse. It was to be a fight to the death, and no half-measures could be countenanced. All the fair suburbs outside the city walls, with their villas and terraced gardens, were destroyed so that the attacking forces might find neither cover nor supplies— all, that is, save one convent which was allowed to remain standing for a good Florentine reason. It contained Andrea del Sarto's fresco of *The Last Supper*.

For ten months the city held out, and but for an ignoble piece of treachery, the Imperial army would have been beaten off. But it was less difficult now than once it had been to find a Florentine who would sell his city. The man was found and Florence fell.

Before they surrendered, the defenders obtained from Clement a promise that the Signoria should continue to rule their city. As soon as the capitulation was effected the Pope had a thousand citizens executed, among them the gallant commander of the garrison. A monk who had preached encouragement to his fellow-Florentines was sent to Rome and starved to death in the Castle of St. Angelo by the Pope's orders. A few months later Alessandro was installed in the Medici Palace, and not long after that the Signoria were

summarily abolished. Such was the value of a Pope's promises
to the city of his birth.

We need not follow in detail the unpleasant tale of Alessandro's few years' rule in Florence. A man of twenty, of low
breeding and vicious life, was placed in supreme control of
a city where every passion could be satisfied. Contemporaries
describe him succinctly as a beast, and the most that well-
disposed biographers of his family have been able to do is
to claim that there was actually no Medici blood in him. At
the age of twenty-six he met the assassin's knife which, had
Florence been less securely fettered, would have found its
mark much sooner. The nightmare of Florence under Alessandro, and his murder at the hands of a younger Medici
whose sister was used to bait the trap, were treated magnificently in De Musset's play *Lorenzaccio*, acted in England as
*Night's Candles.*

For the first nine months of the siege of Florence Catherine had remained with the nuns of the Murate. It was a
terrible position for her. Her own powerful relative was bom-
barding the city, and the defenders could scarcely have been
blamed if they had made reprisals upon her. One member of
the Signoria, indeed, suggested that the little girl should be
hung upon the walls in a basket to meet the fire of the besiegers. For Clement it would have been poetic justice that
he should kill the last precious remnant of his family in this
ignoble campaign. But the Florentines did not fight like that.
They did not even use their hostage when the terms of surrender were arranged.

One July night, however, three senators knocked loudly
at the door of the convent and when a startled sister opened
to them they showed her an order empowering them to take
away the Duchessina. It was the last and most desperate
month of the long siege, and Catherine was sure that the
order meant death. She was eleven years old and she did not
want to die.

Some of the nuns burst into tears, but Catherine did not weep. Stoutly she protested that the nunnery was inviolable and that she would not leave it. The senators insisted that the safety of the Republic overruled all other considerations, but the nuns joined their persuasions to those of their charge. At length a kind of compromise was reached. Catherine was to remain in the convent for the night but the senators would appear again in the morning to remove her.

The heavy door swung into place. The hoof-beats died away along the Via Ghibellina. Catherine ran to her cell, cut short her hair and robed herself like one of the nuns. In this guise she sought out the Mother Superior, saying: "How will they dare now to carry me off in the morning? For in the eyes of all passers-by they will be seen criminally abducting a nun from her convent."

When the senators returned the conflict of wills began afresh. Hour after hour the argument continued, but the girl stood her ground, defying the representatives of the Republic and resolutely refusing to change her nun's habit. At last, despairing of bending her will, the senators were forced to carry her off as she was. Still protesting, she showed no sign of breaking down before the fear of imminent death. But at the Convent of Santa Lucia, in another part of the city, they halted, telling her that this was to be her new home. They were not going to kill her after all, but the Duchessina concealed her relief as she had concealed her terror, and left them marvelling at her firmness and dignity. Long afterwards, when she was the Queen of France, Catherine remembered that the chief of the three senators had shown courtesy and forbearance in carrying out his unpleasant duty. She found that in his old age he was banished from his city and threatened with a heretic's death. Through her intervention his life was saved.

When Florence fell the Duchessina was able to leave the Santa Lucia Convent, and at once she went back to the

Murate to be among her friends again. But in the following spring, when the fruit-trees in the walled garden were heavy with blossom and the Arno was in joyous spate, the Pope summoned her to Rome. He knew how she hated Alessandro, and he feared that the Murate might become a hotbed of conspiracy against the new tyrant of Florence. And for Catherine he had ambitious projects which formed the next item on his programme of diplomacy.

By this time Catherine had made up her mind that she wanted to be a nun. The Murate sisters had been so good to her, their walls so comforting a refuge from the violence and treachery of the world outside. Except for Ippolito, now forced after long resistance to become a cardinal, these kind and cultured nuns were the only people who had shown her real affection. Within the convent there were books and quiet conversation, a bell that told the hour of prayer and a garden where all trouble could be annihilated to a green thought in a green shade. Without was Florence, betrayed and despoiled, losing one by one its treasured liberties to writhe under the heel of Alessandro. What might there be at Rome, sacked by the mercenaries, fouled by the plague, and now again ruled by the cynical Clement? "At Rome," wrote the great Frenchman, François Rabelais, a year or two later, "a world of Folks get an honest livelihood by Poysoning, Drubbing, Lambasting, Stabbing and Murthering." Catherine did not want to go to Rome.

But Clement was the head of the house of Medici and the Duchessina was its last hope. The glittering cavalcade waited for her in the sunlit Via Ghibellina, the horses pawing the stones, tossing their plumed heads and jingling silver bits, the escort sitting in silken magnificence in the saddles. She went with them, and the door of the Murate closed upon her childhood.

In Rome she found again her admired Ippolito, and for a little while her life was sweetened. He was twenty-two now, graceful as an early Pollaiuolo bronze, but his dark eyes held the look of tragic destiny that was in keeping with these latter days of Michelangelo. For he knew himself helpless in the net of Papal politics. Catherine was twelve, and the Tuscan sun brings to swift maturity those who live beneath its beneficence. It was a new kind of affection that she gave Ippolito, the first taste of a love that was to find in all her seventy years of life so few outlets of expression. The two were constantly together, and Rome was not slow to talk of it. The French king had even shown some hopes that they might marry, for the question of the Duchessina's marriage was one that wrinkled royal brows.

But the Pope had other ideas. For this reason among others he had compelled Ippolito to accept a cardinal's hat. Cardinals might not marry, though there was no serious check on the number of their mistresses. And very soon Clement found a means of dissolving this brief companionship.

Catherine was his last card, and he was playing high. The betrothal of Alessandro to the unfortunate daughter of Charles V had sealed the latest bond between the Vatican and Madrid, and the next move was to balance this by a contrary alliance. There were several princely candidates for the hand of the last legitimate Medici. As they pass across this page of history like the show of kings in *Macbeth,* one cannot help but pause and wonder what each union might have meant to Europe. One suitor, for example, was James V of Scotland, and one imagines the Medici blood like a dark stream threading its way among the ravines of Renaissance politics, uncertain for a moment into which inviting valley to turn. One leads to the royal house of England and another to the royal house of France. Under the calculating eye of the impoverished Pope a trifle seems to turn the scale. Posts to Edinburgh were expensive in those days. James V was rejected.

Then there was the Duke of Mantua, but there were unpleasant accounts of his habits, and for once the question of morals was allowed to influence the Pope's policy. And there was the Duke of Milan, but he was old and unlikely to produce an heir. He was also poor, which effectively decided the matter. If Milan were to be added to the Medici possessions it must be by another way.

When further candidates had likewise been found wanting there came an ambassador from Francis I. The French King's second son, Henry Duke of Orleans, was in the market. Craftily Clement sounded the Emperor on the subject, pretending to ask his advice as to how to dispose of Catherine. Charles, confident that Clement would be well snubbed by Francis if he proposed a marriage between Catherine and Henry, encouraged him. But Clement was not snubbed. The betrothal was arranged.

As usual, the Pope kept the terms secret. They included an enormous dowry to be supplied by him, and the presentation of the Duchy of Milan, now in the Emperor's hands, to the bridegroom. For Clement knew that all the treaties in the world would not turn the eyes of Francis from northern Italy. Fortunately, however, this sly device to extend the Medici power from Florence to Milan came to nothing.

The French ambassador sent home to his sovereign a pleasing account of the prospective bride. Catherine was learned, athletic and of irreproachable manners. No longer a child, she had a gaiety and wit that might well commend her to the polished French Court. Her eyes, large and dark, were the eyes of a Medici. Her hair was light brown, not quite of the blonde so rare and so much admired in Italy, nor of the black so characteristic of her family. Her nose was straight, her complexion fresh and her face rather full, though the chin was delicately formed. "She shows a need," wrote the ambassador, "to be caressed and loved." It was an aspect which would appeal to King Francis, but it was the one requirement which marriage was never to satisfy for Catherine.

While negotiations proceeded—while Clement, that is to say, chaffered over the dowry—Catherine was sent back to Florence, with the excuse that malaria was abroad in Rome. Ippolito was sent off to Turkey on a political mission. There was to be no more talk of a match between these two young lovers.

So the Duchessina saw one more spring in Tuscany, and lived again for a little with her dear companions of the Murate. It was 1533. She was fourteen years old, and in a few months she was to go to Marseilles to marry a silent French prince, one year older than herself, whom she had never seen.

One April day during this last brief glimpse of happiness she rode out from Florence to meet another victim of a soul-less dynastic betrothal. The fair-haired twelve-year-old Margaret, engaged to that Alessandro who now rioted in the Medici Palace, was travelling south to Naples, and the two girls met in a wooded valley on the Faenza road. Together they rode back to Florence, and for three days Margaret stayed in the city in Catherine's company. Nobody can say of what they talked. Perhaps it was of the bridals for which each was being prepared like a sacrificial victim, perhaps of the high matters which hung upon the sacrifice. But Catherine must already have learned to keep her counsel where politics were concerned, and Margaret, after all, was not yet in her 'teens. So perhaps they gathered lilies of the valley, and told each other the names of birds, and watched the sheep being folded on the hills at evening like a Giotto fresco. And since it was Margaret's first visit to Italy we may suppose that Catherine walked with her about the city, showing her the marvellous bronze gates of the Baptistery, and the Della Robbia babies on the Hospital of the Inno-cents, and the scar that Michelangelo's colossal David had suffered in the recent disturbances. A sixteenth-century April in Florence must surely have provided material for a nonpolitical conversation, even for the little pawns of politics.

Giorgio Vasari, artist and biographer of artists, was just then painting a portrait of Catherine to be sent to France. On one of these days, when he had left his easel for a short time, he came back to find the half-finished face smeared all over till it looked like that of a blackamoor. The culprits were soon found with their stolen pot of paint, two laughing girls around whom the policies of Europe were revolving. They would, it seems, have blackened Vasari as well if he had not run hastily downstairs, with his sitter and her friend in hot pursuit. And the amiable painter, writing of the incident to an acquaintance, added:

"The Duchessina well deserves that we should wish to keep her portrait among us for her kind and endearing ways. Her sweetness of disposition cannot be painted, and of that my brush can make no memorial."

Then Margaret rode on to Naples and Catherine went back to the Murate. It was said that the match between the Emperor's young daughter and the debauched Alessandro was too atrocious even for Popes and Emperors to bring about. But three years afterwards it took place. Margaret was fortunate in having little more than six months of her husband's company before he was assassinated. Many years later, as the wise and able Regent of the Netherlands, she made a claim on history by her vain efforts to prevent the atrocities carried out by the Duke of Alba.

On September 2 Catherine gave a farewell banquet to the ladies of Florence. For this she was allowed the use of the Medici Palace, and her guests presented her with hangings of cloth of gold embroidered with pearls. The fourteen-year-old Duchessina was now almost a princess, sitting at the head of the table with the beauty and nobility of Florence around her. At three in the afternoon she rode out for the last time under the frowning towers of her native city. That night she spent at Poggio a Caiano, and thence headed for Nice, where she was to meet the Pope.

There was a reason for this arrangement. The overland route from Rome to Marseilles led through Florence, and Clement might have met Catherine there and travelled the whole way with her. He was not a particularly good sailor, but he preferred to go by sea to Nice. It was only one of several occasions on which the Pope put himself to inconvenience, discomfort, delay and even danger in order to avoid passing through Florence. Never once after the siege did he re-enter the city. This was more than tact. It was prudence, the guiding principle of Medici conduct.

# MARSEILLES

THREE hundred guns boomed across the water from the ramparts of Marseilles. The squadron of Andrea Doria had been sighted in the bay, arriving from Nice with Pope Clement and the Florentine bride. The cloth of gold that covered the Pope's galley lifted in the fresh October breeze. It spilled its prodigal splendour in the rippling Mediterranean. Clement sat silent in his carved chair, beneath his golden canopy, listening to the echoes that grumbled away to the horizon. A salute, of course, and a princely one, but was it also a threat? There was bargaining still to be done before he set the ring on his young relative's finger, and three hundred cannon might be regarded as an argument.

Catherine too was silent. She knew the sound of a bombardment. Week after week, for nine long months and more, the stout walls of the Murate had thrown back the menace of the siege guns, and Clement had been behind that grim artillery. They drove her from her nunnery with cannon, and with cannon they welcomed her to her new home. Her lip trembled, but she forced a smile, the smile that had entranced Vasari. Around her was a crowd of excited girls, chattering and laughing until the cannonade struck them dumb and uneasy. They looked to their Duchessina for support, and when she smiled the laughter began afresh. They bore famous names, these gay attendants of Catherine. Palla Rucellai was there, and Catherine Cibo and Maria Salvati. Some were younger than the bride herself, and never before had they been in a ship, and never again would they be in such a ship. Three of them were dark of skin, captured from Barbary in the conflict with Christendom. Marie the Moor, Margaret and Agnes the Turks, had joined the expedition

43

to lend it an exotic air. It was all inexplicable and new, and their distant homes were easily forgotten as they shaded their eyes, eager to be the first to point out the lofty spire rising proudly from its rock above the harbour.

Marseilles was in gala dress to receive the foreigners. It was no common thing to have the restless King Francis in their city, and wherever the King went at least twelve thousand people (says Cellini) went with him. That meant processions to gape at by day, fireworks by night, and a succession of feasts and amusements which would overflow, as often as not, within reach of even lowly folk. Lords and ladies cantered about the city, and a gold piece might be the reward of some trifling service. Scholars and poets and men-at-arms, followed their exalted employers, lingered in the market and swelled the takings at the taverns. Nor did one ever know when the public fountains might not be set to run with wine.

The foremost of the vessels, the captain's galley, was manœuvred to her moorings. Clad in white robes, two equerries stepped upon the quay. They led a white palfrey, and the expectant crowd dropped to its knees—not in worship of the horse but of the transubstantiated wafer, the Body of God which the immaculate animal carried in a pyx upon its back.

Still kneeling, the warrior Anne de Montmorency kissed the jewelled hand of the Pope, who had come to shore with some difficulty from his gilded caravel. Through the rigging of the leading ships could be seen a great sail of purple embroidered with gold thread. Filled with an easterly breeze it had drawn Catherine's galley from Nice, and the sailors sweated and grunted at its rich weight as they hauled at the cords to furl it. The sixty vessels of the fleet were now at anchor, and boatload after boatload was rowed to shore. The Marseillaises craned their necks, giving and taking wagers as to the princely occupants of each boat.

For the Pope and his following a palace had been prepared,

divided from that of the King by a single street, and across this street a covered bridge had been flung, large enough to support a tapestried hall of festival. The glittering procession formed up, and moved slowly towards the palaces through streets hung with silks and velvets, garlanded with the lilies of France and Florence and the wine-red roses of Languedoc, and thronged with wide-eyed citizens who cheered everything they could see.

The Sacrament led the cavalcade. Then came the Pope, carried high on men's shoulders in his chair of office, and attended by bishops and cardinals whose steeds were well-nigh hidden in their flowing robes. Among these rode Ippolito in the suit of mulberry velvet in which Titian had painted him. Alessandro the Moor, if his professed origin were a true one, was a nearer relative of Catherine than the tragic Ippolito, and should have been present at her wedding. But Ippolito was splendid in face and bearing, and there were no tales about him save those of his young romance with the bride. Alessandro was not exactly a good advertisement for the house of Medici, and Clement knew what he was about. This was the last time that Ippolito would see the girl into whose early life he had brought rare moments of happiness. Not long afterwards the people of Florence, outraged by the dissolute tyranny of Alessandro, chose Ippolito as the bearer of a complaint to the Emperor. Alessandro saw to it that he was murdered on the way.

Last in the procession came Catherine, dressed in gold brocade and surrounded by her attendant ladies, some of them young enough to have duennas with them. She rode well, and her emotions were as submissive as the bay mare beneath her. The crowd chattered excitedly: "Look, there she is—the Florentine, the little Italian woman!" To the people of France Catherine would remain for ever "the Italian woman"—spoken sometimes with curious admiration, but more often with mistrust or hatred. But now only the pallor of her round cheeks betrayed the fear that a girl of fourteen might feel in the midst of these staring foreigners. Not even John Stuart, Duke of Albany, her uncle-in-law, who rode beside her, bore himself with greater dignity. "She's proud!" said the Marseillaises, "proud of her Medici money-bags and her kinsman's craft!" And Catherine, wishing herself back in a quiet nunnery garden, rode steadily forward to a life in which humility and patience were to be her only sureties and her strongest weapons.

In the magnificent apartments made ready for him Pope Clement received his host. In a surcoat of parti-coloured silk, with wide puffed sleeves, King Francis knelt to kiss the holy ring of the Vicar of Christ. And in the intervals of junketing and the exchange of elaborate compliments the two astute politicians resumed their bargaining like a couple of Marseilles merchants. Francis was anxious to discover the precise direction of papal policy in Europe, but had he plumbed Clement's cunning to its depths he would have been the first man to do so. Clement, on the other hand, alarmed by recent Turkish victories and well aware that he had tried the patience of the Emperor to a perilous point, wanted Francis to lead a new crusade against the unbelievers, but the Most Christian King, though he did not reveal as much, had already sent his ring to Soliman and would not move an inch. And there was still that unpleasant question of the dowry. For a fortnight the discussions went on, while Catherine assiduously took lessons in the French style of dancing, and even began to learn Greek with an eye to the approval of the scholar-king who was to be her father-in-law.

The marriage contract was ready at last, and duly signed. Of the two parties to the agreement, one had not long before obtained from the other the annulment of solemn undertakings made to a third potentate, while the name of the other was a byword for double dealing. Yet except for a portion of the huge dowry which remained for ever overdue the

*Photograph by A. Giraudo*

## CATHERINE DE' MEDICI IN HER YOUTH
### By François Clouet
(Musée de Versaillcs}

clauses were reasonably carried out. Francis was a sound enough realist to ask for a bigger sum than he had any hope of getting.

On the following day, in a gown of white silk sewn all over with gold and precious stones, Catherine de' Medici was married to Henry of Orleans. Over the kneeling children the Pope pronounced the nuptial blessing, praying this time with more sincerity than was his wont that the vine so carefully planted might prove fertile. Mass was said by the Cardinal de Bourbon, and then came the exchange of gifts. At a time when occasions for tributes both material and rhetorical were of almost daily occurrence this was one of the most important and the presents were appropriately splendid. From Clement, for instance, there was a casket of translucent rock-crystal for the King. It had cost two thousand gold crowns, it was carved with twenty-four scenes from the life of Christ and it contained the sacramental pyx. To Francis Clement further presented the horn of a unicorn, valued at seventeen thousand ducats for its fabulous properties as an antidote against poison. It was mounted in gold to the designs of the Italian Tobbia, whose rival in this commission had been Benvenuto Cellini. To the bride he gave among other gifts three remarkably large and beautiful pearls, which subsequently passed to Mary Queen of Scots, were taken from her by Elizabeth at her execution, and are to this day included in the English crown jewels. The nuptial couch was also provided by Clement, and its value was sixty thousand Roman crowns. The ex-captive of St. Angelo had found means to bleed his ravished capital more completely than any looting army could do. As for Francis, the most singular of the multitude of presents which he showered upon all parties was the live lion wherewith he tried to gain the favour of the ill-fated Ippolito.

A banquet followed, and after that a ball. Little more than fifteen years before, there had been scenes like this at Amboise—the courses served to a blare of trumpets in silken pavilions; costly tapestries walling every room with their insubstantial fancies of pagan festival and allegory; damsels garbed as Hymen and her assistant servitors of the marriage-bed reciting interminable prothalamions; toasts, songs, discourse witty, pedantic and bawdy by turns; jewelled daggers, perfumed beards, plumed caps; silver comfit-boxes passed with prescribed courtesy that the breath might be amorously sweet; the soft opulence of ecclesiastical robes, the frank invitation of women's bodies beneath their rainbow tissues of velvet and satin. That had been in April.

Now the month was October. The Renaissance had ripened towards its red decay. Francis had no longer the face of the handsome young faun. Imprisonment, anxiety and disease had aided the dissipation of his usual mode of life in ageing him before his time. He was still, and would long remain, the brilliant centre of the endlessly revolving circle of pleasure, but the cynicism which had been an amusing affectation had taken root in his nature. He had shaken off the ignominy of Pavia, and France was a great power again. His Court was the most refulgent in Europe. Still the money poured in, he scarcely knew how, and still it poured out again. The retiring Queen who had brought him his throne had died, and he had made an excellent second marriage. The great Humanists whom his gentle sister persuaded him still to support had made France celebrated in the Republic of Letters. A doctor of Lyons called François Rabelais had written a riotous chronicle of wassailing, fighting and philosophising giants, and laughter had rippled round the castles of the Loire. Robert Estienne, Badius Ascensius and Sebastian Gryphius were turning out books from their presses like men possessed. Like the insatiable Pantagruel, like every inhabitant of France in the great drought of the previous summer, the world was athirst and the wine of life was being spilled in such profusion that not even the lees were rejected. And the lees had a bitter taste. There was something that Francis had missed, something that all his squandered wealth, all his theatrical chivalry, all the expert seductions of his deep-bosomed mistresses had failed to give him. Sometimes he thought that his sister Margaret had grasped what he had allowed to slip through his fingers. He had seen her with her Bible or her copy of Plato, talking quietly with half-shut eyes to her eager circle of poets and scholars,—a group in exquisite and enigmatical repose in the midst of a feverish whirlpool of sensations. And once he had come upon her by surprise, sitting at the bedside of a dying waiting-woman, hoping to test those various theories of the soul's destination which so fascinated her. For a moment he had watched her, then fled in sudden terror from the shadow in which all this vivid dalliance must at length be lost. Margaret, he knew, had her hidden griefs, but she had her hidden refuge too. She had not solved the riddle of the universe, but the unceasing search sustained her as it had sustained Leonardo. Had Leonardo found the secret that eluded his royal master? Francis had stared over his shoulder as the pen traced those lambent rhythms that carried the soul with them but left it at last with only one added to its burden of questions. But Leonardo was dead. Only God made artists, and God took them away too soon.

Leonardo was dead. Louise of Savoy was dead. Claude was dead. Louis de Brézé, that mighty hunter and faithful servant, had left Diane de Poitiers a widow. Bourbon had fallen at the gates of Rome and Anne de Montmorency was heading for the post of Constable of France. We shall meet him again, this masculine marshal with a feminine name, a vigorous but not particularly competent warrior, a firm politician who believed implicitly in the absolution of the crown and hated all heretics for their threat to political security. His own usefulness, aided by luck and royal generosity, brought him before his fall some thirty rich estates, and made him Constable, Grand Master, Member of the Council, First Baron of France, Seneschal of Languedoc and Governor of the Bastille. Catherine took note of his majestic figure at her wedding-feast. Here was a man that a Medici must watch.

There were three long tables for the banquet. Catherine sat with the King and his two sons—the Dauphin Francis and her husband Henry—and the cardinals, both French and Italian. Throughout the feast Henry showed his bride every small attention enjoined by courtesy, but he scarcely uttered a word. At fifteen years old his experience as a hostage in Spain and the marked preference of his father for his elder brother had turned him taciturn and melancholy. There were some, accustomed to judge a prince by his conversation, who said that his wits were dulled. His own wishes had been consulted no more than those of Catherine in the matter of this marriage, and he saw no reason why he should pretend to a high-spirited affection miraculously born of a fortnight's acquaintance with the young Italian girl who had just been joined to him in holy union by the Pope. If he thought of any woman at all, it was of Diane de Poitiers, sitting at the third table in the black and white widow's dress that so became her. With his long nose and slanting eyes Henry had something of his father's looks, but nothing of his dazzling vivacity. At his own marriage-feast he remained abstractedly in the background, and Catherine saw at once that her father-in-law, the pivot of the whole complex system, was the one to whose good graces she must find a way. For one of her quick wits the way was easy. She gave Francis jest for jest to his infinite delight. The daring sallies of a girl of fourteen were the best cure in the world for the intermittent boredom that pursued him.

At the head of another table, beside the Pope, sat Queen Eleanor in a gown of jewelled brocade, her hair parted in the centre and drawn back over her ears in the new fashion. Her eyes were brown like Catherine's, and her peaches-and-roses complexion still escaped the pallor of her predecessor Claude. But she too was discovering what it meant to be Queen of France in the reign of the Salamander. To be neglected by her husband was endurable; it was indeed the natural corollary of a political marriage. But she was proud enough to hate the task imposed upon her of drawing back to the Court the ladies whom jealous husbands had forced away from it.

At the third table were the Queen's Ladies, by courtesy so called, though a number of them rendered more service to the King than to Eleanor. Diane was there, thirty-four years old and a widow, but with the face and figure of a girl. Fifteen years ago she had stooped over the cradle of Henry of Orleans at Amboise. Now she was his mistress, and Catherine guessed it. In all that glittering company it was Diane in her black dress with the snowy collar and sleeves whom Catherine's eyes sought out.

Faithful till his death to a husband nearly forty years older than herself, Diane had found a lover nearly twenty years younger. When the boy returned from Spain the habit of silence and introspection had already taken hold of him. His brother, the Dauphin, was rapturously welcomed by the father who had settled on his sickly head such glorious hopes. But Henry was only a younger son, the storm centre of ambitious intrigues which wearied him. It seemed that he had nobody to whom he could turn at a time when his whole being cried out for companionship and support. Diane was ambitious and calculating, and her eyes were wide open when she adopted him. There her detractors would have the matter end. But the most dispassionate view can scarcely deny to Diane at the least a deep and growing affection for the youth whom she so completely enslaved. There was doubtless a maternal element in this affection, but the perfect and lasting satisfaction of body and spirit which she gave him could not have been given by a soulless political schemer, however accomplished in the technique of love. As for Henry, his devotion to her never wavered. "She lapt him round," says her enthusiastic biographer, Jehanne d'Orliac; "with her arms, her bosom, she intoxicated and dazzled him. A bride might come with all her virginal ignorance. She would enjoy social rank and place, she would have nothing of the man enchained for ever." At the ruined château of Anet, in Normandy, a shrine of char-à-banc pilgrimage for all who find romance more heady after a few centuries of bottled storage, the linked initials and devices of Henry and Diane confront the visitor at every turn. Two carven legends among others suggest the nature of their alliance and their love. *Consequitur quodcumque petit,* runs one—"whatsoever she purposes comes to pass." But the other runs: *Sola vivit in illo* —"alone she lived in him."

With that persistent irony with which the gaudy sixteenth-century tapestry is shot, it was at Anet, in the presence of Diane, that the preliminaries to the betrothal of Henry and Catherine had been drawn up. That was two years before the marriage, and Louis de Brézé was still alive, though sinking towards the tomb which Diane was to embellish with her own image. Already there was a bond of sympathy between the Seneschale and the young prince, but as yet there was none of the flesh. De Brézé died, and Diane became the Countess of Saint-Vallier in her own right. Her enemies, fearing her shrewdness and her influence, conspired to emphasise her widowhood and the disparity of age between herself and Henry. But their taunts only helped to throw her into his arms. It was probably in 1533, when the marriage with Catherine was almost certain, that she took the step which bound him to her for ever. Henry was virgin. Diane had at her command the whole Renaissance arsenal of amorous devices. Years later, remembering this first meeting of their bodies, she wrote a set of gay and tripping verses about the fresh morning when she plucked the dewy flower that love held out to her, and found that a laurel of glory was included in the gift.

Catherine knew. As yet there was no scandal on the subject, but when she looked at Henry and Diane she knew. As her watchful brown eyes travelled round the three tables, towards the King, towards her husband, and towards Diane, she began to see the part she would have to play. She turned again to Francis, and her merry tongue made further assault upon that key position.

After the feasting came the dancing. Nowhere in Europe was such dancing as at the Court of Francis, and it was for this that Catherine had written from Italy to her prospective father-in-law, begging him to provide for her instruction in the French manner. Diane, graceful, athletic and completely sure of herself, was an accomplished dancer. So was her great opponent, Anne de Pisseleu, who was the King's new mistress. She was eight years younger than Diane, and never tired of mentioning the fact, though her own beauty and attainments should have been enough to keep her happy without such devices. She was called the loveliest of the learned and the most learned of the lovely, and to give Francis his due her mind appealed to him as well as her body. He had met her in those hectic days of celebration after his return from Madrid, and had promptly found her a husband who could be kept tame with a title. She was the leader of one of the growing factions which, when religious opinions came to divide itself between them, split France into two murderous parties. The King was in her power, and with the King was the Dauphin. Her rivals were Diane and Henry, with the powerful Guise family coming gradually into the open, and Montmorency waiting to see which was to be the party of authority. Behind all the gallantry and lavish display were traps which might well appal the girl who had been brought from Italy with such pomp and circumstance. And as the dancers moved this way and that in the rhythmic patterns of the gaillarde, Catherine saw that she must indeed take lessons before the intricacies of life at this Court could be mastered.

Once more, as at Amboise, a nuptial couch was spread by statesmen for two children who were little more than strangers to each other. With music and torches Henry and Catherine were conducted to a room hung with cloth of gold and silver, to a bed that had wrung the last ducat from Clement's Roman flock, and from the betrayed Florentines as well. In the morning the Pope returned early to satisfy himself that the marriage on which he had spent so much resource and cunning had been properly consummated. It was a question which had cropped up inconveniently in the case of Henry VIII, and he wanted no more trouble of that kind. But Francis was there before him. He had risen still earlier from the arms of Anne de Pisseleu and was standing fully dressed beside the great bed, drawing apart the curtains to watch, with the indulgent eye of an accomplished practitioner, the adolescent novitiates.

The fourteen years of Catherine's girlhood were over. She was entering on the second stage of her education, and that too was to last fourteen years—years that must either make her or destroy her, years that only Medici craft and patience could endure.

# II

# DAUPHINESS

# FONTAINEBLEAU

IN the new palace of Fontainebleau, on the staircases and through the shining galleries, beside the carp-pool and among the great trees of the park, Venus, Cupid, Folly and Time pursued the haunting postures of their ballet.

Always on the move, always planning new castles or embellishing old ones, the King still returned to Fontainebleau, says an ambassador, as if he were returning home. Chambord, Saint-Germain, La Muette, Villers-Cotterets, Les Tournelles, Lescot's Louvre and Madrid in Paris, a new wing at Blois— the passion for building gave Francis no rest. Hunting one day in the Sologne, within convenient reach of Blois and Amboise, he had come upon a shooting-box built six hundred years earlier by a certain Theobald the Trickster. The district was a dismal one, poor in soil and uninhabited. But, partly for this reason, it abounded in game, and the King was seized with the whim to raise a palace in its midst.

It was such a whim as only Francis (or possibly, in a later age, one of the mad Ludwigs of Bavaria) could have put into effect. Fifteen thousand acres were forthwith surrounded by a wall longer than the walls of Paris. Money was drained from nobles and commoners and poured into the vast megalomaniac project. Year after year the building went on in this deserted hunting-forest, and the masons had weapons by their side lest wild beasts should prove too inquisitive when the huntsmen were busy in some other game-belt, at Fontainebleau or Chantilly or in the Forest of Chinon. When Catherine came to France the architects and sculptors had been eight years at their task, and another thirteen years of labour lay ahead of them. There were to be four hundred and thirty rooms and thirteen staircases, one of them the celebrated double spiral wherein two people, the one ascending and the other descending, can keep each other in view without ever meeting. A waggonload of tourists can to-day be lost in the fantastic city of gables and turrets and twisting chimneys which is the roof of Chambord.

Meanwhile wealthy financiers and such landowners as had not been beggared to adorn the royal pageant expressed in stone their own rising ambitions. A stream was diverted and Azay-le-Rideau rose like an opening water-lily from its own reflection. A mill at Chenonceaux was beautified to await the finishing touch of a later and royal hand. These were exquisite dreams, and to this day they retain a lyrical quality, fragile in spite of their endurance. The poet visits them, and the painter, and, of course, the amateur photographer. But Chambord is a specimen for the pathologist, the petrified vision of a gigantic orgiast. Hither and thither in the avenues stray the awed and anxious snapshotters, but their view-finders strive in vain to embrace the infinite ostentation of the Salamander King.

Not even Chambord, nor his favourite Fontainebleau, satisfied him for long. "Never during the time of my embassy," wrote the Venetian Ambassador, "did the Court remain in the same place for fifteen days together." With his retinue of twelve thousand horse, his carriages and his baggage-waggons, Francis roamed the country, giving to every city a glimpse of royalty, seeking, it must almost seem, an impossible escape from the Furies of that ancient age which the Humanists were calling back with all its bewildering implications. How the Court was accommodated on these constant journeys it is difficult to imagine, and Benvenuto Cellini, following in its wake a few years later, wrote: "We had to journey through places where sometimes there were scarcely two houses to be found; and then we set up canvas tents like gypsies, and suffered at times very great discomfort."

To Catherine her new way of life, whether at Fontaine-

bleau or on the road, must have seemed astonishing, and so
absorbed was she in the constant business and amusement of
the moving Court that outside events at first made little impression upon her. In the shortening days she travelled north-
wards towards Touraine and Paris, while Clement left
Marseilles again for Italy, after John Stuart of Albany had
playfully involved him (if we are to believe Brantôme) in a
highly improper joke with three aristocratic French widows.
Well satisfied that the bond with France had been sealed,
the Pope returned to Rome to excommunicate Henry VIII,
a step which French policy for excellent reasons had been
anxious to prevent. And then, not quite a year after Catherine's marriage, he died, thus discounting to a great extent
the political advantage to France of the match. Even in death
Clement had played a trump card. His successor was the
Farnese Pope Paul III.

It does not appear that Catherine grieved overmuch at
the loss of her kinsman, nor even at the news of the murder
of her former lover Ippolito which reached Fontainebleau in
the following year. She had other things to think about, and
the dazzling scene around her was sufficient to occupy all her
attention.

The study of the reign of Francis is a study in chiaroscuro,
and at Fontainebleau the high lights and subtle colouring
can be recognised. For the grim, presageful shadows we must
look elsewhere. One such shadow fell across the unfinished
canvas a year after the wedding at Marseilles. On October
18, 1534, the King was at Amboise. Fixed to the door of his
chamber that morning was found a placard denouncing the
Mass in violent terms. Throughout the cities of the North,
in Paris, Rouen, Orleans, Blois and Tours, similar placards
had been posted in the public squares—a foolish gesture by
irresponsible extremists of the Reforming party, or possibly
by Catholic *agents provocateurs*. Guided by his sister Margaret, Francis had so far maintained at the least a tolerant

attitude towards the Reformers, who numbered amongst them nearly all the great scholars whom he delighted to honour. But this challenge to authority could not go unanswered, and the answer was prompt and unequivocal. A penitential procession in which the King himself took part was followed by the burning of a number of heretics, the maiming in tongue and hand of supposed contumelious persons, and the banishment of two hundred citizens of Paris with confiscation of their property. Only the intervention of powerful protectors of learning prevented the entire suppression of printing, and, as it was, all writers and publishers became subject to the closest invigilation. It was violent reaction, precipitated by an anonymous piece of bravado.

With grave eyes Catherine watched that solemn procession through the streets of Paris. She had heard King Francis remind the Venetian Ambassador of Maximilian's saying: "The Emperor is king of kings; the Catholic King is king of men; the King of France is king of beasts, because, whatever he commands, he is instantly obeyed, like men by beasts." And now here was this all-powerful sovereign walking with a lighted taper in his hand, openly humbling his magnificent person because religious opinion had been outraged. Two months before, Ignatius Loyola had enrolled in a chapel of Montmartre the first recruits in his counter-Reformation campaign. Calvin had fled from Paris to Geneva, where he was preparing to strike his blow for the Reformers with the *Institution Chrétienne*. Everyone in the capital was talking of religion, and when evening drew on the lurid flames of burning dissentients added to the stern object-lesson that Catherine was facing.

But in the pleasure-palace of Fontainebleau, on the edge of the ancient hunting-forest, religious controversy was still avoided. The subject of the soul might be raised, and Plato or Pythagoras invoked for evidence, but Francis and Margaret did all that was possible to prevent any opportunity for bitterness. Fontainebleau was not built to be the house of discord. The lovely masque must go on, with its nymphs and its satyrs and its learned allusions. Venus, Cupid and Folly still held their revel, with the brigand Time looming ever more threateningly above them, ready to shroud their transitory sports in his blue cloak of infinite oblivion. The Florentine Bronzino had painted this subject, and his picture hung in the room that led into the King's bathing-hall, with other masterpieces beside it—Leonardo's *Virgin of the Rocks*, Raphael's *La Belle Jardinière*, Michelangelo's *Leda and the Swan*, Andrea del Sarto's *Charity*, and many more.

Catherine was in the midst of it all, but she was not of it. Hers was to be the new age, the High Renaissance as it is usually called, though it represented in so many ways a retreat from a perfection that could not possibly have been prolonged. For a year or two she did not know that she would one day be Queen of France, though that possibility was distant only by one remove. But she saw the spreading web of intrigue that Francis and Margaret tried so hard to check, and like the Medici she was, she resolved to be in at the spinning, for she guessed that a time might come when she would have to choose whether to be the spider or the fly. She was young, and her glance was ever forward towards the day when these superbly dressed voluptuaries would be in their sculptured tombs.

Henry meant very little to her. He was her lawful husband, he was civil and considerate in this Court where the King would permit no breach of manners, whatever experimental tricks might be played with morals; and he was attractive in a quiet and distant way. But he wore the black and white favours of Diane, and though many believed that only a Platonic bond attached him to this woman who was old enough to be his mother, Catherine knew better. She knew that nothing was to be gained from attempting to make him love her. From his father, on the other hand, much was to be expected, and from day to day the Medici princess strengthened her position under the indulgent eye of Francis. Their relations were friendly to the point of tenderness— *"ma fille"* he called her, and to please her he would sometimes talk to her in Italian. Like a lover who begs for news of a distant mistress he made her tell him of the cities of Italy, set among the vines and olives of their hills, ringed about with their battered bastions, filled with the works of their incomparable artists. He gave her a rainbow for her device, with a Greek motto signifying: "She brings light and serenity." It was his answer to the ambitious *Plus Outre* of the Emperor Charles, for the marriage of Catherine and Henry had been intended above all things as a brake on the Imperial power.

Thus life ran by in hunting and dancing and diplomacy, and in each castle and town and city that the Court visited in its endless peregrinations, Catherine saw little but the Court itself. She knew that Jacques Cartier had sailed back to St. Malo with the description of a great river whose mouth he had discovered in the Western continent. The St. Lawrence he had called it, and Francis was delighted with the success of the expedition. But discoveries were happening every day, New France had not yet become Canada, and how could the men of the sixteenth century look forward to the Heights of Abraham? In the outside world storms were gathering that Catherine would one day have to face, and the secret intrigues of the Court, into which she entered with all her family aptitude, were to breed open struggles and pitiless bloodshed. Already men were dying by the sword and the axe and the faggot, fighting and fleeing, printing books and burning them, bearing themselves like heroes and like savages, stamping the bright colours of the Renaissance into a muddy war of creeds. She would be ready for the conflict when it came, but now she was content to view world-issues microcosmically in the mirror of her immediate surroundings. She had distressed herself little at the deaths of Clement and of Ippolito, who had been her relatives, and one of them her lover. Why, then, should we expect her to spare much thought for these others, some of them perhaps quite unknown to her, whose deaths were to be milestones for historians? Three years after she had come to France the Inca Atahualpa was slain by Pizarro, and Fisher and More by Henry VIII. Only the Massacre of St. Bartholomew would stain the century more darkly than the execution of More, whom Erasmus called "the supreme judge of that kingdom, whose heart was whiter than any snow, and the like of whose genius England never had and never will have again." Not long afterwards Erasmus himself died, leaving partisan chroniclers to wrangle for centuries as to the state of his soul in his last moments.

There was one death in that year 1536, however, which deeply concerned Catherine and her future. On August 10 the twenty-year-old heir to the throne of France, the idol of his father and a prince of some promise, succumbed to a sharp attack of pleurisy following a draught of cold water— a drink of which he was unusually fond. Such, at all events, is the view of the Dauphin's death generally accepted to-day, though at the time it was not found satisfactory.

It happened in this way. A defensive campaign against the Emperor was being conducted in Provence, and the Court was at Lyons. The Dauphin, after a strenuous game of tennis in the hot sunshine, drank ice-cold water from a well, and shortly afterwards fell ill. Four days later he was dead.

How could the terrible news be broken to the King? At last it was decided that his oldest and closest friend, the Cardinal de Lorraine, should attempt the task. But even this ready statesman found himself tongue-tied when he came before Francis. Knowing that his son was unwell, the King bade the messenger speak if he had news of the Dauphin.

Brokenly the Cardinal stammered that the boy was worse, but that they must place their trust in God.

"I understand," said Francis. "You dare not tell me that he is dead, but only that he will shortly die." Then with a bitter cry he turned his back upon the distress of the Cardinal and the courtiers who stood in silence around him. At last, unable to control his emotion, he faced them again, doffed his plumed cap and raised his hands towards heaven. "Ah, my God!" he cried, "I know that I must patiently receive whatever it pleases Thee to send me; but if not from Thee, from whom then can I seek fortitude and resignation? Thou hast burdened me already with the diminution of my kingdom and the defeat of my army; and now Thou hast added the loss of my son. What remains, save to destroy me utterly? If that be Thy pleasure, at least give me warning, that I may know Thy will and not rebel against it, Almighty God, who strengtheneth the human frailty that is natural to me!"

Now there was a certain Count Sebastiano di Montecuculi in the service of the Dauphin. He was an Italian who had come to France with Catherine and Clement, and except for the page who had handed the Prince the cup of water, he had been the only witness of the fatal draught. It was natural —in those days it was inevitable—that suspicion should fall upon him. He was immediately arrested, and a search of his house revealed that, like many of his countrymen, he had interested himself in arsenic and other dangerous substances. He was put to the torture, and a confession was extracted from him involving two Imperial generals in the guilt, and suggesting the intention to poison both the King and Henry of Orleans as well. A few months later the unfortunate Italian was torn asunder by wild horses, in the presence of the King and all his Court—not excepting the ladies. It is well to remember, when we attempt to assess the characters of some of the more sinister women of the Renaissance, that seventeen-year-old girls were accustomed to sit stiffly in their rich clothes while living bodies were burned or torn in pieces before their eyes.

Not till Montecuculi had paid this terrible penalty for what was almost certainly a natural accident, did Francis publish the accusation against the Imperialists. The charge was indignantly denied, and met with a counter-charge against Catherine herself. For Catherine and Henry (and thereby Diane) were the only people who could possibly profit by the removal of the heir to the throne. The accusation was a false one, but it was not very difficult to accept. It is the first of a long tale of poisonings, swollen by legend to fantastic proportions, to be laid to Catherine's account. The Italian woman—a daughter of Florence and a daughter of the Medici—was by inference the most natural author in the world of a crime of this kind. Had Clement been alive at the time, one would indeed be inclined even now to suspect that there was a Medici behind it all. But whatever murders must be traced to Catherine—and there are a handsome number of them—she must be absolved, at the age of seventeen, from this too easy suspicion. The story, at any rate, percolated through France and found plenty of ready hearers, and at Court Catherine already had sufficient enemies to circulate it. But with Francis on the throne it might have cost a courtier his life to speak the charge aloud. He, of all men, would never have believed it.

So now Henry was Dauphin, Catherine was Dauphiness, and Diane was a step nearer the postion of uncrowned queen. When the season of mourning was over, Fontainebleau resumed its fairy-tale gaiety, the hunting-horn was heard again in the forest and the artists continued their labour of filling each ceiling and panel with some symbol of vanished beauty. As Dauphiness, Catherine was worth a castle of her own, and an architect and painter of her own race was commissioned to design it. This was Primaticcio, already busy enough at Fontainebleau. The new castle was to be at Ancy-le-Franc, and would take eight years to perfect. One more to add to the necklace of stone jewels that the Renaissance hung upon the neck of impoverished France.

Blois, Chambord, Saint-Germain, La Muette, Villers-Cotterets, the Louvre, Les Tournelles, Fontainebleau. If the colossus of Chambord typifies too vividly the malady of an ageing sybarite, Fontainebleau recalls the royal Humanist, the scholar and patron of scholars, the acolyte who trims with such loving care the lamp of the Renaissance, the thurifer who scatters its incense in ever richer profusion among his courtly fellow-worshippers. The despots of Western Europe who have left such startling monuments of their wealth and power have not invariably been able to convince us of their taste. Sovereignty too frequently demands of the artists who stand about the throne the sycophantic scene-painting of a Louis David. But Francis could recognise a Leonardo, though Leonardo never flattered his person. He could recognise a Cellini, overlook his indiscretions and laughingly refuse to be turned against a great artist even by the complaints of his royal mistress. He could recognise an Erasmus and continue to honour him when he refused to sell his services. He could recognise a Rabelais and find mirth where his advisers insisted there was disaffection.

It is at Fontainebleau that one remembers Castiglione's high hopes for Francis when he was still a prince—his delighted praise for his "most noble conditions, greatness of courage, prowess and liberality," his "handsomeness of person and beauty of visage, and in his countenance so great a majesty, accompanied, nevertheless, with a certain lovely courtesy." Fontainebleau was built and furnished and occupied as the expression of a new cult, enthusiastically, if imperfectly derived from ancient thought and manners. The Château de Madrid in Paris, raised by Girolamo della Robbia to celebrate the King's return from the Spanish captivity, must have been a lesser Fontainebleau, but not a stone of it remains to us since the Revolution.

The French were learning now to rival the Renaissance art of the Italians, and Francis, though his eyes were still on Italy and the fair duchies that he had signed away in more than one faithless treaty, was not slow to encourage the craftsmen of his own race. Jean Goujon, mason, architect and sculptor, designed supple, fleshly bronzes, and Germain Pilon raised noble memorials to the exalted dead. The prodigious young Philibert de l'Orme, who had written a notable treatise on architecture and at the age of eighteen had had three hundred men working under his direction in Rome, had put the best of his fertile brain into Fontainebleau, and had still enough ideas left to be of service later on to Catherine de' Medici. Leonard Limousin had made Limoges famous with his cunning work in enamel, François Clouet had succeeded his father Jean as official portrait-painter, and with Corneille de Lyon was engaged on that enormous output of portraits which so vividly suggests the new importance of individuals in the sixteenth century.

Nevertheless, the Italians were at Fontainebleau in force, and Catherine, watching them at their work, or sitting near them when they took their honourable places at the board, was happy to talk in her native tongue. Primaticcio was chief of them all. With French and Italian assistants he decorated the King's bathing-hall with the story of Calisto, and the apartments of his mistress (now graced with the title of Duchesse d'Étampes) with the story of Alexander and Campaspe, allegorically portraying the love of Francis and herself. Primaticcio's cartoons were copied, too, in the royal tapestry factory which had just been set up at Fontainebleau to revive an art in which the Flemings had of late years had all their own way. And then there was Rosso, a tall, florid, temperamental Florentine, whose sensual realism haunts one with something of the uneasy power of Michelangelo's enigmatic figures in the Sistine Chapel. Rosso had had a wild life in Italy. He had suffered gravely at the hands of the invaders of Rome, and later injuries had been caused by the fall off a roof. Probably he was not quite right in the head. He killed himself at length, poisoned himself after a quarrel with a friend about a debt.

Endlessly the artists strove to fix for the restless eye of their master the beauty that was so seductive and so elusive, beckoning and again retreating like a wanton hamadryad, while death came relentlessly nearer. Soon Cellini was to join them at Fontana Belio—as he calls Fontainebleau in his autobiography—setting the Court by the ears with his follies, antagonising the Duchesse d'Étampes, showing to the delighted sovereign the waxen sketches for the silver Jupiter, the golden salt-cellar, the bronze Nymph of Fontainebleau, returning to his forge for the casting, choosing his models with the eye of a connoisseur and using them, as he tells us frankly, for his pleasure. The sensuous prose of Lemaire de Belges, the poetry of Clément Marot and a few *rhétoriqueurs*, the tales of Despériers and Margaret's *Heptameron*, the remaining tithe of the pictures and statues, majolica and metalwork and tapestries—it is only through these that we can find our way into the life of Francis and his Court. With a new world open to them, the men of the Renaissance knew only too well how swiftly it must pass. The skull grinned through the myrtles, the moving finger traced out its menace, the elaborate clocks—those clocks which absorbed the last despairing years of Charles V, those clocks which Rabelais would not admit in his Abbey of Thélème— reiterated their inexorable message—one more hour of the world's loveliness has been tasted, one less remains to taste. Desperately wealth was gathered and spilled that something tangible might survive. "I am smothered in gold," said Francis to Cellini. But still it went on.

With a new master and a new impulse, the artists brought

to their work the accumulated lessons of an older tradition
and an older patronage. For centuries Jesus had been painted
on the cross. Now, for a little while, Marsyas took his place.
For centuries the Church had attempted, often with astonishing success, to canalise the force of sexual attraction into the
worship of Mary, and slowly the physical beauty of the Virgin
had unfolded, bursting first the Byzantine sheath and then
the Gothic, until at a breath it blossomed into Venus. Mary
the makeless maiden, *Stella Maris,* Star of the Sea, looked
down from window and altarpiece with all the tender mystery
with which each artist invested his own vision of woman-
hood. And now there was Botticelli's Aphrodite, foam-born,
her body slender as man's hope of peace, her hair blown free
like thought released from dogma, innocence in her curved
lips and all experience in her dreaming eyes. Latona's children were slaughtered now in place of the Innocents, and
where the Angel had touched the hollow of Jacob's thigh
Hercules now lifted Antæus from the earth that gave him
strength. The old fleshly subjects which the Scriptures had
provided merged almost imperceptibly with the new. Susannah and the Elders, Diana and Actæon, David and Bathsheba,
Nessus and Deianira, Judith and Holofernes, Jupiter and
Ganymede—there is a place for each in the Renaissance
hierarchy. And still the perfect parable is the favourite one,
the story of Eros and Psyche.

With our acute modern sex-consciousness we read our
Brantôme or our Marot and make sly jokes at the venery of
Francis and his Court. We visit castles and museums, testing
the springs of royal and ancient four-posters when the guide's
back is turned, as if the occupations carried on in those
lordly beds were fundamentally more exciting than similar
occupations carried on in furniture from the Tottenham
Court Road. It seems that each generation must learn afresh
the dreariness of the mere repetition of the act of love.
The very number—almost invariably quoted inaccurately—

of the paramours of a long-dead monarch, has an inexplicable glamour about it, a mathematical significance capable somehow of arousing twentieth-century erethism. At Fontainebleau and Blois and Les Tournelles the body was not indulged more frequently, or with greater technical resource, than in a modern hotel. In some respects, indeed, amorous idiosyncrasies were more limited four centuries ago than they are to-day, and Cellini was tried by jury for using his mistress "after the Italian manner"—a phrase that scarcely calls for elaboration. In the circle with which we are dealing, money was more plentiful, manners for the most part more scrupulous, furniture more beautiful, conversation more intelligent, and longevity less probable. And that is about the sum of it.

*"En France il fait bon faire l'amour!"* exclaimed Brantôme happily. But it has been held pleasant to make love in other countries and at other times, admired men of letters instance the pursuit as one of the few sources of delight in this vale of tears, and human beings of every condition continue to practise it to the limit of their consciences, opportunities or capacities. We cannot all hang Bronzinos on our walls, nor commission a Primaticcio to paint our mistresses' bedrooms, but there is no lack of good artists with different names, and pictures are as cheap as motor-bicycles, with the advantage of being less lethal. We cannot all afford black satin sheets as was done by several sixteenth-century notables for the better display of feminine nakedness, but we can turn the electric light on and off at our bedsides, which would have delighted Francis.

And yet there is a difference between the elaborate system of Venetian mirrors whereby Francis watched the ladies of his Court bathing in the grotto of Fontainebleau, and a pair of binoculars trained on the *figurantes* of the Folies-Bergère. For love to be tolerable in any great quantity, a ritual and a mythology are necessary. The *Kama-Sutra*, the Courts of Love of twelfth-century Provence, and the archetypic plot

of the modern film-romance are all instances of the adapta-
tion of this principle. It happens, moreover, that the Renaissance ritual and mythology are particularly well-developed
and particularly attractive. It is, as it were, the trimmings
of love that fascinate us, its philosophic landscape and its
intellectual decorations. And well they might. Perhaps at no
period of history—not even in Periclean Athens—have the
body and the mind been so perfectly and harmoniously cul-
tivated as they were in the immediate circles of the greater
Renaissance despots.

But still the sand slips through, and there will be no one
left to turn up the hour-glass. They knew themselves both
the beginning and the end of an epoch. So much would
die with them, mouldering more quickly than their bones
beneath those huge and sumptuous tombs which they were
continually raising, as if the arch-enemy death were worthy
at last of the richest tribute that a chivalrous victim could
pay him. A century later, when the Renaissance had crossed
the Channel, Andrew Marvell would write:

> But at my back I always hear
> Time's wingèd chariot hurrying near.

And at Fontainebleau they heard at each moment, in the
rustle of their rich tapestries, the splashing of their carved
fountains and the murmur of the autumn wind in the forest,
the music of those approaching wings. A lady once said to
Brantôme, as if the Day of Judgment were upon her: "In
these days we must waste no time, nor make the least delay,
but the sooner assaulted the sooner we shall be taken and
captured." And the assault of feminine citadels was only one
of so many exciting things that must be crowded into the
hurrying years. They were all discoverers, launched upon a
new ocean that offered unlimited possibilities to the adventurous. There were intellectual heights to be climbed,
philosophic seas to be charted, and women's bodies were

islands of pleasure to be invaded, while the poets in endless anatomies mapped out their contours and tabled their properties.

With a passion, for proportion learned of Greek sculptors and dialecticians they drew up the recipe for their ideal of feminine beauty. The mystical number three was borrowed from the same ancient source from which Christian theology had already derived it. Here are the thirty articles of their formula:

Three things white: the skin, the teeth and the hands.
Three black: the eyes, the eyebrows and the eyelashes.
Three red: the lips, the cheeks and the nails.
Three long: the body, the hair and the hands.
Three short: the teeth, the ears and the feet.
Three broad: the bosom, the forehead and the space between the eyebrows.
Three narrow: the mouth (both the one and the other), the waist and the ankle.
Three delicate: the fingers, the hair and the lips.
Three small: the nipples, the nostrils and the head.

Their interest never flagged, and they added zest to the game with academic discussions on the virtue of chastity. They glorified their girls with a persistence worthy of Mr. Samuel Goldwyn, but from different motives and with profounder demands. The breadth of forehead required by these early connoisseurs gives a hint of the difference. Nearly three centuries were to pass before the Renaissance delight in learning was to give place to an organised boycott of the brain.

And these ardent young painters' models, with their firm bodies, their classical coiffures, and their lips parted to show teeth and tongue, were the measure for all artistic endeavour. Man was the microcosm wherein the ordered complexities of the natural world were studied, and the perfection of feminine beauty was the standard for all proportion and harmony. Poems and palaces followed the same rules of classical construction, and just as variety in womankind emphasises the excellence of the pattern, so austerity was avoided in the arts by the liberated human element, the privilege of educated individualism.

Thus did Venus, Cupid, Folly and Time keep their revel, and the master of the ceremonies held death at bay for fourteen years after Catherine had come to France. Much may be learned in fourteen years, and in Bronzino's picture there are two other figures not named in the title. They have the faces of Furies, and one of them holds the cloak for Time while the other twists bony fingers in her hair. They are malevolent shapes to intrude on this scene of dalliance, and the one might be taken for Ate, goddess of discord. Perhaps Catherine, gazing at the picture in the King's chamber, saw its moral more clearly than most men. For whether she welcomed the growing conflict or whether she dreaded it, she certainly prepared herself steadily to meet it.

"Dullness," wrote Margaret in her *Heptameron*, "is an incurable malady." But at least it could be allayed. Catherine judged her King rightly. It was distraction that he needed, and she provided it by every means in her power. Much could be done by conversation, for he was a brilliant and a tireless talker, and looked eagerly for a like talent in those about him. And in other directions Catherine showed herself equally resourceful. She invented new games, new dances, new entertainments when the weather kept the royal Nimrod from his favourite pastime, and when it was fine she practised with the cross-bow, or watched him at tennis until at length she ventured on the sport herself. She stood on the horse-shoe staircase in the court-yard at Fontainebleau when he clattered off in the early morning to the sound of the baying of his hounds and the fanfare of his liveried hunts-

men. And one day she begged to be allowed to join the chase
with him.

There was more in this than the mere desire for sport and
exercise, more even than the wish to be at the King's side.
When Francis went hunting he was accompanied by his
famous *Petite Bande*—twenty-seven ladies chosen above others
for their beauty and their accomplishments, and led by the
royal mistress, at this time Madame d'Étampes. Wherever
one meets the ghost of Francis—in the glades of Fontainebleau, in the gardens of Amboise, in the old streets of Tours
and Paris, in the court-yard at Blois, on the double stairway
at Chambord—these lovely, fragile shades accompany him.
Physical perfection was only one of the qualifications required
of them, and a moment's sadness the worst offence they
could commit. Latin and Greek entered into it, and the
ability to dance like Herodias and talk like Vittoria Colonna
after a day of strenuous exercise. The hunt balls of the
English counties would scarcely furnish twenty-seven candidates to pass muster with the *Petite Bande*. The King himself
selected and paid for their gowns, which, within doors, were
designed to tone with the furnishings of the palace, and
without changed their colours in accordance with the variable
royal livery. From the old account books we learn that ten
ells of material were an average measure for each dress,
though sometimes eleven ells were needed. And for a certain
Madame de Canaples, whose beauty was of the ample type of
Juno, the books show an indenture for sixteen ells.

To be a member of the *Petite Bande* was to enjoy the
highest honour and the most intimate confidence that Francis
could bestow, for he preferred his twenty-seven beauties to
any privy council. As yet the company had not reached its
greatest significance, for while he lived the frank nature of
the King held in check the forces of internal political intrigue. But Catherine saw at once the possibilities of the
*Petite Bande,* and she was not prepared to allow Francis to

go off for eight or ten days with them, as was his custom,
unless she were of the party. He granted her request, and
thenceforward she never left him. Even among those fanatical
equestrians she rode well, and she was the first of them to
sit with her leg over the saddle-bow. By all accounts it was a
very handsome leg that was thus revealed. Catherine had
already made a friend of Madame d'Étampes, the leader of
the troop, and both women had a tendency to play with
wires, the one from what she conceived to be necessity in
a royal mistress, the other perhaps largely by family instinct
and upbringing. The time was to come when the *Petite
Bande,* transformed into Catherine's own Flying Squadron,
should be a power to be feared.

Catherine's motive in securing for herself a place in this
troop of goddesses, as Brantôme calls them, was certainly a
political one, but she did it under colour of her affection for
the King and her fondness for riding. It was the nearest she
ever came at this time to the appearance of pushing herself
forward, for humility was the best, indeed the only card she
could play. Diverting Francis, deferring to Diane, earning
the alliance of Madame d'Étampes and the sympathy of the
warm-hearted Margaret, she skilfully relieved an intolerable
situation and watched every change of the political weather
with an attention that Clement himself, the master of guile,
would have admired. But a major difficulty was threatening
to ruin her. She had been married nine years and had produced no child.

Ever on the watch for such details, Brantôme relates that
Henry had the reputation for a physical peculiarity which
might have been responsible for this problem. But in 1538
Diane de Poitiers had borne him a daughter who became
Diane de France. The relations of Henry and Diane were
still believed by some to be Platonic, and a putative mother
was found for this infant, a Piedmontese, who was forthwith
hurried away to a convent. But there can be no doubt that

Diane was the mother, and Henry at all events is thereby exonerated from Brantôme's suggestion. Catherine, however, was still barren, and that was a serious matter now that she was Dauphiness. So serious was it that there began to be talk of a divorce. It was urged by Catherine's opponents that Henry ought to repudiate her, a step for which there was ample precedent.

It was not Diane who started this hare, though many have held her responsible. Her word would have carried no weight with the King, beside that of the all-powerful Duchesse d'Étampes, her rival and Catherine's friend. Nor would a repudiation serve Diane's purposes in any way. If Catherine were divorced a new wife would have to be found for Henry, and it would certainly not be Diane. Probably it would be somebody very much less submissive than Catherine. It was in Diane's interest that Catherine and Henry should reach the throne in safety, with herself as the left-handed Queen.

Who first made the suggestion? Probably it was Montmorency, the First Baron of France, Conservative and Catholic, allied with the rising family of the Guises, admired by Henry but suspicious of Catherine. He had no love for Italians, and he wished them as far as possible from the throne of France. He had no love for heretics, and the faction led by the learned Duchesse d'Étampes was to his way of thinking altogether too liberal-minded in face of the Protestant danger. If this were his idea he was to pay for it, for thereafter Catherine and the King's mistress did not rest until they had had him disgraced.

It was well for Catherine that she had so sedulously pursued the favour of Francis. For however much he disliked the proposal as her father-in-law, he was bound, as King, to see points in its favour. The cunning little Medici did not wait for him to make up his mind. She went to see him, dissolved in tears. Tenderly Francis asked the cause of her distress. She told him between her sobs that she had heard she was to be sent away from Fontainebleau for the good of France. She was ready to do whatever her sovereign asked of her, to retire into a convent if he thought fit. But she had been so happy here. Could she not, whatever he meditated, remain humbly in his service in some other capacity?

Two centuries later, at the Court of St. Petersburg, another Catherine was to find herself in the same position and use the same device. And in both cases it worked admirably.

The King was conquered. He kissed the weeping Dauphiness on the brow. "Have no fear, my daughter," he said kindly. "It is God's will that you should be my daughter-in-law and the Dauphin's wife, and I would not have it otherwise. It may please Him to grant to you and me the blessing that we desire above all else in the world."

From the Court of Navarre, where she was now, by a second marriage, Queen, the gentle Margaret wrote to Catherine to add her comfort:

"My brother will never allow this repudiation, as evil tongues pretend. But God will grant to Madame la Dauphine a royal succession when she has reached the age at which the women of the House of Medici ordinarily bear children. The King and I will then rejoice with you, in spite of these miserable slanderers."

It was a signal victory, but it still remained to consolidate it by fulfilling the hopes so kindly and piously expressed. It is said by some that Catherine resorted to the black arts in order to conceive. There is no proof of this, but it would not be in the least surprising in that age when necromancy went hand in hand with philosophy and so learned a person as Margaret herself was fain to believe that the soul of a swan took longer than other souls to leave its body on account of the length of its neck. And in these days of what we are pleased to call the exact sciences the division between knowledge and presumption, medicine and magic, faith and superstition, is often too arbitrarily drawn. Later in her life Cath-

erine interested herself in the arts of Nostradamus, and if at
this crisis of her early years she resorted to a very common
expedient, it may well be that among the charms she tried
were some of the following, listed by Jehanne d'Orliac on
the assumption that she used them:

"According to Albertus Magnus, the herb known as
shepherd's rod, periwinkles pounded to powder and mixed
with earthworms, gives women the desire to conceive. The
ashes of a frog, the genitals of a wild boar, produce the
same effect. According to Photius, a glass of mule's stale
drunk every month by a barren woman will make her fertile.
The middle finger and the anus of a fœtus born two months
before its time make excellent amulets. Another author
affirms that hare's blood, and the left hind paw of a weasel
steeped in vinegar are very efficacious. Lastly, according to
Blérien, a girdle made of goats' hair, steeped in asses' milk
and worn above the navel by the woman who wishes to
conceive, will make her the mother of a male child."

However this may be, the more natural device was not
neglected, and it was Diane herself who sent her lover regularly to sleep with his wife; her assistance in this connection
was afterwards used as a pretext for a handsome present
from Henry to his mistress, "in consideration of the good
and praiseworthy services she formerly rendered to the
Queen." Irony could scarcely go further.

Margaret had been right in her estimation of Medici
fertility, and on February 10, 1543, Catherine gave birth
at Fontainebleau to a son, the first of her ten children. It was
Diane, in her dress of black and white, who held the infant
Francis on her lap, as she had held his father at Amboise,
twenty-five years before. Diana, moon-goddess, daughter of
Latona, sister of Phœbus, fleet huntress, patroness of streams
and wells and forest glades, was also the protectress of the
Roman mother, the goddess of children and of child-bearing.

## PARIS

THREE years before the birth of Catherine's son, King
Francis had stood with his Queen at a window in Paris,
to watch the Emperor Charles pass in splendid pomp through
his capital. This powerful and life-long enemy of France
had been granted permission to travel through the country
with his suite on his way to do some fighting in Flanders,
and in every town and city he had been received, by the
orders of Francis, with the ceremonies usually reserved for
the newly crowned kings of France. It was the most extraordinary gesture imaginable, and there had been many to
warn Francis against it, or to laugh at his persistence. But
it was seventy years too early to use the word "quixotic."

This was the manner of it. After the death of his dearly
loved son Francis endeavoured to forget his grief in the
vigorous prosecution of the war in Provence. Perhaps he
hoped for another Marignano to restore glory to his declining
years, and with the aid of Montmorency, now Constable of
France, he certainly achieved some notable successes. By the
merciless expedient of laying waste the countryside of his
own people, Montmorency checked the advance of the Imperial troops on all fronts. He was a terrible soldier, this
Constable, feared by his own men almost more than by the
enemy, and Brantôme describes him in the field, muttering
his prayers and at the same time giving such orders as:
"Hang me that man! Bind that scoundrel to the tree! Run
him through the body with your pikes! Burn yonder village!"—all without interruption of his devoutly orthodox
orisons.

By one means and another the Emperor was at length
driven to a treaty. In July, 1538, Francis and Charles met at

Aigues-Mortes, and with every mark of affection made a peace for which the French King, advised by the Constable, changed his foreign policy in several respects. Concessions were really unnecessary on his side, for he had the power at that moment of pressing his advantage by force of arms. But the crafty Charles dangled Milan before him, and Milan had never yet failed as a bait. Moreover the Pope was in the background, encouraging the reconciliation of the two mighty monarchs so that each could turn his attention more thoroughly to the extinction of heresy in his own dominions —an object very close to His Holiness's heart, and one which he felt to be more deserving of the assistance of the sword than were mere squabbles between nations.

Next year, with all the courtesy which should exist between chivalrous sovereigns, Charles asked permission to make his way through France. It was a chance for Francis to play the paladin, and Montmorency had no need to add the reminder that the gesture might at last secure Milan, which coveted duchy was at the Emperor's disposal. The King gave his word. Charles was welcome.

The invitation did not appeal to the Duchesse d'Étampes, who knew that neither Francis nor Montmorency was a match for the Emperor in diplomacy. She urged the King to take Charles prisoner when he had him in his power, and thus avenge the captivity of Madrid, dictate his terms, and make sure of Milan. The story is told that Triboulet, the King's jester (whose services were the subject of unpleasant gossip), was present at this interview between Francis and his mistress, and was observed to be writing busily upon a tablet. The King asked him what he was about.

"Sire," said Triboulet, "I am here making a list of all the greatest fools in the world. For many call me fool who should themselves wear the cap."

Taking the tablet, his master saw the name of Charles

upon it. "How?" he cried. "Are you so much in love with
the whip that you have the insolence to write down my
Imperial brother as a fool?"

"Assuredly, sire. He deserves a place in the fraternity if
he sets foot in France."

"And how will the list continue, Fool?"

"If the Emperor should suffer an accident in France his
name will be struck off, for I am concerned only with living
fools. But if he should return safe and sound to his own
dominions—why then, Sire, I shall perforce have to write
your name in his place."

At this Madame d'Étampes laughed heartily, but the King,
with all that majesty of voice that so forcibly impressed
foreign envoys, said only:

"I have given my pledge."

It was his favourite rôle—the pattern of chivalry. Not for
the world would he have gone back on the promise that he
had made to his inveterate enemy. And Charles, wishing
to get through France as quickly as possible on account of a
chill that he had caught while crossing the Pyrenees, found
his progress held up by elaborate pageants. Montmorency
and the King's two remaining sons—the Dauphin Henry and
the young Charles, now Duke of Orleans—met him at the
frontier with a splendid cavalcade and conducted him north-
wards; and Montmorency used every opportunity of further-
ing his crazy policy of alliance with the Empire. At every
stopping-place the extravagant mummery had to be gone
through, gentlemen and burgesses coming out to welcome
the party, processions and banquets and carnival, and long
speeches to which the bored Emperor had by courtesy to
listen, shivering with ague beneath his furs in the wintry
weather. It was December 10 when they reached Loches,
where the King and Queen met him and feasted him. Thence
the whole party continued up the Loire, through Amboise,
Blois and Orleans, with more feasts, richer spectacles, longer

speeches. And at last, on the afternoon of New Year's Day, 1540, came the state entry into Paris, and the procession which Francis watched from the Constable's mansion in the Rue Saint-Antoine.

The vision of Milan must indeed have been a dazzling one to blind the King's eyes to the folly of the scene upon which he was gazing. The *Parlement,* having protested in vain against the reckless extravagance of this entertainment of an enemy, had the honour of leading the procession. Then came the fierce Constable, bearded like the pard, clad in cloth of gold holding the rein of his richly-caparisoned steed in one hand and in the other his unsheathed sword of office. The Emperor rode between the Dauphin and the Duke of Orleans, his secrets locked beneath a furrowed brow. He was growing weary of the endless solemn ceremonies that made up his public life, weary too of guiding the fortunes of an Empire that stretched from Mexico to the Danube. These Frenchmen were too easy to fool and he was anxious to hurry on to dispose of the rebellious burghers of Ghent. Moreover, he had a nasty cold. But as he passed the Duchesse d'Étampes he did not forget to let fall at her feet, as it were by chance, a diamond of great price. She stooped and picked it up. Charles had made one more friend in France.

And so it went on: a speech from the sheriffs at the Hôtel de Ville, together with the present of a gold and silver figure of Hercules "of the height of a tall man"; more speeches from the governors of the prisons, who delivered up to him their keys; a Mass in Notre-Dame; and then a whole week of festival. Not till January 24 did he at last reach the Flemish border, and there take leave of his escort with many gifts and expressions of cordiality.

And after all this Francis did not get Milan. Charles had never intended him to have it, and had seen to it that every subject but that one vital one should be discussed while he was in France. War broke out again on a new front, to the north-east, in the region that would one day become the chief theatre for the greatest war in history. The Imperial troops penetrated as far as Épernay, and a fresh treaty was forced on Francis. There were rumours that Madame d'Étampes, and Catherine with her, were by secret diplomacy serving the Empire better than France. It may well have been true, for it was what Francis and the Constable had been doing publicly for three years. And then the English, allied with Charles, took Bordeaux, and fresh terms had to be sought.

But Catherine and Madame d'Étampes were firmly entrenched. The moment for Montmorency's fall had clearly arrived, for the King was by no means pleased with the outcome of his tactics. A pretext was found, and the mighty Constable, the first Baron of France, was requested to retire. It was a victory for the Left. The Dauphin Henry had conceived a deep affection for the fire-eating Constable, who had taught him his first military lessons. With Henry was Diane, and with the Constable were the Guises. It was a formidable clique at which the King's mistress and the King's daughter-in-law struck this blow, and Catherine realised that the swiftly growing rivalries were going to make it more difficult than ever to swing from one to the other. But while Francis lived she had her chance of revenging herself upon the man who had counselled her divorce, and she took it like a Medici. From that time forward, though Catherine retained by every art the favour of Francis, Henry fell further and yet further in his father's estimation. He had made serious mistakes as a soldier, and it was said that he appeared a little too eager for his father's death and his own accession. The split was widening rapidly.

## RAMBOUILLET

T HE King," wrote the Venetian Ambassador in 1546, "is now fifty-four years old: his aspect is entirely regal, so that merely to look at him, without any previous sight of his face or portrait, one would say at once 'He is the King.' All his movements are of such nobility and majesty that no prince could equal him . . . He affects a certain elegance in his costume, which is laced and braided, rich in jewels and ornaments of price; even his doublets are beautifully worked and woven with gold."

Francis was making a brave end. A year later, in the last days of March, 1547, he lay dying at Rambouillet. The pudendagra which for years he had been fighting intermittently with the unskilful help of his doctors had at last beaten him. A legend was later to gain currency that the disease had been deliberately transmitted to him through La Belle Ferronière—one of the supposed casual loves of his later years—by her jealous husband. Others said that political enemies, agents of the Empire, had brought about his infection. These are not pretty stories, and they are not true. His blood had been poisoned long ago.

In February the news had arrived of the death of Henry VIII. It had upset Francis badly, and thereafter he smiled almost as seldom as the Dauphin. These two monarchs, of the same age, and with such similarity of appearance, character, and significance in history, must inevitably have felt a certain kinship. Francis, moreover, trying to find some way out of the political impasse into which the fallen Constable had let him slide, had based high hopes on a new alliance with the English King. Now Henry was dead, and Francis knew that his own star must be setting also.

There had been other deaths to hasten his decline. Charles, Duke of Orleans, had been the third son to predecease him, and only Henry was left. After the death of the Dauphin Francis he had transferred his affection to his youngest son, for never in his life had he had much love for Henry. And when Charles died he turned, needing still some comely and gallant youth to remind him of his own early manhood, to the young Duke of Enghien, a dashing soldier who was looked upon as a formidable opponent of the Guise influence upon the Dauphin. There came a winter's day, with heavy snow upon the ground. Francis suggested the diversion of a snow-ball fight among the youngsters of his suite. "During the combat," says the chronicler, "some ill-advised person threw a linen chest out of a window, and it fell on the Sieur d'Enghien's head, inflicting such injuries that he died a few days later." Historians have suspected the Guises, and even Henry himself, of arranging this unhappy accident. But one of Henry's biographers, Mr. Noel Williams, makes the following comment:

"That, notwithstanding the suspicious circumstances attending it, the death of Enghien was due merely to one of those acts of brutal horse-play so common at this epoch is scarcely open to question. Those who scattered the feathers from the beds of the plague-stricken over themselves and their companions, who were only prevented from strangling their friends by some one cutting the cord in the very nick of time, who placed the corpses of felons who had been hanged in the beds of court ladies, were quite capable of throwing furniture at one another's heads without the least homicidal intention."

To this we may add the courtly Castiglione's disapproval of those who "hurl billets and bricks, one at another's head. . . . Then at table, potage, sauce, jellies, and whatever cometh to hand, into the face it goeth." And Brantôme, between instances of sophisticated chivalry and polished manners, describes the most disgusting practical jokes. High spirits were continually breaking free in this Court where pleasure was the rule of life, and at first it seems impossible to reconcile such stories as these with the elaborate codes of conduct which were formulated at the same time. But if the age is to be understood, that reconciliation must be made.

Francis preserved till the end of his days, says a contemporary, an excellent memory and complete intellectual powers. He retained also his life-long passion for the chase. As a young man he had slain a wild boar single-handed in circumstances that left no doubt of his personal bravery. No feat of his save the victory of Marignano had been celebrated so often and so enthusiastically as this. Poets had written of it in heroic verse, and Primaticcio had painted the exploit in a gallery at Fontainebleau. The classical example was not hard to find, and the boar, of course, was the boar of Calydon. For Guillaume Budé, royal secretary and one of the greatest scholars of his brilliant epoch, Francis had found no more honourable task than the replacement in Latin and Greek of the mediæval terms of hunting, and Diane de Poitiers owed much of the glory that surrounded her to the cult of her namesake as the lissom goddess of the chase.

And so, when he felt his end upon him, the dying hunter took to the forests with a feverish vigour that belied his wasted strength. From Fontainebleau to Saint-Germain he travelled, from Saint-Germain to La Muette with the baying of his hounds in his ears, from La Muette to Villepreux with the horns echoing behind him, from Villepreux to Dampièrre with the fresh cheeks of his *Petite Bande* stung by the wintry weather; thence through the leafless woods of Chevreuse, Limours, Rochefort, following the track of deer and hare and boar in the deep snow. "When I am old and sick," he told his courtiers, "I will be borne to the chase in a litter—when I am dead I may yet go in my coffin."

But at Rambouillet he became too ill to move. He took to his bed towards the end of March, and he did not live to see April. He could scarcely speak, but his eyes followed his mistress, his daughter-in-law, his Minister Tournon, as they quietly entered and left the room. He was not afraid to die, but his thoughts were melancholy as his mind travelled this way and that over his past life—recalling the day when he had knelt to receive knighthood from Bayard, the perfect chevalier, and then that later day, only two years ago, when Étienne Dolet had been burned with his books in the Place Maubert in Paris. He had shone in the reflected glory of Dolet's learning, and he had allowed him to be burned alive for three words added as explanation to an obscure passage in Plato's works. Dolet dead at the stake, Marot dead in exile, Bonaventure Despériers dead by his own hand. These were not comforting thoughts for the royal patron of literature.

From the corridor the sound of singing reached his ears. Always those psalms! Clément Marot, hiding in Italy, had scored his last and greatest success with these renderings of the psalms into metrical French. For some years now it had been fashionable to sing or recite them at the Court. Everybody had his favourite one, and the warring factions found them useful slogans. Catherine, the humble little Catherine, was fond of one which began:

*Vers l'Eternel, des oppressés le Père,*

and Francis had often thought, when she sang it, how unhappy her life must be, for the graceless cub Henry had no eyes for anyone but Diane. But Catherine would come through it, she was clever. It had been a back-handed blow of fortune for Pope Clement to die just when the alliance had been so carefully secured, but it had been pleasant, with or without an alliance, to have the little Medici about the Court.

But these psalms. Francis had had his own psalm, like everyone else, but he knew the whole thing was insincere. It had not been like the Bible readings that Margaret had arranged. Margaret was serious, a little heavy at times perhaps, but exquisitely witty when she had a mind to it, and with more ideas in her head than the rest of the Court put together. If it had not been for Margaret he would not be feeling so calm now, in pain and in the face of death—not frightened or resentful, only rather wistful for the wonderful days long ago, and bewildered by the new currents that had left him powerless even to save his friends from death. It was not everyone who chose such humble expressions of resignation as Catherine. The comminatory psalms were the most popular, anything with hatred in it. They were good, sonorous psalms, but hatred was going to take a terrible toll of French blood. It had begun already. There was the Vaudois suppression, Cardinal de Tournon's job. Three thousand men, women and children massacred in cold blood, two hundred and fifty-six summarily executed, six hundred sent to the galleys, children sold as slaves. Thank God the soldiers who had been sent for the purpose had refused to carry it out! They had been replaced, of course, and when the letters patent approving of the butchery had been brought to Francis he had signed them. How could he have refused? When men got this virus in them they were beyond control. Better to let them kill a few hundred heretics now than have the whole country reeking with civil war. And the Pope had been pleased. That might be good for France when all was forgotten. Or it might not, for Popes were slippery allies. Francis did not know, and he was tired of it all. And though there had been other massacres, and treachery, and botched trials, and unjust edicts, in these latter years, his conscience was not greatly troubled. He had shown his people the glory of a cultured monarchy, he had protected the scholars and poets who were giving France her place in the Republic of

Letters, and if men turned and preferred to hunt heresy he did not see that he could be blamed.

But those psalms. Francis would not be the last to smell bloodshed in them. There were Puritans and Covenanters to come, and in his own country the Florentine Dauphiness would before long find less humble psalms to sing.

At last he knew that his fifty-four years' masquerade was over. Death was close upon him. He sent for his successor.

Like young English Harry, the Dauphin had already tried on the crown. It was of little use for Francis to warn him against the Guises and Montmorency, for Henry fully intended to restore the Constable as soon as he was King, and the Guises were his friends. Speaking with great difficulty, his father tried to show him the perils of religious controversy into which he was too eager to rush, the danger of affording ambitious men a cause for which to fight. He urged him to reduce taxation wherever possible, to labour to restore the confidence of a nation which would bear any impositions so long as it had the glory of national expansion in return, but would turn rebellious at the first failure in foreign policy. He commended the Duchess d'Étampes to his protection, for he was persuaded that she had never acted against the interests of the monarchy. Again it was "Beware the Guises!" and then the dying King took his son in his arms and blessed him. The chaplain approached the bedside, and Francis repeated the name of God until he could no longer speak. Still making with his fingers the sign of the cross he lay back and died.

It was no ordinary king who died at Rambouillet. He has been extravagantly praised and extravagantly vilified, but he remains somewhere in the company of Louis XI, Henry IV and Louis XIV. All had their glaring faults, and only Louis XI can be commended for his thrift, for thrift is a rare virtue among kings. In the last years of his reign Francis made conscientious efforts to economise, but the damage had already been done. Not till the trade expansion of the eighteenth century did the country recover its credit, and then there were the Bourbons to pay for. France subsisted, and would continue to subsist, on her soil, and the peasants were mercilessly taxed to assist the luxury trades of other countries. In 1542, five years before the end of the reign, Matteo Dandolo wrote to Venice that in Normandy "the peasants are fleeing with their children on their backs, not knowing where to go, hopeless refugees, rendered destitute by the taxes." There had been serious riots in different parts of the country in protest against the salt tax—that notorious *gabelle* which was later to become a battle-cry; and distress and disorder were increased by the disbanded troops that roamed the countryside, unpaid, hungry and armed.

It is by no means a vision of national contentment. But behind those glittering façades which tend inevitably to become the stuff of history there were similar scenes to be witnessed all over Europe, and our own glorious Elizabethan age does not look quite the same from both sides. The people pay and go on paying, and will do so, perhaps, to the end of time. The question is what do they get in exchange?

They got from Francis a monarchy developed to such a pitch of absolutism that while it lasted everything would depend upon the character of the sovereign. Weak rulers like the sons of Catherine and Henry would leave France at the mercy of palace intrigue. A strong man like Henry of Navarre, with nothing but his sword, his white plume and his energy to recommend him, would have the chance of saving the country and would take it.

Francis himself was too easily influenced to be the great king that he might have been and that France needed. Guizot called him a "brilliant spoiled child." Treated from his earliest years almost as a god, it was only to be expected that he would sometimes fail to be a man. "My Cæsar, my son!" murmured Louise of Savoy, bending over his cradle, and his sister Margaret wrote to him: "I was yours before you were born. You are more to me than father, mother and husband. Compared to you, husband and children count as nothing." His most devoted friends were all women.

Yet he managed to survive two things which might have wrecked lesser characters—the triumph of Marignano and the disaster of Pavia. His knightliness was not all a parade. He loved honour and plain dealing, he hated treachery and cruelty. But treachery and cruelty were part and parcel of the dazzling epoch in which he lived, and weakly he allowed himself to be led into them, sincerely believing that he was thereby avoiding worse evils. He foresaw the suffering that France was to undergo as the battle-ground of the Reformation, but he cannot be blamed for it.

If he remained too much under feminine influence, he was more fortunate than later monarchs in his choice of women. Among his male advisers were two of the noblest servants that France ever knew—the brothers du Bellay,—and though he recognised too late the folly of Montmorency, his judgment of the Guises was correct from the start. In foreign policy the Emperor again and again made rings round him, but it was small disgrace to be beaten by the cleverest politician in Europe. The alliances with the Turks and with the Lutheran Princes of Germany were bold and intelligent measures for which Francis earned the obloquy of Catholic historians.

Louis XII had steered France out of the Middle Ages. Francis helped her to take her place as a modern power. His concordat with the Pope, his foundation of the Royal College, the rise of schools and hospitals, the development of silk, printing and banking in Lyons, were all pointers towards the France that was later to emerge from the civil wars. By centralising social and political life in his own Court he dealt a shrewd blow at feudalism and made much easier the later work of Richelieu in hammering down the power of the nobles. From the reign of France began the steady severance of the link between lords and lands, which may be regarded as beneficial or otherwise according to one's view of the feudal system. Two and a half centuries later these superb aristocrats, as distant from their ancient subjects as heaven from earth, went to their arrogant deaths at the hands of a class on whom they had scarcely deigned to set eyes since Francis had summoned their titled ancestors to his side.

The aspect of the King's character which chiefly commends itself to modern sensation-seekers has already been dealt with at perhaps excessive length. But in order to avoid the charge of partiality it may be well to add the terse verdict of one who did not approve. Miss Julia Pardoe, in her standard biography of Francis, wrote:

"We dare not comment upon this frightful feature of the reign of Francis I; but as faithful chroniclers we are compelled to record that while the highest honours of profligacy were unanimously awarded to the King himself, the second were conceded to the Cardinal of Lorraine, one of the first prelates of the kingdom."

A medal in the Victoria and Albert Museum bears on one side a portrait of Francis in profile, and on the other his athletic figure seated upon a leaping horse, in the attitude of the English St. George, bearing victoriously down, not upon a dragon, not upon the Calydonian boar, but upon a beautiful girl. "The sooner assaulted, the sooner we shall be taken and captured."

At Saint-Cloud an effigy was made of the dead sovereign and placed upon a bed covered with cloth of gold edged with ermine. On the head was a velvet cap and crown, in the right hand a sceptre, in the left a hand of justice—a somewhat sinister arrangement. The body of the effigy was clothed in a shirt of crimson satin, and a tunic of blue satin sprinkled with the royal lilies of France. From the shoulders was draped a mantle of violet velvet, embroidered likewise with fleurs-de-lis and trimmed with ermine. "Morning and evening," wrote a Venetian spectator, "at the usual hours they brought wherewith to dine and sup, with the same ceremonies and forms as they use with the living person of the King. And when this had continued for some days they took off the royal robes and clothed it in mourning. And forty-eight friars stood beside it, singing Mass every day and all day long, and performing other holy offices for the salvation of his soul." Meanwhile the real body was placed in a coffin and carried in solemn procession to Saint-Denis, last resting-place of the Kings of France. Those notables who were unable or unwilling to be present at the obsequies sent effigies of themselves instead. And while the waxen figures played out the last act of the passing pageant, the men whom they represented plotted and planned the new order.

The great courtyard at Fontainebleau is called nowadays the *Cour des Adieux,* because it was here, on the horseshoe staircase of Francis I, that Napoleon stood to take leave of the Imperial Guard on his abdication. With the year 1547 comes the first farewell of Fontainebleau—farewell to its creator. The palace was to witness many historic scenes—the arrest of Biron by Henry IV, the Revocation of the Edict of Nantes, the abdication of Napoleon. Catherine de' Medici would still walk its shining galleries, and the Valois kings, and the gallant Bearnais, and the *Roi Soleil,* and Mme. de Maintenon, and Pope Pius VII, and Marie-Antoinette, and Louis-Philippe. But Francis had ridden out for the last time on his last and lonely hunt. Farewell, with his splendid talents and his disastrous faults, to the salamander King.

# III

# QUEEN-CONSORT ··

## SAINT-GERMAIN-EN-LAYE

I T was midsummer of 1547. The new reign had opened
with customary pomp, and King Henry had had all the
robes and ornaments of consecration renewed for his anoint-
ing at Rheims. His own royal garments, and even the festive
hangings, were sprinkled with that significant cipher upon
which Catherine had perforce to school herself to look with
outward calm—the double D linked with an H. With the
exercise of a charitable imagination, it was possible to con-
strue this D as a C, for the monogram was thus:

But nobody chose to take it that way. There were no two
opinions about it. The Italian woman might be consort in
her legal right, but the ruler of Henry was the shrewd
Frenchwoman Diane. Everywhere those linked initials of
the King and his mistress spread their confident challenge.
We find them carved on stone balustrades, painted on the
margins of portraits, woven into tapestries, embroidered on
church hassocks, printed in the dedication pages of books,
signed at the foot of the letters that passed between Henry
and Diane. Occasionally, very occasionally, we come upon
some portrait painted to the order of the Queen, and on its
frame another cipher, one that clearly shows the difference.
For here the C is shown unequivocally:

97

From a platform constructed to the design of Philibert de l'Orme, Catherine looked on while the crown was set upon the head of the husband who cared nothing for her. She was twenty years younger than Diane, and she had been pregnant six months with her third royal child. The reign of her rival could not last for ever. Catherine must wait, and the waiting helped to make her into the Medici monster of legend. It was a trial from which few women could have emerged unembittered.

Now it was midsummer, and in a meadow beside the château of Saint-Germain the stage was set for one of the strangest spectacles of the age—the last full-blooded judicial combat in history. Feudalism had been called back to satisfy Renaissance rivalries.

In the royal tribune, richly hung with silks and banners, Diane sat beside the King. The quarrel was partly hers, as will presently be seen. The ladies and gentlemen of the Court were present in full muster, among them the Constable de Montmorency, restored by the new sovereign to the rank and position in the national counsels from which Francis I had degraded him.

To right and left were the tents of the respective combatants, with their gonfalons scarcely moving in the still air of summer. And below the Constable's seat stood five figures masked and draped in black—the executioner and his assistants. Their task would be, if either combatant were slain, to drag his corpse to the gibbet as that of a felon.

Behind the barricades a vast crowd had been waiting since early morning for the unusual spectacle that was promised them. They had streamed out from Paris in their thousands, lesser gentry, rising bourgeois, unemployed soldiers, students, artists, market-women, pedlars, whores and vagabonds, and the archers of the Royal Guard had had hard work to keep them off the field of combat. Quacks, conjurers, thieves and enterprising vendors of fruit and fish and love had found the occasion as good as a fair, and the taverns of Paris were expecting brisk business that evening. Already it was six o'clock, and most of the spectators had been waiting all day under the hot sun, among the jests and smells of their neighbours.

But now at last the Herald of Guienne stepped forth, magnificent in his silken tabard. A hush fell upon the crowd. Things were beginning.

The Herald paced the length of the lists, and at each end he proclaimed in a loud voice:

"This day, the tenth of the month of July present, our sovereign lord the King hath ordered and granted free and fair field for mortal combat to François de Vivonne, Sieur de la Châtaignerie, assailant, and to Guy Chabot, Sieur de Monlieu, assailed, to resolve by arms the question of honour which is at issue between them. Wherefore I make known to all, in the King's name, that none may turn aside the course of the present combat, neither aid nor hinder either of the combatants, on pain of death."

Those are the combatants, Vivonne and Chabot, the latter more usually known by his other title of Jarnac. And while the long ceremonies of preparation are being solemnly enacted—the honouring of the field by the *cortège,* the *concordance des armes,* the oaths taken in the presence of a priest by each combatant that he has no charms and incantations for the injury of his enemy—while these are lasting their full hour, we may examine the issue for which the champions are met.

It had happened in the reign of Francis, but that notable

hater of brawling had refused his permission for the fight to take place. Jarnac, a man of about thirty-six, had been brought up in the King's household, and though a studious, quiet and relatively unathletic courtier, had earned honour in the wars. He enjoyed not only the favour of Francis but also, it is said, that of the Duchess d'Étampes, and there was a story that only the sacrifice of the reputation of one of the serving-ladies of Mme. d'Étampes had saved the pair from discovery by Francis *in flagrante delicto*. The King's mistress, at all events, had found Jarnac a convenient wife in her own sister, and he was further protected by his stepmother, a wealthy heiress who assisted his meagre fortunes in the matter of keeping up appearances in the luxurious Court. One day at Compiègne, Jarnac replied to a question put by the Dauphin Henry that his stepmother kept him, meaning simply that she provided him with very necessary funds. The admission was deliberately misconstrued, and the whole Court was soon aware that Jarnac had boasted of being the lover of his stepmother.

This was much more serious than the ordinary gossip of *Messieurs et Mesdames les Belles-Bouches,* as the Court scandal-mongers were playfully called. It was a blow struck at the all-powerful Duchesse d'Étampes, and either Henry or Diane de Poitiers, or more probably both of them together, must have purposely spread the calumny.

Jarnac made a public repudiation of the charge and demanded redress. But the Dauphin, debarred by his rank from duelling, was awkwardly placed. If nobody came forward to defend the matter he must accept tacit humiliation.

In this situation Vivonne de la Châtaignerie perceived an opportunity of advancing himself by serving the cause of the future sovereign. He was ten years younger than Jarnac, who was one of his closest friends, but he threw the friend-ship aside in the interests of his ambition, and declared that it was to him that Jarnac "had cynically boasted of the

HENRI II ROY DE FRANCE

HENRY II
By François Clouet
(Louvre)

culpable conduct which he had later thought proper to
deny." Henry and Diane had found a formidable champion,
for Vivonne was unanimously accounted the best swordsman
in France.

But Francis, advised presumably by his mistress, who saw
no hope of Jarnac emerging alive from a meeting with
Vivonne, was adamant. Not only did he refuse permission
for the disused feudal right of judicial combat, "the issue of
which could bring no profit to the kingdom," but he forbade the quarrellers, under the strictest penalties, to indulge
even in an ordinary duel.

From his tomb in Saint-Denis, however, Francis could no
longer prevent a fight upon which not only Jarnac and
Vivonne, but the rival interests which they represented, continued to insist. Henry was on the throne, Diane in the seat
of Madame d'Étampes, and the fallen royal favourite banished to her estates. Vivonne renewed his challenge and
Jarnac announced his readiness to disprove by force of arms
the accusation that had been brought against him. The King
granted the necessary approval, and the crowds gathered at
Saint-Germain to witness the historic trial by combat.

And now the champions are in the field, and their seconds
have retired to their pavilions. *"Laissez aller les bons com-
battants!"* cried the Herald of Normandy.

Vivonne has boasted openly that he will make mincemeat
of this clumsy miscreant who is rash enough to oppose the
shrewdest sword-arm in the land. Nobody in that vast throng
of excited onlookers can be found to take a wager against
him, and in his pavilion a great banquet is already spread
to await his certain victory. But Jarnac has a burning wrong
to avenge, and he has had ample time to prepare himself.
He has taken lessons from an Italian fencing-master, he has
thought everything out, and his friends have been busy with
suggestions. As the one assailed, he has the inalienable right
of choosing whether the combat shall be on horse or on foot,

and of specifying the weapons. He has chosen cunningly, so cunningly that Vivonne held up the proceedings for some time with an objection, but was overruled by the Marshals. The fight is on foot, and the armour, shields, two-edged swords and short daggers are of the ancient type, heavy and hampering. Vivonne has a celebrated trick of leaping upon his opponent like a bear, throwing him to the ground, and there dispatching him. But this terrifying method of attack is now made exceedingly difficult. Vivonne has also, as Jarnac knows, an ancient wound in the right arm. With his iron *brassards* and gauntlets, his enormous sword will not be easy to wield.

Nevertheless, Vivonne strides forward with raised weapon as if a single blow will finish the matter. Jarnac advances more slowly, in a crouching attitude, his shield and sword on the defensive. The spectators hold their breath. It is the most thrilling moment they may ever know.

Vivonne relies on his well-tried tactics. With a terrible slash at Jarnac's head he leaps upon him. It looks like the end, and a beautifully bloody one for the crowd.

But Jarnac was ready. The blow has struck his shield, and his own sword is free, free as he stoops to thrust viciously at his opponent's knee. Vivonne staggers, not badly hurt, but completely surprised. And in that fatal moment Jarnac has brought the other edge of his sword across the same mark, a back-handed cut which severs the tendons and brings his man to the ground in a pool of blood.

The spectators can scarcely believe their eyes. The fight is over but the result is a miracle. A great shout goes up from the Constable's tribune, for Montmorency is on Jarnac's side and he is surrounded by his friends. Henry and Diane stare straight in front of them, deathly pale.

"Vivonne," cries Jarnac, to his fallen enemy, "give me back my honour, and commend yourself to the mercy of God and His Majesty for the evil you have done!"

Vivonne tries to rise, but sinks back again, and Jarnac, approaching the royal tribune, salutes the King, begs for the restoration of his good name, and formally surrenders his opponent to his decision, death or life.

But Henry has no word to say. Three times Jarnac appeals to him, while Vivonne, bleeding profusely, refuses to retract. All eyes are turned upon the King, and the Constable approaches him, urging that only he can save the life of his defeated champion.

At last Jarnac, indignant at the injustice put upon him, can contain himself no longer. To the King's sister he cries in a bitter voice that all can hear: "Madame, you told me that it would be thus!"

Now it is exposed to all the world. Jarnac had been warned that not even his victory would turn the royal prejudice. The murmur of the crowd rises. King Francis would not so have sullied his honour.

In face of that sinister cry Henry must break silence. His voice is cold and perfunctory as he says: "You have done your duty, Jarnac, and your honour must needs be restored to you." Then, turning to the Constable, he gives orders for the disposal of the stricken Vivonne, now in his last extremity.

The formalities must be gone through. Jarnac has the right to a triumphant march from the lists, but wisely he forgoes it and submits himself humbly to the King, who grudgingly pays him the conventional tribute that he has "fought like Cæsar and spoken like Aristotle."

It is not only Vivonne who is struck. The party of the Guises, who rely upon Diane and the King, has suffered a blow. The Constable is louder than Jarnac in delight at the victory. It is the first bloody engagement of a terrible feud. Feudalism has opened the lists for the religious wars of the Renaissance.

The stands are empty. The King and his Court have retired to the château in the fading light of this memorable June evening. And the crowd, bursting the barriers that have hemmed it in all day, streams across the field of combat to the pavilion of Vivonne, where the banquet awaits the victory that was to be. "The soups and entrées," says Vieileville in his memoirs, "were devoured by an infinite number of harpies, the silver plate and the handsome sideboards, borrowed from seven or eight households of the court, were broken or carried off, amid indescribable tumult and confusion; and for dessert there were a hundred thousand blows from halberds and staves, distributed by the captains and archers of the Guard and the provosts, who fell upon them unexpectedly." It had been, at all events, a marvellous holiday.

Meanwhile, in another tent, the doctors have done their best for François de Vivonne, Seigneur de la Châtaignerie. They think, after all, that he will live. But he will not live. He tears the bandages from his wound and bleeds to death.

.    .    .    .    .    .

"As to what may come of the rivalry between the Grand Constable and the house of Lorraine," wrote an Italian observer at the beginning of the new reign, "all things are possible and even easy, seeing the natural tendencies of the nation, and the ordinary ways of the court. . . . The Constable and the younger members of that house, every day and every hour, give expression to their mutual affection. I have seen the Archbishop of Rheims make court to his Excellency, and go to meet him, and accompany him to table, and dine with him. Yet all are of opinion that in the end the house of Lorraine will beat him to the ground, though it cannot happen at once."

The house of Lorraine is the Guise family, and the younger members of that house, between whom and the Constables such honeyed words were now passing, were those Guises against

whom the dying Francis had vainly warned his son, telling
him that their aim was "to strip him and his children to
their doublets, and his people to their shirts." They were
the six sons among the ten children of Claude, Duke of Guise,
whose brother, John, was that Cardinal of Lorraine who had
been on such good terms with the late King. If Francis were
the secular leader of those pagan revels that have alternately
shocked and intrigued historians, then the Cardinal was their
high priest, and Brantôme tells us with an unusual and
probably ironic delicacy of language, that the gay churchman examined the qualities of each lady who entered the
court and initiated her into the cult of abandon in which she
would thenceforward participate.

Both Claude of Guise and his brother the Cardinal were
now old, and the interests of the family were in the ambitious
hands of the younger men, among whom the Archbishop of
Rheims mentioned by the Italian correspondent was to take
over the Lorraine Cardinalate when his illustrious uncle
came to die. It was a family rich in mitres and cardinals'
hats, a family whose power was essentially clerical. The elder
son, Francis of Lorraine, was a brilliant soldier, and these
Guises, proud, ambitious, Catholic, loose-living, but always
energetic, were eminently suited to be the cynical champions
of the Church Militant.

With the Guises was Diane, the key to power over King
Henry. Always conservative in mind, it consistently suited
Diane's interests to protect the Catholic cause, and the Guises
were her natural allies. She was accomplished as all high-
born women of her time were accomplished. She interested
herself in medicine, and a French doctor dedicated to her,
as to a fellow-practitioner, a treatise on feminine ailments.
She founded schools and orphanages, and she was responsible for the printing of *Amadis of Gaul*. But there her literary patronage ended, and the countless works of art which
are associated with her name owe their origin rather to the

implications of that name than to any direct effort of her own. When Philibert de l'Orme built the Château of Anet for her it was she who supervised the domestic arrangements, the orchards and gardens, for she was ever homely, a careful housekeeper, a gracious hostess, a good businesslike country lady of France. But it was her lover—who in lesser degree had inherited his father's artistic tastes—who took the deeper concern in the planning and decoration of Anet.

Diane was certainly no Margaret of Navarre. Such intellectual leanings as she had would never have been sufficient to turn her favour towards the Reformers, and she was confirmed in her reactionary attitude by the long years of enmity with the Duchesse d'Étampes, who was genuinely scholarly and had ably seconded Margaret's liberal influence with Francis I. When the new reign turned the tables on the former favourite the tables were turned also on the cause of the Reformers. The wisest and most pacific statesman could not henceforth have disentangled the religious issue from the palace rivalries.

Over against Diane and the Guises stood the restored Constable de Montmorency, and in this camp, naturally enough, was Catherine de' Medici. With the Duchesse d'Étampes she had connived at the disgrace of the Constable under Francis I, but that did not matter now. By the same token it was of no consequence that Montmorency had been friendly with the Guises when Henry was Dauphin. It was now necessary that he should oppose the predominating Guise influence on the King. The constantly shifting balance of power in the French Court carried religion with it, this way and that, until the whole country was involved in civil war. With Marot's psalms on their lips and murder in their hearts, caring not a rap for truth or religion or anything but their own advancement, the rival factions spat defiance at each other, manœuvring for position with diplomatic marriages of their young children and nephews and nieces, until the opportunity should come to turn upon each other the swords that were at present fully occupied against the Emperor.

Montmorency, as we have seen, was by conviction a staunch Catholic, but the present circumstances threw him with no great difficulty towards the Protestant side. Not only did op-position to the Catholics constitute opposition to the Guises, but there were among his own family some notable support-ers of the Reforming idea. The elder branch of the Mont-morency family was the house of Coligny, led by the Constable's nephews, the Three Colignys. One of them was a Cardinal, for Montmorency, as well as the Guises, could count a few cardinalates and bishoprics in his cards. This Cardinal Odet de Coligny was sufficiently advanced to have been the patron of Rabelais, who dedicated his "Fourth Book" to him, calling him "a second Gallic Hercules in Learn-ing, Prudence and Eloquence, and Alexicacos in Virtue, Power and Authority"—with other high-sounding titles worthy to be borne by one who protected an honest writer in those days of persecution and suppression. The liberal Cardinal had indeed, Whitehead relates, his Rabelaisian moods. "In 1547 he and his uncle, with the King, and the Cardinal of Guise, took part in what the shocked Ambassador of Ferrara called a revel of Sardanapalus; the Cardinal of Ferrara, more virtu-ous or more seemly, refused to be present. Five years later he was still a participant in pleasures which, if comparatively in-nocent, were at least unclerical. Thus in December, 1552, he was awakened at the dead of night, and swept along in a rout of churchmen and courtiers. . . . In the Farnese collection at Naples is to be found an odd leaf in Spanish without name or date, but evidently written before the fall of the Constable in 1541. It gives a not unrealistic sketch of two bathing scenes where the Court disported itself with the unforced gaiety of Pan and the Nymphs."

The Coligny on whose account the name is remembered was another of the three, a brother of Odet and nephew of

the Constable. At the Court of Francis Gaspard de Coligny
had not only tasted the Valois feast of pleasure but had
applied himself to study and made the acquaintance of
the leading Humanists. He was ready for Protestantism, the
cause that was to lead him to Saint Bartholomew. At the
accession of Henry he was twenty-eight years old, the same
age as Catherine. At once he became Colonel-General of the
French Infantry, and within five years Admiral of France.
With the Constable in supreme command of the army and,
as Grand Master, first Minister of the Crown, the powerful
Guises had here to face an opposition so well supplied with
estates and offices that for the first ten years of Henry's reign
the balance was evenly maintained.

Jarnac had won his fight. *Fifteen-love* to the Constable.
But a year after that thrilling combat in the meadow of
Saint-Germain, a royal galley put into the tiny Breton port
of Roscoff, and a fair-haired girl of six, in stiff brocaded
bodice and hooped skirt, stepped for the first time upon
shores of France. *Fifteen-all.*

This was Mary Stuart, the little Queen of Scotland, and
she had come to be betrothed to the Dauphin Francis, Catherine's sickly five-year-old son. From château to château she
travelled with her four Maries and the rest of her glittering
escort until she reached the Court at Saint-Germain, a
progress full of strange delights for the beautiful, wide-eyed
girl who at last would have to make another progress and a
terrible one, through Carbery, Loch Leven and Carlisle to
Fotheringay.

Mary had Guise blood in her veins. The marriage of Mary
of Guise to James V of Scotland ten years before had been
a shrewd political gamble. Two sons had been born to the
pair, and neither had survived infancy; and then, while
James turned his face to the wall at Falkland to die, a girl
was born at Linlithgow, "a very weak child and not like to
live." *It cam' wi' a lass and it'll gang wi' a lass.*

Storms raged round her cradle in Scotland as they had done round that of Catherine in Florence. Henry VIII had wanted her safely in England, where she could be married to Edward, Prince of Wales. He tried to kidnap her, but his agent in Scotland had to write to him that there was "some jugglery here." And so there was. After much sleight of hand the child was tossed out of Scotland into the waiting arms of France. The English bid to close that awkward Scottish back door which France was so fond of using had failed.

King Henry was away when Mary arrived in France, making with his mistress and his queen a tour of his southeastern possessions. But he had left full instructions as to the lodging of the little Queen at Saint-Germain. She was to be brought up as one of the Valois children, with his daughter Elizabeth, now three and a half years old, as her chief companion. Catherine de' Medici, after her hesitant entry into maternity, was proving remarkably prolific, and one remembers grimly the rôle that Diane played in this connection. "It is owing to her," writes Guiffrey, "that the King loves the Queen. It is owing to her he decides to fulfil the duties of a husband. At night, she urges him towards that bed to which desire cannot draw him. And perhaps Catherine de' Medici should owe some gratitude to Diane de Poitiers for this odious intervention, since it is thus that she will be able to become the mother of a whole line of kings."

We may reasonably doubt whether Catherine, in her intolerable position, spared very much gratitude for her rival. But the game that she was able to play with her progeny was an astonishing one even in those days of dynastic chess. In thirteen years she brought ten children into the world, of whom three died in their cradles. Of them all only two survived her and only one lived beyond the age of forty. This one, Margot of Navarre, who died at sixty-two and left a name to conjure with, was the only one who was at all robust, for the old Medici weakness, reasserting itself in alternate generations, cropped up again in Catherine's children. And yet this is the record of her family: three successive Kings of France, of whom one was for a year King of Poland, one Queen of France (Margot married Henry of Navarre), and a Queen of Spain (Elizabeth married Philip II). It was very much more than Diane could promise herself.

At Saint-Germain, therefore, which in the early part of his reign was Henry's favourite residence, the royal cradle was seldom empty, and Mary Stuart was assured of a succession of playmates worthy of her rank. The King decided at once that she must be allowed to take precedence over the Valois princesses, both in view of her own high station and of her betrothal to the Dauphin. Suitable apartments were prepared for her, and ladies and gentlemen-in-waiting appointed for her service. Her Scottish escort was sent home again, all but Lady Fleming, her governess, who had contrived to make an immediate and favourable impression at Court. She was thirty-five, and a widow, but she seemed to have Diane's secret of perpetual youth, and when the King returned from his progress he paid her much gracious attention, to such a point that at length she was indiscreet enough to exclaim in the general hearing, "God be praised, I am with child by the King!"

And so she was. Infatuation for Diane and the performance of the marital duty for Catherine had not prevented Henry from yielding to the peculiar charms of Lady Fleming. It was evidently a brief passion, inspired most probably by a sudden wayward thirst for physical novelty, and if we except the doubtful story of the Piedmontese woman while he was still Dauphin, this seems to be the only occasion on which he strayed from the path that he had chosen between wife and mistress.

It led, at all events, to the only case of concerted action between Catherine and Diane, who both exerted instant pressure on Henry. Lady Fleming was banished and her son was brought up quietly as the Bastard of Angoulême. We shall not meet him again until the morning of Saint Bartholomew.

It was not jealousy which so strangely united the Queen and the concubine on this occasion. Diane was too sure of her power to succumb to jealousy, and Catherine had learned in a hard school not to give way to it. They were actuated above all by fear of a scandal which might prejudice the political aims of both. Lady Fleming had been foolish enough to boast of her affair with the King, and that was unforgivable. For Diane throughout her life maintained a curious dignity in her relationship with her lover. She allowed their joint monogram to scatter itself through France, but neither Henry nor herself permitted any indelicate references to their love in this Court that lived on scandal. Poets and painters perpetually called in allegory to sing their praises, and though nobody in France was unaware of their true connection one might be forgiven, for all the public reference to it, for imagining that they found nought but philosophy in each other's arms. Henry, the unpromising youth whom Diane made into a poet as well as a ruler, was her troubadour. Their relation was of that extra-marital variety which the troubadours held to be the only pure love. And just as the old Counts of Toulouse had thrown gold to the troubadours who made their courtly advances to their Countesses, so Catherine was expected to smile complacently at the romantic devotion of her husband to his mistress. This was the superficial remnant of that Platonism which the learned Margaret, now dead with her brother Francis, had so rapturously embraced. Smile Catherine did, but it was a Medici smile, the smile of one who awaits with superhuman patience the advent of her hour.

The Lady Fleming affair proved another point to the Guises. For Diane was convinced that the Constable de Montmorency had had something to do with it, perhaps that he had led Henry to the Scotswoman's bed as she had led him to that of Catherine. Hitherto, in consideration of the King's great affection for the Constable, she had not thrown the whole of her weight into the Guise side of the balance. But henceforward she was whole-heartedly of their party.

"Madame (Diane) complained bitterly," says the Italian Contarini, "and the King had to offer many apologies. For a long time the Constable and Madame were not even on speaking terms. At length, at His Majesty's entreaty, they made a semblance of a peace, but at bottom their hatred is as bitter as ever. Hence have arisen the two parties which are like two factions at the Court, and he who draws near to one knows assuredly that he must expect nothing but hostility from the other."

This was the atmosphere into which Mary Stuart was plunged at the age of six. It was the atmosphere that made her tragedy, for in an age of cynicism sincerity courts tragedy, and Mary, growing up swiftly and precociously, soon showed that she had that dangerous quality of sincerity. Coligny had it, too, and his end was terrible. The faith which he learned to embrace with all the honesty of his noble temperament was Protestantism. Mary's was Catholicism, and almost alone among the great men and women of her day whose lives were conditioned by religious struggles, she loved her faith. In this sixteenth century which opened with a burning enthusiasm for a new philosophy and a new freedom of the senses, and closed in cold-blooded civil strife in which religion and love were nothing but political instruments, Mary's character seems as though it had been deliberately brought in by the hidden playwright to add poignancy to the drama and bring down the curtain on a tearful second act. For she was warm-hearted. She loved by instinct and not by deliberation. Her straightforward sexuality was incomprehensible in a period of expediency-worship. While Catherine de' Medici played with marriages as if they were a pack of cards, and Elizabeth of England continued to hold the trump of her virginity until the end, Mary gave her body as her heart directed her. It is for this reason that she has left a legend unchallengeable by her more skilful and more successful contemporaries. It is for this reason that men still love her in spite of her crimes, and women still envy her in spite of her fate.

# LYONS

SECURELY set upon the confluence of two great rivers, Lyons was a proud city, proud of its long history, its learned men, its four annual fairs that attracted merchants from the whole of Europe and from Asia as well, its silk-looms and printing-houses and banks and hospitals; proud, too, of the traditional splendour with which it welcomed distinguished visitors, so that a Lyons triumph was second only to a triumph in the capital of France. When Francis I had made his progress through the city in 1526 his reception had been such as to form matter for an enormous descriptive volume which can still be read. In May and June, 1533, he had again established his Court there, while the negotiations for the marriage of his son to Catherine de' Medici were in progress. And now, in September, 1548, while Mary Stuart was making her way to Saint-Germain, Lyons decked itself afresh for its new sovereign.

The Emperor Agrippa had made the Roman colony of Lugdunum the point of intersection of four great highways. The Emperor Nero, whom posterity has not celebrated for salvage work, had given money for its rebuilding after the disastrous fire of A.D. 59. The Merovingian Childebert had founded, it was said, the hospital on the banks of the Rhône in which the beloved physician Rabelais became house doctor. Rabelais was but one of many giants of arts and learning who, esteeming it an honour to know Lyons in the sixteenth century, honoured it in their turn by their own accomplishments. Corneille de Lyon, who was to paint a portrait of Catherine de' Medici and her daughters, took his name from the city of his birth. The architect Philibert de l'Orme, the poets Mellin de Saint-Gelais, Clément Marot and Maurice

Scève, the antiquary Guillaume du Choul, the Hebraist
Sanctes Pagnini, Calvin, Béza, Dolet, Despériers—all had
recently helped to make Lyons a notable colony of the Republic of Letters. Most of them were dead now, for the
splendid days of learning were over. Dead, too, was Erasmus,
to whom all men of culture had looked as to a father. He
had known Lyons, and his secretary Bertoul had stayed long
enough in the city to provide his master with the material of
his inimitable "Colloquy" upon the local taverns.

But perhaps the most famous glory of Lyons was its women.
It was a city of wise and liberal government, beautiful
architecture and sumptuous living, for it lay on the high road
from France to Italy, speeding Frenchmen to the wars and
welcoming Italian scholars, artists, jewellers and bankers.
Its free-thinking atmosphere was to serve in punctuating its
history with exciting heresies and terrible massacres, but it
served also in making this Athens of France the nursery of a
remarkable creature—the woman of the French Renaissance.
To this topic we shall shortly return, and in particular to
Louise Labé, *La Belle Cordière,* or, as Miss Sichel calls her,
the George Sand of the Renaissance. At the moment it is
sufficient to mention her evocative name, and those of some
of her beautiful and learned companions—Claudine and
Sybille Scève (sisters of the gifted Maurice), Jacqueline
Stuart, Jeanne Gaillard, Pernette de Guillet, Clémence de
Bourges. Poetesses, musicians, lovers, their very names have
a lost magic in them. And the most fascinating woman of
her age, the royal Margaret of the *Heptameron,* had lived
often in Lyons, where lived and died so many of the great
men who gathered at her feet. It was her favourite city, and
she wrote a sad and lovely lyric to the rose tree in her garden there.

Lyons numbered many Florentines among its citizens,
and Catherine looked forward to the entry she was to make
with her husband as she seldom looked forward to such

elaborately empty shows. There was Florentine money in the great houses of exchange, there was Florentine influence in the architecture of the palaces of merchants and nobles, and there were Florentine cakes in the pastry-cooks' shops—cakes so succulent that their fame reached England, where an Elizabethan poet, addressing George Thornley on his translation of that delicious morsel *Daphnis and Chloe,* referred to them in his metaphor:

> Custards, Tarts, Puf-paste, Florentines of wit,
> For to refresh the Palate of thy mind.

Such refreshment Catherine hoped to find in Lyons, where the epithet of "the Italian woman" might be expected to shed its opprobrium. Diane, it was true, was of the party, but she was well accustomed to her presence, and in so progressive a centre as Lyons it might well be that Protestant influence would be strong enough to dispose the citizens against the staunchly Catholic mistress of the King.

On September 21 Catherine and Diane were joined at Ainay by the King, who had been busy with Montmorency suppressing with savage severity the insurrection against the taxes in Guienne—an insurrection which, it is true, had been responsible for almost equal barbarities towards officials and private persons. Two days later the three entered a vessel of state with their suite and sailed down the Rhône gorge to Vaise, where the first part of their reception took place in a gorgeous pavilion.

Again the grim monogram, the interlacing H and D! It was embroidered on the saddle-cloths of horses and the pennons that fluttered above the tent of honour. Where Catherine walked, she trod the symbol on thick carpets; when she sat down to receive the high representatives of the city, the letters were behind her on her chair of office, above her on the canopy. Yet all this might be borne as it had been borne before. The Lyonnais, generously-minded towards

Italy, might put upon the cipher that alternative interpreta-
tion of H and C. Catherine refused to be discouraged so early
in the ceremonies.

But at the next moment she knew that she had nothing
to hope from Lyons. The municipal dignitaries, after kneeling to pay their duty to the King, turned not to Catherine
but to Diane, to kiss the long fingers, white and well preserved, which held with such unassailable confidence the
reins that should have been in Catherine's own hands. That
homage done, the officers turned to Catherine, who sat pale
and upright in her chair, her brown eyes giving no sign of
what she was enduring. It was only a formality, but it would
have broken a weaker woman. "Never," says a biographer of
Henry II, "had a Queen of France to submit to so cruel a
humiliation; not even the long-suffering consort of Louis
XV."

*The magnificence of the superb and triumphant entry into
the noble and ancient city of Lyons accorded to the Most
Christian King of France, Henry the second of that name and
to the Queen Catherine his wife, the XXIII of September,*
1548. That is the title of the account of the fêtes printed at
Lyons in the following year. No mention of Diane. All is
carried through with the strictest propriety, but it is obvious
to every eye which of the two women is being honoured by
the Lyonnais.

In the midst of the city an artificial forest had been planted.
Lightly attired for the chase, the loveliest girls of Lyons make
their way between the trees. The leader of this bevy of
nymphs steps briskly forward in the buskins of the goddess of
hunting, her young, athletic body scarcely covered by the
chlamys of the ancients, one breast bared to view. The crescent gleams in her hair, the quiver hangs from her shoulder,
and in her left hand is a golden bow. With her right she
leads on a silver chain a live lion, representing the trophy
of her chase. King Henry is her Actæon, observing with a

gracious eye the supple curves of the goddess, but visited with no punitive metamorphosis. Instead he receives an address in verse, spoken in a clear voice by the lion-taming nymph. The captured beast which she begs him to accept is the symbol of the city of Lyons, offering itself submissively to its august sovereign. A pretty conceit, charmingly carried out, and greatly enjoyed by the onlookers.

But the symbol which impresses itself upon every memory is not that of the lion but that of Diana, the goddess of the hunter's moon whose earthly prototype rides behind her royal Endymion in her robe of black and white.

On the following day a second entry was staged, this time specifically for the Queen. Catherine was carried in a richly decked litter through the city, her clothes ablaze with diamonds, her dark eyes wide and watchful. Cheers echoed from the tall houses, caps were flung in the air, flowers were scattered from window and balcony—but not for Catherine. Behind her rode Diane de Poitiers upon a black palfrey. Diane was by no means universally popular in France. The literature of the time, for all the courtly references to her beauty and her power, shows us also a good store of attack. Many called her an old hag who by magic incantations was able to keep the love of a witless king; others called her a harlot. The Protestant pamphleteers were particularly venomous, and between them and the chivalrous eulogisers it is often difficult to find our way to the real woman. But she had a power which Catherine, if she had ever possessed it, would hardly have cared to use. With her calm and self-assured smile she could rule every pageant and move a crowd of idle spectators to tumults of applause.

From the balcony of her house in the Rue Notre-Dame de Confort, overlooking the meeting of the two rivers, Louise Labé had watched the royal processions pass and had not failed afterwards to present herself to the King and Queen. She was twenty-two years old, with an intellectual brow, a lovely, sensual mouth, dark eyebrows and golden hair. The big house at the riverside corner was well known to the people of Lyons, and many a glance was cast up at the balcony by passers-by. For on this balcony, at certain times and seasons, the intoxicating Louise appeared at the request of the wise City Fathers, in order that the citizens, gazing upon her, might be confirmed in their love of beauty.

Louise had met Henry before. It was said, indeed, that she had lost her heart to Henry when he was Dauphin. For at the age of sixteen, when the French army passed through Lyons with Henry in the van, she had put on full armour, mounted a mettlesome horse, and ridden off with them to the siege of Perpignan, returning to Lyons only when the French had won the day.

Now she lived with her husband in that celebrated house, with its balcony and its library and the big room downstairs where she received her friends and admirers and ruled her circle of polished intellects; and behind the house was a shady garden, with lawns and flower-beds, fountains and pleached alleys. Her husband was a cordwainer, as her father had been—hence her popular title of *La Belle Cordière*. He deserves well of posterity, this honest ropemaker, content to look after his wife and receive from her a purely formal affection, while she lavished her passion on a brilliant succession of lovers and her conversation on the first *salon* of France. Cuckoldry has for so many centuries been a staple jest that it is seldom indeed that the wearer of the horns can hope for justice. But when the noble history of complacent husbands comes to be written, the good *cordier* of Lyons will have his honourable place in it.

Not yet had Louise Labé met the man who was to stir her deepest emotions and inspire her poetry till it rose from the rigid correctitude of a Petrarchan scholar to the passionate lyricism that has come down to our own day as fresh and moving as when it was written in that vanished garden of

Lyons. He was a poet himself, Olivier de Magny by name, now almost forgotten save for a few poems cherished by the erotically curious, for they deal in scrupulous detail with the beauty of his mistress. Yet, during the period of their love, before it was shattered by a misunderstanding, de Magny too wrote sonnets which are worth rescuing from neglect for their simplicity and personal feeling. But when it was all over he turned against her with a bitterness that injured more than her. For the cruel verse which he wrote in his revulsion of emotion was quoted everywhere and turned the ladies of Lyons from her company. When she died at the age of forty, however, the city whose glory she had so greatly enriched showed that she was still beloved. "Her funeral was a sort of triumph," Miss Sichel quotes a chronicler as saying; "she was carried through the city with her face uncovered, and her head crowned with flowers. . . . Death could do nothing to disfigure her, and the people of Lyons covered her grave with tears and with blossoms."

Under a date a few years later than that of the entry of the King and Queen into Lyons there is a letter from Louise Labé to Clémence de Bourges, her Sapphic friend. "I can do no more," writes Louise, "than implore virtuous ladies to raise their minds a little above their distaffs and their spindles. It is for them to rouse themselves and to show the world that, even if our sex were not born to command, we ought not to be despised as companions (whether in public or in private) of those who *are* born to rule: to rule and to be obeyed."

It is the woman of the early Renaissance who speaks here, the woman who was content to use her emancipation as an influence upon man rather than as a means of usurping his position. Repression is always based upon fear (or, as we were told in our schooldays, "the bully is always a coward") ; and two institutions—husbands and the Church—combined to produce the mediæval subjection of women. Both were ab-

jectly afraid, not only of women as individuals, but of the
woman-principle formed of man's desire, the Aphrodite
whom Christianity had perforce to make into a witch. The
ecclesiastical laws of marriage, neatly dovetailed into the
feudal property system, survive with but slight variations
to-day, and the history of sexual morals in Western Europe is
the history of man's escape from his own self-defensive laws
and of woman's use of his escapist impulse.

The Renaissance brought woman her opportunity, and the
emancipation which she achieved in the sixteenth century was
greater than anything she has achieved in the twentieth. But
the Renaissance was little more than a vast speeding up, aided
by the coincidence of a number of important circumstances,
of movements which can be traced much farther back in
history; and for centuries woman had been preparing herself
for the place which she was now to occupy. The very ceremonies of the religion that feared her had been turned to her
advantage, and at a time when the distractions of life as well
as its duties began and ended with the Church, an appropriate background had been found for the display of feminine
beauty of face and dress. White hands moved dazzlingly in
the rich gloom, praying and making the holy sign and sprin-
kling the holy water. Often a gallant would seize a swift opportunity of serving a lady with the water, or would pick up
the perfumed and jewelled glove that she had dropped at the
cathedral door, or pass her a *billet-doux* as she knelt beside
him at her devotions. The Pauline injunction—born of a custom localised in time and space—that woman's head should be
covered in church, bred a store of trouble for Paul's successors. Of all the feminine fashions stormed with clerical shot
and shell, and stormed quite ineffectively through the Middle
Ages, the headdress holds pride of place. Nations could be
excommunicated and emperors sent on barefoot pilgrimage
across the Alps, but the louder the objurgations of the bishops, the higher grew the fantastic headdresses of the women,

rearing their challenge of lechery under the eyes of the preachers who thundered that "the women that were so horned were like to be horned snails and harts and unicorns." Countless mediæval moralities of horned women torn by demons, and red-hot needles thrust into the brains of those who had plucked their eyebrows, testify to the Church's recognition of the erotic basis of fashion; and a knowledge of feminine nature is revealed in the direction of ecclesiastical attacks chiefly against the leaders and innovators of style. "The bishop," says the fourteenth-century Chevalier de la Tour Landry in his delightful and significant book of instruction for his daughters, "bad them leave these quaintnesses, for it is the sin of pride, and engendereth and kindleth lechery . . . and therefore it is great folly for any woman to bring up any new novelties of array . . . for they that take such arrays first shall be with God most blamed and have least pleasure and worship in heaven." In like manner were treated all measures for adornment and even for physical cleanliness, and the bath remained for many centuries a storm-centre of conflicting opinions. Saint Clement of Alexandria had permitted bathing in private provided it were undertaken solely in the interests of hygiene, but added the rider that to derive any pleasure from it was to be involved in sin. And as late as the fifteenth century Friar Olivier Maillard, a last representative of mediæval morality who drew crowded congregations by the picturesque vigour of his sermons, thus addressed ladies who took baths: "Ye women who stew yourselves, I summon you all to the stewpots of Hell!"

But no objection to baths could survive the revival of classical learning, and this favourite custom of the Romans became an important institution in the Renaissance courts, though we have the testimony of Montaigne that the habit fell away again at the end of the sixteenth century. Diane de Poitiers, like Poppæa, was credited with a bath of asses' milk,

and it is in her bath that Clouet has painted her in the celebrated picture belonging to Sir Herbert Cook—the parent-
painting of numerous imitations. She is shown in a charming
domestic setting with two children who may be those of
Henry and Catherine. One of them reaches a hand towards
the fruit beside her and the younger one is at the nurse's
breast, while in another room revealed in a mirror and taste-
fully decorated with a unicorn-screen (a Diana symbol?) and
a fine Venetian looking-glass, a serving-maid is busy about
her task. For the bath, as in Roman days, was held to provide
an excellent setting for conversation.

And at that word "conversation" the Renaissance rises
before us with its peerless women. In her long period of
waiting for this apotheosis woman had taken such opportunities as were allowed her for the development of this
pacific art, and had earned a reputation dear to mediæval
farce, the reputation of one who with her tongue and her
brain could capture or deceive the sex which relied for its
superiority upon physical strength. The knights went off to
Palestine for the masculine duties that were their perpetual
glory and solace, leaving their women behind them to ply
the distaff and make their orisons and chatter to their hearts'
content. Not infrequently the Crusader locked up his wife's
body as he locked up his other earthly possessions when he
departed to fight for the Sepulchre. But the *ceinture de
chasteté* was nothing more than a challenge to a locksmith,
and even where virtue resisted the advances of those despised
males who, more cunning with a lute than with a sword,
were left behind when warlike business was afoot, the long
months of waiting were an invitation to the practice of conversation, music, poetry, study and all such pursuits as might
be undertaken with a moderately clear conscience.

In the reign of Louis XII, Miss Sichel relates, there was a
lady with political ambitions who earned a royal reproof
for her bold interference. "In the times," she replied, "when

Lords and Princes went to the Crusades and achieved great feats, there was nothing for us poor women to do but to pray and watch and fast and make vows, so that God might give them a prosperous voyage and a safe return. But nowadays, when we see that they accomplish no more than we do, it is quite right for us to talk about everything. For why on earth should we pray God for them, considering they are no better than ourselves?" It was an embarrassing question to answer, and one which Louis had invited by helping to open up to France the glories of Italian art and learning.

For the Renaissance provided a field in which women could at last compete on an equal footing with men. The newly discovered classics were open to all who had the money to buy books and manuscripts and the diligence to study them, and although woman must apparently remain second to man in point of creative genius, she had in some ways an advantage over the sex that had hitherto been so deeply engrossed in physical pursuits. The feminine cunning which in the mediæval stories so easily deceives the pitiful stupidity of a jealous husband, is given at the Renaissance the chance of becoming feminine scholarship.

In Castiglione's *Courtier,* the greatest book of conversation since Plato's *Symposium,* the gentleman who wishes to perfect himself is urged to give long hours to study, "for beside the contentation that he shall receive thereby himself, he shall by this means never want pleasant entertainments with women which ordinarily love such matters." Already the Renaissance woman is setting a standard. Music was higher as an art than poetry, painting, embroidery, all of which were necessary accomplishments, but conversation was the highest art of all. It was in conversation, which Erasmus sportively labels an insidious vice "wherewith I am more often drunken than with wine," that women wielded their greatest power.

In all this ceaseless flow of talk there was doubtless much

that was trivial and much that was too stiffly rhetorical. But one could wish that some adventure like that of the Frozen Words which befell Rabelais' Pantagruel and his companions might give us back the best of those lost conversations. Pantagruel's experience is based upon a phenomenon first mentioned by Plutarch. There had been, it appeared, a great battle on the confines of the Arctic Ocean, and the words and cries and boom of guns and trampling of horses that issued therefrom had been immediately frozen, to be released from their cold storage by milder weather long afterwards in the hearing of the astonished voyagers. Such a miracle, in terms of modern scientific discovery, might recapture the sweet cadence of sixteenth-century French and Elizabethan English and Risorgimento Italian, falling from lips that every poet in Europe praised. Much has come down to us of this conversation. We can still read, though we may not hear, the discourse of Boccaccio's noble refugees in the walled garden of Fiesole, of Castiglione's friends at the Court of Urbino, and of the company of the *Heptameron* on one side of their hedge in France, while the monks listen so long on the other side that they arrive at vespers quite out of breath. But much also is irrevocably lost.

The great individuals detach themselves one by one from the bright throng of laughing, dancing, chattering nymphs who could write a sonnet, sing a ballad, take a lover, gallop over the frontier, gently argue a doctor to a standstill on the subject of the Aphorisms of Hippocrates, a scholar on the Aristotelian and Platonic cosmogonies, a theologian on the nature of vice and virtue. There is Margaret of Valois, of Angoulême, or of Navarre—which you will—with her coterie of eager intellects. There is Louise Labé with the body of Aphrodite and the mind of Athene and the lyre of Sappho; there is Vittoria Colonna, who enslaved the titanic passion of Michelangelo, so that we read: "He for his part so loved her that I remember to have heard him say that he regretted nothing except that when he went to visit her upon the moment of her passage from this life he did not kiss her forehead or her face, as he did kiss her hand. Her death was the cause that oftentimes he dwelt astonied, thinking of it even as a man bereft of sense." There is Botticelli's *Bella Simonetta,* whose eyes, laden with the world's love and the world's sorrow, gaze at us perhaps from his Anadyomene; and there is the mistress whose bed Giorgione would not forsake even when she fell ill of the plague, so that he too died. Most remote of all from our own exhausted civilisation there is Tullia d'Aragona, the courtesan who for her great beauty and learning was excused the wearing of the yellow veil which was otherwise obligatory for her calling. She is the *hetaira* of Periclean Athens reborn in more perfect form, the woman who satisfies the new and immeasurable yearnings of men's minds as she satisfies their bodies, and is honoured for it by rich and poor. When she reaches the Court of Ferrara it is matter for the Mantuan envoy to send off a dispatch. "I have to record," he writes, "the arrival amongst us of a gentle lady, so modest in behaviour, so fascinating in manners, that we cannot help considering her something divine; she sings impromptu all kinds of airs and motets; she keeps herself in touch with the events of the day, and we cannot suggest a subject with which she does not appear conversant. There is not one lady in Ferrara, not even the Duchess of Pescara (Vittoria Colonna) that can stand comparison with Tullia."

For these women of the early Renaissance their rôle in life is clear, and willingly they make their contribution to their age. In Castiglione's book it is decided by the debaters that "man has for his portion physical strength: all doing must be his; all inspiration must come from woman. . . . Without women nothing is possible, either in military courage, or art, or poetry, or music, or philosophy, or even religion. God is truly seen only through them." And in the time of Francis I it is said that "a Court without women is like a garden without flowers."

For a time, in a garden so beautiful, they were content to be flowers, for it was a very different proposition from that which confronted the women who went before them. They had the power now, and perhaps they could keep it for ever. They used it well, toning down blood-sports, alleviating the horrors of war, and by their artistry and wit preventing a joyous freedom of manners from degenerating into coarseness. They gave liberally the pleasures that were sought of them and received with a gentle smile the wealth that was poured at their feet. If Plato and Macchiavelli were the good and evil angels of the Renaissance, then theirs was the side of Plato.

But it did not last for long, and the fruit was not worthy of the blossom. To the age of Margaret of Valois succeeded the age of Catherine de' Medici. In the early Renaissance it is the women who modify by their influence the political excesses to which the men are tempted, but it is the men who rule and accept the responsibility. Charles V, Francis I and Henry VIII stamp their personalities upon their period. But in the succeeding age the women themselves are the leaders. It is the age of feminine diplomacy. Mary of Scotland is broken by it. Elizabeth of England triumphs. In France Catherine de' Medici, her heart dried up by the long years of ignominious submission to Diane de Poitiers, places her sons on the throne in front of her and stands above them to manœuvre her pieces on the board. In the Escurial sits the moody Philip II, a man in body, but as feminine as any of them in the processes of his crafty mind. And so the Renaissance reddened to its inglorious autumn, with religious wars in France and *autos-da-fé* in Spain, till James I of England wreaked his perverse fury on the witches and Pope Paul IV put fig leaves on Michelangelo's nudities.

It is to this autumn that Catherine belongs, and in its

slanting light she must be judged. Her Medici birth had planted in her a taste and a talent for chicanery. Her troubled childhood in Italy had left her with no religion save her belief in expediency. As the wife of Henry of France she had to bear what no woman can bear with generosity. She was to emerge therefrom into a period which demanded of those who rule just that cold and guileful attitude which she had inherited and acquired. Intensely of her age, intensely of her race, intensely motivated by her peculiar circumstances, she was to leave a memory with no quality of feminine charm, but one which posterity cannot disregard. She may be called a monster, but she must be understood as a woman.

So Catherine rode out of Lyons with the King and his concubine, and left Louise Labé to wait for the lover whom destiny had chosen for her. Louise has left us only her poems and the testimony of her admirers. She belongs to that earlier age that promised so much and passed so quickly. The conversations in her garden are no more recoverable than the song the sirens sang, nor are such things, alas, the stuff of history.

# PARIS

PARIS waited to receive its new sovereign, for each town in succession had to stage its state entry, as suited the convenience of the King. Nor had Catherine yet been crowned, for in France, by the Salic law, no woman could be more than a consort, and consorts did not share the ceremony at Rheims with their kings, nor were they anointed with the holy oil. Her coronation took place in Paris, at Saint-Denis, on June 10, 1549, nine months after the Lyons festivities, and on the 16th and 18th of the same month Henry and herself made their respective entries into the city.

Paris was a strongly walled, mediæval city, with the Gothic towers and spires of Notre-Dame and the Sainte Chapelle rising from the island in its centre, and a few Renaissance buildings scarcely holding their own among the cluster of old churches and the feudal bastions of the Bastille and the Conciergerie. The south bank, with colleges and convents climbing up the hill of Sainte Geneviève was then, as now, the recognised quarter of the students and artists, whose tumultuous amusements were regularly joined by a rabble of rogues and vagabonds. Here Villon, the "poor little scholar," thief, murderer and the greatest poet of France, had lived out most of his brief and stormy existence; here Marot had known the inside of wine-shop and prison and the swift alternation of poverty and success; here Erasmus had received his early education in the Collège de Montaigu—that "lowsie Colledge" as Rabelais called it; here Rabelais himself had abandoned for a time his monastic habit, an offence for which he took the opportunity of obtaining absolution when he visited Rome; and here Rabelais' great creations, Gargantua and Pantagruel, had passed student days, and Panurge had played his gigantic practical jokes on the watchmen, the lawyers, the theologians and the lady who resisted his advances. Rabelais had watched the strengthening of the walls of Paris when there was a threat of Imperial invasion, and from his writings, merry and serious by turns, we can discover much that went on within those walls. The roast-meat shops, the printing-presses, the libraries and colleges, the church ceremonies, the taverns of the *Magdalen,* the *Pineapple,* the *Castle* and the *Mule,* the scuffles between students and watchmen, the lurking cutpurses, the hatchet-faced notaries, the fur-gowned City Fathers, the mules of the sheriffs, the pages playing dice on the steps of the palaces, the liveried processions, the tolling of bells from fifty steeples, the very dogs and sparrows—the whole pageant of sixteenth-century Paris comes alive as we read.

Later to become the city of barricades, Paris was always ready for a riot; and ready, too, to throng to any spectacle from a cock-fight to a coronation, "for the people of Paris," says Rabelais, "are so sottish, so badot, so foolish and fond by nature, that a jugler, a carrier of indulgences, a sumpter-horse, or mule with cymbals, or tinkling bells, a blinde fidler in the middle of a crosse lane, shall draw a greater confluence of people together than an Evangelical Preacher." The population turned out in force to see the brave show of the royal triumph.

Into what sort of a King had the dreamy Henry grown, the silent youth over whose development Diane had watched so carefully? The best answer comes from the least biassed observers, foreign travellers, and in particular the Venetian ambassadors and their suites. We can hardly do better than let them speak, one after another, in their own words. In details they sometimes conflict with each other, but the composite portrait that results must in the main be as faithful a one as we can hope to have.

"His Majesty is in his twenty-ninth year (1547), and al-

though I formerly described him to your Excellencies as a
prince of a pale, livid countenance, and so disposed to melancholy that those about him said that they had never known
him laugh heartily, to-day I must assure you that he has become gay, that he is ruddy in complexion and in perfect
health. He has but a scanty beard, but nevertheless he trims
it; his eyes are rather large than otherwise, but he keeps them
lowered; his face across the jaws and across the brow lacks
breadth; his head is on the small side. His body is very well
proportioned, tall rather than short. In his person he is full
of courage, very bold and enterprising; he is exceedingly
fond of the game of tennis, at which he never misses a day
unless it be on account of rain, for he plays under the open
sky, sometimes even after hunting a stag or two at top speed,
which is the most fatiguing kind of exercise, as your Excellencies are aware. On the same day, after these exertions,
he will indulge for two or three hours in military exercises,
at which his fame stands high."

At tennis "he was clad all in white, with white shoes also,
and with a fine straw hat upon his head. He wore his doublet
for playing. He has a good figure, perhaps a little heavy, but
well proportioned on the whole. When one sees him thus
at his game one would scarcely realise that it is the King who
is playing, for even his errors are openly discussed, and more
than once I have heard him taken to task."

"Henry is the sovereign lord of a great kingdom, being
now aged thirty-two years and eight or nine months (1551).
Tall in stature and of proportionate girth, hair dark, forehead handsome, eyes bright and black, nose large, mouth undistinguished, and beard pointed, of the length of two finger-
joints. . . . In body he is very healthy, though his teeth cause
him pain. . . . He desires good and strives for it, he is easy
of access and never refuses an audience. While he is at dinner
he always has people talking to him of their own affairs and
he listens and replies with the utmost courtesy. He is never

surprised in anger, except occasionally while at the chase. . . .
On the whole he is temperate, and as for the delights of the
flesh, in comparison with the late King, his father, and some
other Kings now dead, he may be esteemed very chaste; and
such amours as he has are so conducted that there can be no
great scandal about them, which was not so with King
Francis; hence the Court, which was formerly very licentious,
is now regular enough. . . . King Henry loves good stories
as well as the Kings who preceded him, but he dislikes shock-
ing ladies with them. . . . He eats and drinks with moderation. He is looked upon as less generous and less magnificent
than his father, but that may be because he gives largely to
a few. . . . His Majesty fails not of his religious observances,
he hears mass every day and vespers on the saints' days; he
walks in procession at the appointed annual festivals and at
all the principal feasts he lays his hands patiently and rever-
ently upon numbers of the scrofulous sick, who declare themselves healed by his very touch. The King is of an intelligent
turn of mind and nimble in memory. He speaks French,
Italian and Spanish well."

We learn, furthermore, that after dinner Henry "devotes
himself to reading and study," that he "loves music dearly
and has admirable notions on the subject," that riding is his
chief passion, and that he rises in summer at dawn, in winter
when it is a little lighter. And we learn also, of course, that
his great delight is in the conversation and company of Diane
de Poitiers, whose symbol and favours he always wears.

Undoubtedly Henry managed to make himself popular,
particularly in his capital city, and the enthusiasm at his
formal entry into Paris, two years after his coronation, was
as sincere as such demonstrations can be expected to be. It
was an immense procession. Two thousand pages walked
in front of him, all clad like so many magpies in the black
and white livery that spelt homage to Diane. The Parlement,
the municipality, the university and every trade of Paris

were represented, and a curious feature was the company of printers to the number of three thousand five hundred, all dressed in black and equipped with armour—"a gentle hint," suggests one commentator, "that they would be prepared to resist any undue interference with the liberties of their trade." King Henry, who was always seen to advantage on horseback, rode a white charger, as yet scarcely broken in. It was not one of his stable favourites, whose names we know—the gentle, highly bred Hobère, the war-horse oddly named Le Bay de la Paix, the high-stepping Mireau, the famous sire Gonzague, Quadragant that would kneel before his master like a circus-horse. His steed for this occasion was white to match the prevailing tone of his costume, and its caparison was of cloth of silver. A white plume mounted in pearls rose from the King's cap of white satin and silver lace. A tunic of cloth of silver covered his white armour, and his sword-scabbard was of silver wherein rubies and diamonds were set to catch the June sunlight. Behind him followed the whole of his Court.

Less than three weeks later occurred an incident which throws a curious light upon the character of Henry, and although the fullest account of it is from a sympathiser with the Reformers, there is sufficient corroboration for us to accept it as essentially true.

It had been reported to the King, who was still in Paris, that among persons imprisoned in the city was a number of adherents to the Protestant faith. As was witnessed by the Italians, Henry had a familiar habit of allowing the poorest of his subjects an audience if they requested it, and in this instance he conceived a wish to see one of the captive Reformers and hear his case. The Cardinal of Lorraine was commissioned to bring such a man into the royal presence, and from fear that a learned representative of the new faith might unduly influence the King, he selected a poor tailor who, as he thought, would be so ignorant and so terrified as to present a very unimpressive argument. To the astonishment of King, Cardinal and Court, however, this humble subject ("strengthened," says Theodore de Bèze, "with power from on high") , held forth with great skill and eloquence, confidently answering every question put to trap him. It became, in fact, the old situation, familiar in the scriptures and the lives of the saints, of "almost thou persuadest me. . . ."

But then it was the turn of Diane to speak. She had suffered a good deal from vindictive Protestant attacks, and her aim was rather to confound the fortitude of the tailor than to promote any very profitable discussion on faith. She had her questions ready. Yet no sooner did she turn to address the ragged man who stood so boldly in the midst of all that magnificence than he stopped her mouth with: "Madame, be satisfied with having corrupted France, and do not intrude your filth upon a thing so sacred as the truth of God!"

The King was furious. Perhaps no Italian envoy was present to observe this lapse into a passion to which he was said to give way only when out hunting—or perhaps heretic-baiting was held to be a branch of the chase. It can readily be understood, at all events, that Henry did not relish the charge of filthiness against the woman whom he had loved for some fifteen years or more. The Protestant's words "so greatly enraged him, who loved nothing in the world so much as this lady, that he wished to see the tailor burned alive in the Rue Saint-Antoine, after a general procession."

Needless to say, the royal wish was put into effect, and three more heretics were found to keep the tailor company at the stake. From an open window Henry looked on while the defamer of his mistress endured the slow torment of the flames. But the tailor made a good end. Catching sight of the King he proceeded to regard him so steadfastly that even the increasing pain was not able to divert his gaze. While his fellow-victims cried out in their agony the eyes

of the courageous tailor remained fixed accusingly, through
fire and smoke, upon the author of his death until the ghastly
business was over. Henry was "so horrified that he often said
afterwards how it seemed to him on the following night that
he could still see this person, and that even during the day
the fear came upon him that he was following him about;
so that he vowed that never again would he witness a burning, so dearly had he paid for his pleasure." He kept his
oath, which did not at all mean that there were to be no
more burnings.

It must be understood that such an incident as this is
perfectly compatible with the contemporary description of
Henry as a king who genuinely desired the good. It was,
indeed, to be counted in his favour that he was humane
enough to dislike witnessing the practical expression of the
royal duty of punishment, a duty which he nevertheless did
not forbear to carry out. So far from sullying his reputation
in the eyes of the majority of his people, he had substantially
enhanced it, and it may well be thought that the Paris mob,
if robbed of the familiar spectacle of burning offenders, would
have taken matters into its own hands and found human
fuel for itself. It was an age in which physical courage was
the highest virtue, and hideous cruelties were perpetrated
every day without protest. Women were just as well accustomed as men to the spectacle of deliberately inflicted
suffering, and the application of humanitarian principles to
our estimate of the great figures of the period would mean
the sacrifice of nearly every hero and heroine dear to romance. To use a modern phrase, one got away with murder
in the sixteenth century as one gets away with manslaughter
in the twentieth, and the burners, slaughterers and rapers
would probably have regarded with horror a civilisation
which does its killing in high-powered vehicles on the roads.

Like his father, Henry was by nature less cruel than many
other prominent men of his time. Like his father also, he

was easily led. His mistress was the natural and circumstantial enemy of the Reformers; Catholicism was the life-blood of the Guises; and as for the Constable, who was so loved by the King that at one time he appeared to some observers to be a rival in that respect to Diane herself—as for Montmorency, he remained as fiercely opposed to heretics as political intrigue and the Protestant commitments of his family would allow. Yet at the beginning of his reign Henry wore a tolerant aspect. There were two reasons for this, more important reasons than any personal inclinations. One was that he needed the help of the Protestant Princes of Germany against Charles V, and the other was that his policy included the discrediting of his father's advisers. Simply on this account the leaders of the bloody campaign against the Vaudois that had stained the last years of the reign of Francis were arraigned before the Parlement, a circumstance which gave the Protestant interests unwarranted hopes. For the matter was talked out and allowed to drop.

Political developments soon persuaded Henry to a severer attitude. His negotiations with Germany were followed by the threat of a charge of heresy against him, and although by French law no such excommunication, as had been used against England, was possible against France, it yet seemed necessary to take some step which should clear the air of suspicion. The step on which the King decided was the Edict of Châteaubriant, a decree aimed directly at the Protestants, and the institution of a special chamber in the Paris Parlement to deal with cases of heresy. This court was given the sinister name of *Chambre ardente,* or burning chamber, and made full use of the power vested in it.

There was yet another factor to keep alive the fires of persecution, for the death of a heretic meant the confiscation of his property, which was a plain temptation to avarice. It was not necessarily the Crown which benefited by the burning of a wealthy Protestant. More usually it was the courtiers, to whom actual promises were made of certain lands held by suspected persons. All that they then had to do was to discover or manufacture the evidence required to secure a conviction, a process which naturally led to corruption, not only in the Court, but also among lawyers and justices.

A state of affairs such as this must qualify the rosiest estimate of Henry's character and reign. The briars of intrigue which his father, at all events until his later years, had striven from genuine motives, and with some success, to keep down, sprang up and flourished with renewed vigour when Henry came to the throne, effectively choking those more precious cultures which Francis had tended. The very praise showered upon the King in respect of his private life is indicative of the new atmosphere. Of a typical notable of Henry's reign it might be said, as Edward Armstrong said of Charles V: "if he sported with Amaryllis it was in the shade." There are two ways of regarding the change. Sixteenth-century diplomats, brought up to the art of dissembling, rejoiced that the licentiousness of the Court was now kept dark, instead of being the "open scandal" that it had been in the previous reign. But a twentieth-century observer may justly feel that the frank and unashamed enjoyment of Francis was preferable to the policy of discreet concealment which followed it. The healthy laughter of Rabelais had given way to the curtained vice of Brantôme, for it is less with the reign of Francis than with the succeeding period that Brantôme deals. The fact was that Henry, completely subservient to Diane, yet under the political necessity of recognising Catherine, was from the very beginning predisposed to an attitude of dissimulation and surface smoothness; and the Court followed to a man—and woman—the new incentive to secrecy. Sex, like religion, like politics, like everything else in an age of decadence, was being driven into underground channels.

It need hardly be said that Catherine throve on this air,

an air to which she had for so long been conditioned. She was foremost of the Court in condemning scandal, and already, though her power was so restricted, her tongue was remarked as a formidable weapon. By the restriction of gossip no interests were served better than hers, for her unhappy position invited malicious and damaging talk. The outward friendship displayed between herself and the hated Diane was matter for admiring comment by the Venetians and other observers, and political sympathy with the opponents of the Guise faction gave her a reputation for Protestant piety which an examination of her inward thoughts would scarcely have substantiated.

And still she waited for her hour.

# ANET

"FINDING myself near the road to Anet I made my way thither, for I have ever been a lover of the beautiful, and eager to possess or to behold things curiously and exquisitely fashioned; and without exaggeration I reached the conclusion, having seen everything here, that the Golden House [1] of Nero was neither so rich nor so lovely."

Thus the Florentine traveller Simeoni, writing in 1557, and his praise is borne out by Sir William Pickering, the English Ambassador, received at Anet by King Henry a few years earlier. "So sumptuous and prince-like as ever I saw," says he, and an English Ambassador in the sixteenth century may be regarded as an experienced judge of the sumptuous. Hyperbolically, sycophantically, or in sincere bursts of lyricism, the poets add their tribute—Joachim du Bellay, Mellin de Saint-Gelais, and Olivier de Magny, lover of Louise Labé.

At Anet the first steps in the negotiation of Catherine's marriage had been taken. To Anet her husband hurried three days after the birth of his son, who was to be Charles IX, breaking all royal precedent in leaving his wife at such a time. But never in her life did Catherine cross the threshold, although on one occasion, after the death of Henry, she promised to visit Diane there in her retirement.

For Anet was the temple of the moon-goddess, the vast and lovely symbol of her union with Endymion. Henry returned thither from his campaigns to be with Diane. The royal children played there in the bright gardens, and the little Dauphin Francis has left a letter in which he expresses delight in the comfort of the great bed in which he slept at

[1] The *Domus Aurea*, built after the fire of 64 A.D., and recently excavated by order of Signor Mussolini.

Anet. None would have imagined, to see them in that magnificent yet essentially domestic setting, that Diane was not their mother, that their mother sat nursing her wounded pride and laying her schemes in Amboise or Blois or Saint-Germain. For the lovers even had their homely differences, so swiftly made up, over the children at Anet. Despite Catherine's policy of outward friendliness towards the royal mistress, it is not surprising that she never went the length of Diane-worship. A, visit to Anet meant just that.

As for Henry, he was never so happy as at Anet. Whenever he could do so he transacted the business of the kingdom there, and "given at Anet" appears on many of his edicts. He played tennis there, and hunted in the nearby woods, or simply rode all day across the country with Diane riding beside him, silent for long stretches of time in that complete intimacy which was theirs. There he could lie at full length in the sunshine, on the smooth lawn, beside the cool fountain of Diane, dreaming as he had done in his youth before his mistress drew out his royal qualities, or composing the tender, elegant poems, for which only she had discovered his talent. Hither he summoned from Fontainebleau or from wherever the Court was in residence his Italian lutenist, Alberto de Ripa, to beguile him with the music that he dearly loved. Here he would hear the melodies of Palestrina, or the liturgical settings of the Fleming Jehan Ockeghem, once Master of Musick to Louis XI. And the verses of Ronsard, the Prince of Poets, arranged for four voices moving in plain chords, or contrapuntally decorated by Pierre Certon, Jannequin or Goudimel, would be sung for him—"*Bel Aubepin*," "*Marie, levez-vous*," or "*Mignonne, allons voir si la rose.*" Pierre de Ronsard himself was passionately fond of music, though he was afflicted with deafness and could not sing a note. He had come back to France from Scotland with the little Queen of Scots, and now with Joachim du Bellay, Remi Belleau, Pontus de Tyard, Jean-Antoine de Báif and the rest of his glittering *Pléiade* was accomplishing for French poetry a Renaissance of its own, a sort of promontory of the Renaissance mainland that had already been won by colonisers now dead. Never was poet more certain of his immortality than Ronsard, not even the Shakespeare who wrote:

> Not marble, nor the gilded monuments
> Of princes, shall outlive this powerful rhyme.

For the *Pléiade,* and principally the great du Bellay, had realised at last that Rome's language had survived and would survive the destruction of its material symbols, its battered Colosseum and broken pillars and overgrown aqueducts. The men of the early Renaissance had pitted their sculpture and their architecture against death. Their security against oblivion had been stone. Taking over their heritage in times that threatened war and spoliation the Pléiade forged a subtler armour of imperishable words.

Anet has, in fact, proved more defenceless against time than Chambord, Blois, Fontainebleau, Azay, Chenonceaux and the rest. The Revolution did not leave much of it. Diane's tomb was rifled and the hair cut from her corpse to be distributed as souvenirs to the crowd. A later owner sold stone by stone the remainder of the château, and it was only by the intervention of an archæologist that the *Diane Chasseresse,* Goujon's marvellous figure of an idealised Diane, the presiding deity of Anet, found its way to the Louvre. Two ruined wings, after some praiseworthy attempts at restoration, are all that we see to-day.

When Diane's Anet was built she was probably the richest woman in Europe. Avarice is the term used by her enemies for what was certainly a very shrewd head for business. Henry showered gifts upon her in money and in kind, and she was involved in frequent litigation for the defence of her estates and those of her dead husband or for their increase. The writs remain to-day, together with numerous letters and

documents testifying to the minute care with which the great
lady watched over her multifarious revenues. It is perhaps
better not to enquire whence came the money for the building of Anet. Sequestration of the property of impeached
Protestants certainly accounted for some of it, and the sale
of galley-slaves might also be set down in the books. Yet
such money, however tainted, might well háve been—and in
most cases was—diverted to very much worse ends than the
building of a stately château.

The estate of Anet had been in the possession of the Brézé
family since the twelfth century. Diane had lived there with
Louis de Brézé, in the old days when Francis I was a frequent
visitor. Her daughters, now profitably married, had been
born here (with the exception of Diane de France, Henry's
mistress bore him no children). When Louis de Brézé died,
the Duchesse d'Étampes had put in a claim for Anet as a
perquisite of the Crown, but Francis did not much care to
be a party to this move, and the suit had not reached a conclusion when he died. And then, of course, with the accession
of Henry, Anet belonged irrefutably to Diane, now created
Duchesse de Valentinois. It was then that the new château
came to be built.

Only the greatest architect in France was good enough
for the job. Philibert de l'Orme not only planned the immense range of buildings and court-yards and the lay-out
of the gardens and heronry, but contributed a number of
ingenious details not usually entrusted to the architect. Here
is an extract relating to Anet from his celebrated treatise
on his craft:

"You may see over the highest pitch of the great door a
decoration of fine Vernon stone and black marble, with
panels for sculpture. In the same place is a clock to mark and
show the hours both inside and outside the château, also
with a face and figure of an astrolabe and planisphere with
the zodiac, accompanied by the twelve signs and the daily

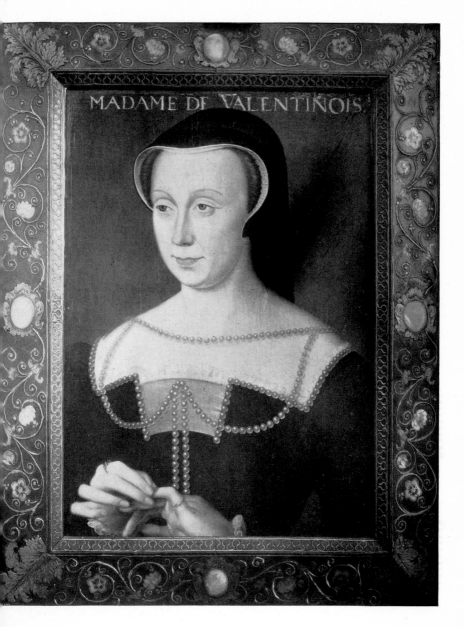

MADAME DE VALENTINOIS

*Photograph: E. M. Eadon*

## DIANE DE POITIERS
### FRENCH SCHOOL
(Graves Art Gallery, Sheffield)

motion of the moon, likewise of the planets. Beside the two-
hour dial faces there is a chime, which before the hours,
half-hours and quarters, sounds the baying of four hounds
instead of the quarter-bells, seeming to bay against a stag,
which is set up above the said dial faces. And since it is
the nature of the stag to strike with his foot when he hears the
baying of the hounds, it has been so fashioned that after the
said hounds have sounded the hour-chimes, the stag strikes
with his foot to sound the hour. Also I caused to be made
at the Château of Anet, among many fine works, a stairway
shaped as a crescent, which stands in the garden, in front of
the cryptoporticus, to ascend to the terrace and the garden-
pavilion above the said cryptoporticus."

Always the crescent and symbols of the chase. The sculptor
Goujon, the goldsmith Cellini, the enameller Léonard Limousin, the master fountain-maker, Jean Nicole, the royal
embroiderer, Robert Mestays, and many other foremost
workmen of their day gave of their best, under the direction
of de l'Orme, to make Anet the outward and visible sign of
the indissoluble bond between Diane and Henry—and everywhere the interlaced initials of the King and his mistress
were repeated.

That monogram has never ceased, from that day to this,
to engage the attention of historians. For while it is still
debated whether Diane really loved Henry, and whether love
for Henry had any part in Catherine's hatred of Diane, no
doubt has ever been cast on the patent attitude of Henry
himself. Nor can the historian, however dispassionately he
may seek a middle way among the biased opinions of the
time, and however coldly he may view the intrusion of romantic passion upon his researches, by any means escape the
historical fact that Diane made the King what he was. And
not this alone. Diane made Henry kingly, but she also made
Catherine revengeful; so that at the very least she made her
mark on history.

This is how the royal lover wrote to his mistress at Anet. The letter is from Fontainebleau, undated:

*"M'amye,* I entreat you to send me news of your health for the distress I am in since hearing of your illness, and in order that I may act according to such news; for if you continue to be ill I should not wish to fail to come to you to be of such service as I may; for in such straits I could not live long without seeing you. And since in times past I was not afraid to lose the favour of the late King in order to be with you, so now I will spare no pains to render help to you; and I assure you that I shall not be easy until the bearer of this letter returns to me again. I beg you, therefore, to send me a true word of how you are in health and when you will be able to depart. I think that you understand full well how little pleasure I have at Fontainebleau when I may not see you, for it is very hard for me, absent from her with whom rests all my welfare, to find happiness; which makes me now sign this letter from fear that it may be too long and weary you in the reading, offering my humble recommendations to your good grace as one that would fain keep it for ever

☒ ."

And from the army in Alsace, in 1552, he writes:

*"Madame m'amye,* I shall not write a long letter, for I have given the bearer all information, and also because I have not the leisure, being now about to make the passage of the River Sarre. I beg you to believe that my army is in fine condition and of an excellent heart, and I have confidence that if we are opposed at the crossing Our Lord will aid me by His grace, as He has done from the beginning. I will write nothing else to you, but leave full news with M. d'Aranson, who will return immediately; meanwhile I entreat you to keep remembrance of him who never knew but one God and one love, and assure you that you will not have cause for shame

to have granted me the name of servant; which name I beg
you to keep for me for ever.  ▨  ."

Not only was Henry the chivalrous champion of Diane.
He was also her troubadour. There exist some verses, written
with the corrections unquestionably in his own hand, and
addressed to his lady. They begin something like this:

> Never swore vassal truer faith,
> My Princess, to a Prince new-crown'd,
> Than my love's pledge, that shall be found
> Steadfast in face of time and death. . . .

And Diane, too, would versify with a certain pagan facility
when occasion offered. Henry has gone off to the wars again,
wearing her favours like a true knight. Until he return to
the blessed retreat of Anet her bed will be lonely and her
board cheerless. She takes leave of her lover thus:

> Farewell my heart's prolong'd delight,
> Farewell my master and liege knight,
> Farewell true scion of nobleness.
>
> Farewell full many a royal feast,
> Farewell the dish of subtle taste,
> Farewell superb festivities,
> Farewell sweet kisses, pigeon-wise,
> With lip and tongue; farewell again
> The secret sports betwixt us twain,
> Farewell, farewell, lov'd long and well,
> Incomparable joys, farewell!

There was something here so fixed and secure that all the
intrigues and all the gibes of political opponents spent their
force upon it and made no inroad. The fashionable simile
of a fortress trenched about and invulnerably bastioned slips
easily to Henry's pen as he composes his verses in camp, and
it recurs quite naturally as we examine the facts of this remarkable alliance that was to mean so much for France.
We cannot know for certain whether Diane retained until

well past fifty those outward graces of form and feature which made the flatterer Brantôme exclaim: "Her winter was more glorious than the spring and summer of any other." Such tributes as these must be accepted with caution, and the discrepancy between the portraits of the middle-aged Elizabeth of England in pen and in paint should be a warning to the hasty romanticist. But it is no more possible to share the view of those contemporaries of Diane who, in vulgar diatribes, ridiculed the King's passion for an old, hideous and painted face. For, at the same time, there were other enemies to give away their case by accusing Diane of the use of enchantment to keep herself young and beloved. We know, at all events, that she had a more natural and more efficacious prescription. To the end of her life she maintained a habit of rising as early as three o'clock in the morning for a ride before breakfast, and in spite of the story of the asses' milk she bathed regularly in ice-cold water. Perhaps, too, while conforming to all other social refinements, she eschewed many of those feminine devices which are said to hasten age though they beautify youth. For the women of the Renaissance, without being hypnotised into it by advertising campaigns, had recourse to those aids to beauty which are as old as Eve and yet earn afresh, in each generation, the laudatory or opprobrious epithet of "modern." The contemporaries of Diane and Catherine used lipstick and powder and eye-black, and in Gabriel de Minut's pleasant and painstaking book De la Beauté, which he dedicated to Catherine, there is a reference to the use of cosmetics for parts of the body not usually exposed to more than one admirer at a time— a point which Brantôme, of course, is not behindhand in elaborating. They plucked their eyebrows, these exquisite ladies of the sixteenth century, and they wore high-heeled shoes, though it seems to have been an unwritten law that the higher were the heels the lower were the morals. Italian prostitutes of the time, at any rate, are shown upon heels which in extreme cases become pattens or even stilts. Yet with the vision of Tullia d'Aragona in our minds it is dangerous to generalise about the morals of prostitutes. Let us return to Diane, and to the only recorded instances, during Henry's lifetime, of Catherine's loss of temper with the favourite. Perhaps the weather had been oppressive or perhaps Catherine, whose health was not invariably good during her dozen years of child-bearing, had a sick headache. Diane found her deep in a book, and asked her what she was reading. There are moments in everybody's life when a question so simple as that can be intolerably irritating. Catherine raised her eyes to those of her rival and replied: "It is a history of France, and I find that not seldom the rulers of this land have themselves been ruled by whores."

It was a slip, perhaps the only one in all those weary years. It was patience that she needed. There is another picture of Catherine at this time, and a more characteristic one, though since it is Brantôme who gives us it, a certain allowance must be made for the poetic licence of that egregious chronicler of situations painful or intoxicating. Perhaps the scene is Fontainebleau.

"There was a king who, in his time, bore great love to a very fair and estimable lady that was a widow, so that he was thought to be bewitched by her, for he had little care for others, or for his wife, save on rare occasions, for the said lady had always the plucking of the fairest flowers in his garden; insomuch that the queen was greatly incensed, deeming herself as beautiful and as pleasing and as worthy to be well served and to have morsels as dainty as that other, so that she was exceedingly angry at the affair. And having complained to a certain noble lady, one of her favourites, she plotted with her to find some means whereby she might spy through an aperture at the sports in which her husband and his lady might together indulge. She had accordingly a number of holes pierced in the ceiling of the said lady's bedchamber, to see what manner of life they led there. And they put themselves in order to watch the spectacle, but they saw nothing that was not very meet, for they perceived a very beautiful woman, white, exquisite and very fresh, half-clothed by her shift and half-naked, lavishing upon her gallant every sort of caress and wanton embrace, the which he returned. Thereafter the two would quit the bed, and lie beside it on the thick carpet and there play together, to avoid the heat of it and to have pleasure where it was cooler. Then this lady of rank, who had witnessed everything, fell to weeping and groaning and sighing in her distress, saying that her husband never used her in this fashion, nor played such frolics as she had seen him do with the other. The lady who was with her forthwith consoled her and chid her for having such grief, saying that since she had been so curious to see these matters she had what she must expect. And the queen said only 'Alas, it is true! I longed to see that which I should not have longed to see, since the sight of it tortures me'; yet when she had been soothed she took good cheer and ceased to brood upon it, and renewed this pastime of watching as often as she could, and turned it to matter for mirth and perhaps for something else also."

It is a cruel contrast, the lady of Anet and the eavesdropping queen; on the one hand the middle-aged Frenchwoman, calm with the confidence of perfect sexual poise, hard of head and soft of heart, heaping up her treasures both tangible and intangible, with all her calculating talents doubled by brilliant luck; on the other the Italian, young in body but old in mind, fighting implacable adversity with the only weapons left to her, patience and cunning. It was rather like the combat of Jarnac and la Châtaignerie, for only an adroit thrust from below could avail against the heavy armour of Diane.

# VAUCELLES

JARNAC and la Châtaignerie at Saint-Germain, Henry and Diane at Anet, and now Charles V and Coligny at Vaucelles. It is still a hidden part that Catherine de' Medici plays in history, and to give her greater prominence in this period of subordination would rob of its true perspective our view of the procession of events. Time runs on. She is there, always in the background, hating and waiting. Unseen, she holds a watching brief. Later she will walk in disguise through the streets of Paris with her daughter the Queen of Navarre, listening to gossip, testing the wind of favour. Even now she is disguised, for none would know her for a queen, so unapparent is her power. In the euphuistic phrase that so greatly impressed the fond old Polonius, Catherine is the mobled queen, her secrets scarfed about; the mobled queen, hooded like the snake that awaits the moment to strike, the Medici cobra with the curious markings that might be mistaken for a smile.

At Vaucelles, near Brussels, Gaspard de Coligny met the Emperor Charles in February, 1556, for the conclusion of a truce. Charles was exactly fifty-six years old, in failing health and weary of the cares of the great office he had held for so long. Coligny was exactly thirty-seven years old and by no means weary of the multiplicity of offices that he had acquired. He was acting Colonel-General of the French Infantry, Admiral of France, Governor of the Ile-de-France and Governor of Picardy, and the Truce of Vaucelles for which he was about to obtain the Emperor's signature was a triumph of able diplomacy. In a small house in the midst of a great park the representatives of two ages were facing each other.

Charles had already begun the lengthy and delicate negotiations which were necessary to his resolve of resigning the
Imperial crown and retiring from the turmoil of politics
to end his days in peace, a resolve which had been of great
assistance to Coligny in obtaining favourable terms for
France. Abdication from the control of the various dominions
of the Empire had to be carried out step by step, and his
two successors introduced no less gradually into their various
inheritances. His son Philip was to have Spain, the Netherlands and the Italian provinces; his brother Ferdinand the
Imperial title and Austria. The Netherlands had already
taken their leave of Charles in a celebrated scene at Brussels,
the lachrymosity of which is eloquently described by the
English envoy, Sir Thomas Gresham: "And here he broke
into a weeping whereunto, besides the dolefulness of the
matter, I think he was much provoked by seeing the whole
company to do the like before; being in mine opinion not
one man in the whole assembly, stranger or other, that during
the time of a good piece of his oration poured not abundantly
tears, some more, some less." A little later the kingdoms of
Spain and Sicily had been formally resigned to Philip, and
this meeting with Coligny at Vaucelles was a third step on
the road to the monastery of Yuste where the last of the great
Emperors was to beguile with his clocks the brief twilight
between life and death. He had journeyed, as he told the
Estates at Brussels in the speech which caused such emotion,
"nine times to Germany, six to Spain, seven to Italy, ten
to the Netherlands, four to France, either in peace or war,
two to England, and two to Africa, in all some forty journeys,
without counting numberless visits within his other kingdoms, countries and islands, nor yet laying stress on his
journey across France to remedy the troubles in the Netherlands, which was not the least of his exertions. Eight times
had he crossed the Mediterranean, three times the ocean."
And with all this he had not succeeded in obtaining the

political and religious unity within his vast Empire for which he had striven. No wonder he was tired.

Gaspard de Coligny, a black-bearded, vigorous figure in velvet cloak, doublet, slashed breeches and trunk hose, his hand lying lightly on the jewelled hilt of his dagger, had climbed to the Emperor's chamber with a feeling of embarrassment such as he never exhibited in the face of physical danger. For the past few days he had accustomed himself to looking at Spanish tapestries proudly woven with the victory of Pavia, but now there was no more of this arrogant colour to affront his patriotism. The prevailing note was one of deepest black. The staircase was lined with silent Spaniards, dressed all in black. The antechamber was hung with black curtains. So was the Imperial chamber, and the Emperor's table and chair were draped in the same sombre hue. Charles was in mourning for his mother, but to Coligny and his suite, the richness of whose costume was emphasised by these melancholy surroundings, the *décor* must also have seemed to signify the Emperor's resolve to be henceforth dead to the world, and his atrabilious fits that some called madness.

Charles sat huddled in his black chair, his rheumatic hands clasped on the black table in front of him. He was dressed in the dark and humble clothes which for years he had affected—"a little suit of Florentine serge like that of a common citizen, cut above the knee, his arms passing through the sleeves of a black coat made of German stuff; he had a cap trimmed with a narrow silk cord, and a shirt with a simple collar." But his melancholia was relieved by a playful vein of banter of which he soon gave evidence.

Coligny approached the table, bowed low, and presented a letter from King Henry. Charles struggled for some minutes with his crippled fingers before he could break the seal. "What think you of me, Sir Admiral?" he asked. "Am I not a fine knight to charge and break a lance, I who can open a letter only with such difficulty?" And while the envoy was framing a polite reply he went on to enquire after the health of the French King.

"Very well, sire," answered Coligny.

"Indeed I am glad of it. But I am told that he is already turning grey. Surely there cannot possibly be anything younger than he is? Why, it seems only three years since he was a child in Spain, without a hair on his face."

"It is true, sire," admitted the Admiral, "that the King has two or three white hairs." And forthwith the frail little Emperor wandered off into reminiscences of his own first signs of age, and of the barbers of Naples, and of the ladies there also. He rallied the French jester who was present, reeling off his pleasantries as if to postpone the State business that had become so fatiguing to him. Tears rose to his eyes when at last he forced himself to consider Henry's letter and the terms of the truce. There was scarcely need, he told Coligny, for his oath to the compact, since he was beyond the age for campaigning and had no wish but to die in peace. Yet he would give the signature that was requested of him.

And so the Truce of Vaucelles was signed, and Coligny departed from the black audience-chamber, leaving Charles gazing wistfully through the window at the bare trees of the park. When the Admiral saw his King again, he reported that the Emperor who had harried France for so long was weak and shrivelled into an old man, but that behind the careworn lines of the Hapsburg brow there lurked still a rare wisdom and a harmonious judgment.

The treaty which Coligny had carried through with no little skill confirmed the position that had been reached by the hostilities throughout the reign. It left in French hands the three strongholds of Metz, Toul and Verdun that had been captured on the eastern frontier from the Imperialists. But it did not last long, and it did not gain for Coligny the smallest advantage. The history of the war with the Empire under Henry is a history of continual jealousy be-

tween the Guise faction and that of Montmorency and
Coligny. If one party scored a success against the enemy its
importance was immediately belittled by the other, and even
on the field of battle opportunities were found for the exchange of sneers and threats. Perhaps the Guises must be
given the greater responsibility for this state of affairs, but
the Constable, whose sharp tongue we have already heard
in the Piedmont campaign of the previous reign, could be
a fire-eater in his own camp even if he hesitated to take
decisive action against the enemy; and Coligny had already
suffered enough from jealousy to engage briskly where he
felt his honour was concerned. There was only one kind of
warfare that would satisfy these bitter captains, and that
was civil warfare; nor was it long in coming.

It was to be expected that the Guises would have no good
word to say of the Truce of Vaucelles, and they speedily
found an excuse for persuading Henry to break it. The family
ambitions had always pointed to Italy, where the greatest
Guise exploits had been performed, and as the Catholic
party they now demanded support for the new Pope Paul
IV. Paul detested and mistrusted Philip of Spain, to whom
Charles's Italian possessions had been made over, and the
Guises urged an immediate Italian campaign. Henry had
at first welcomed the Truce of Vaucelles as a triumph. Before
the year was out he had sent the Duke of Guise with one
army into Italy and the Constable (who had been won over
to the policy) with another into the Netherlands, whither
Coligny unwillingly followed him. The Constable made
blunder after blunder. In spite of heroic fighting by Coligny,
Saint-Quentin fell to Philip and was sacked with horrible
cruelties. Guise hastened back from an Italian defeat and
recaptured Calais from the English by a stroke of military
genius which, as we are so often told, wrote the name of
Calais on the heart of Mary Tudor. Then came the Treaty
of Cateau-Cambrésis between Henry of France and Philip

of Spain. It was the Truce of Vaucelles writ large, with ex-
changes of conquests and prisoners, and all those other items
common to peace treaties which make war look so silly that
the marvel is that anyone should think it worth while to
wage it.

On his deathbed in the monastery of Yuste lay a withered
man who for nearly forty years had been Master of the Two
Worlds and had reached the conclusion that very few things
were worth while in this world, and those only the delicate
and unregarded things—music and flowers and country food
and the love of children, and perhaps ... yes, perhaps, after
all, religion. Around him in his chamber ticked the clocks
of curious craftsmanship which, like the kingdoms of the
world, could never by any skill or patience be made to run
in unison. *"Ay, Jesus!"* murmured Charles, and fell back
dead.

# PARIS

YET another show for Paris, this time the most magnificent of all. For more than two centuries no Dauphin had been married on French soil, and the fact that the nuptials of Francis and Mary were to be celebrated in Paris rather than in Edinburgh or Stirling or Falkirk was a tribute to the skill of the Guises in subjecting Scotland completely to French influence. This was a Guise triumph, and they saw to it that it was a splendid one.

So for the first weeks of early spring of the year 1558 the *parvis* of Notre-Dame and the Palace of the Louvre were loud with the saws and hammers of armies of workmen labouring under the direction of the pageant-masters to erect stands and galleries and amphitheatres. Laden with bales of rich stuffs and crates of valuables, the boats put in every day at the Seine wharves, and the shopkeepers of Paris, the mercers, the goldsmiths and silversmiths, the jewellers, the costumiers and embroiderers worked overtime to satisfy the throngs of purchasers, each of whom was ready to beggar himself in order to eclipse the finery of his neighbour.

On April 19, in the great hall of Lescot's Louvre, took place the first ceremony of betrothal. It was the Guise churchman, the Cardinal of Lorraine, who witnessed the troth of the two children over their clasped hands. Mary was led to him by King Henry, Francis by the foppish and mercurial Antoine de Bourbon, first prince of the blood and no enthusiast for Guise supremacy.

And while they kneel there, hand in hand, the fifteen-year-old Scots girl and the fourteen-year-old French boy, let us examine them more closely; or as Montaigne would say:

"and sithence we be falne into this subject let us a little follow it I pray you."

There were now seven surviving children of Catherine and Henry, all of them, of course, quite young, and none of them very strong in health. Francis had suffered an attack of small-pox in his fourth year, and his recurrent ailments are constantly referred to in the correspondence of the Court. But he seemed, in the circumstances, a cheerful youngster, and though he never showed any intellectual promise he made brave efforts to develop and exercise his sickly physique. At eight years old he demanded to learn the art of the cross-bow, and butts were set up for him at Blois. Whenever he could do so he followed his father to the hunt, and even begged to be allowed to follow him to the wars. In appearance he was more of a Medici than a Valois.

Of one thing there is ample testimony: "He dearly loves her Most Serene Majesty of Scotland, a very pretty little girl"; "for his part, M. le Dauphin was desperately in love with her"; "it sometimes happens that—caressing one another the while—they like to retire a little way, into a corner of the room, that none may disturb their little secrets."

The bewitching northern child, who sent home for Scottish ponies and "erth-doggs" (terriers) to give to her playmates, captivated more than her fiancé. She captivated the King, whose delight in her and in his own children, and his understanding of them, are among the pleasantest traits of his not unlikeable character. As Catherine had been when she came from Florence to the French Court, Mary was among strangers and under the necessity of pleasing them. Like Catherine, she pleased the King. But their situations were not really similar. Catherine was fourteen years old when she came to France, and already rich for her years in experience of diplomacy. Mary, though she, too, had been a storm-centre of policy from the moment she came into the world, was only six when she reached the Court of Henry. Catherine

MARY STUART AS QUEEN OF FRANCE
FRENCH SCHOOL
(National Gallery, London)

found a bridegroom whose affections were already irrevocably engaged; Mary found one whose affections were willingly yielded to herself. From the moment she set foot on French soil Catherine had to find and keep her own friends, but there were powerful relatives waiting to do all they could for Mary's advancement. She was important to the Guises and they looked after her well. Within a short time after she had left Italy, Catherine's last kinsman died, including the Pope who had sent her to France. Mary had a mother in Scotland anxiously watching over her interests. Mary, in short, started with everything on her side, and died by the axe at the age of forty-five. Catherine started with everything against her and died in her bed at the age of seventy.

This is how Brantôme, who knew Mary in France and had heard her praises sung by Ronsard and du Bellay, wrote of her after her death:

"She had this further perfection, the better to set the world afire; a very sweet and true voice; for she sang very well, accompanying her voice with the lute, which she touched so prettily with that fair white hand, and with those fair and shapely fingers which yielded in nothing to those of Aurora. What remains to be said of her beauties save that which was said of her?—that the sun of Scotland was very little like her; for on several days in the year it does not shine five hours in her country, whereas she shone so brightly that she made her land and her people to share in her rays— a land and people that had more need of light than any others, since the clime is so distant from the great sun of heaven. Ah! Realm of Scotland, I think that now your days are yet shorter than they were wont to be, and your nights yet longer, since you have lost the princess who illuminated you!"

Scotland was still a land of mystery to these Frenchmen, a bleak and inhospitable country that bred tall archers and lovely princesses, and Mary was treated far more as a fascinating curiosity than the Florentine Catherine had been. Brantôme alludes not only to the sunless climate of the north, but to the strange, uncivilised and unmelodious language of the Scots, which nevertheless, when Mary chose to use it, lost its rudeness on her lips. And among the many dazzling costumes which the young Queen wore with such effect we are told that she sometimes adopted "the barbarous fashion of the savages of her country, and thus appeared, a mortal body in a dress uncouth and rude, a very goddess." They called her, indeed, "the little savage." It was a term of delighted affection, a name very different from that of "the Italian woman."

In spite of the power of Diane, the Italian woman managed to have her say in the education of her children. When they were quite young, indeed, she taught them herself, and her letters contain minute details of their regimen in health and sickness. And Mary, as we have seen, was, by command of the King, to be brought up in the royal nursery with the Dauphin and the two little princesses Elizabeth and Claude. But the Guises, with Diane in alliance, had no mind to allow Catherine to influence their protégé in her formative years. For a time all went smoothly between Mary and Catherine, for Mary had a store of charm and sympathy which she was ready to distribute among all around her, and Catherine for the most part was tactfully unobtrusive. But there came a day when the little Queen—prompted, no doubt, by the Guises—lost her temper with her prospective mother-in-law, and called her a merchant's daughter. It is easy to see how she picked up the slighting phrase, which must have been a commonly whispered aside at the Court. From that moment Catherine made no further attempt to ingratiate herself in this direction. The Guises had scored another point, and she could only retire to nurse this fresh wound.

The history of the royal children from the arrival of Mary

in France to the death of King Henry deserves a whole
volume to itself, for these little princes and princesses, in
their voluminous and splendid clothes, with their armies of
servants and their famous tutors, are the more fascinating
to-day for our knowledge of what was to happen to each of
them. The Dauphin who had the fortune to love the girl he
would in any case have to marry, and the misfortune to die
less than three years after his wedding; Mary Stuart who, as
Catherine herself said, "has only to smile to turn every
Frenchman's head," and who can still turn heads three and
a half centuries after Fotheringay; Elizabeth, shortly to be
Queen of Spain, to whom the attentive Constable sent "a
piece of the horn of an unicorn" to cure an attack of small-
pox; Claude, who was so naughty as to drink excessively
before going to bed one evening, and of whom Catherine
wrote: "the King and I are of a mind that she be fed upon
toast and water rather than anything else, since it is healthier
for her than broth—wherefore pray send for some for her";
Charles, later to be Charles IX, "eating and drinking very
sparingly, and losing all his breath at the least exertion,"
thin, pale, violent and impulsive; Henry, later to be Henry
III, the apple of Catherine's eye, with his delicate hands, his
charming manners, his Medici craft and his lapdogs; Margot,
in whom all the vitality of the stock seemed to have been
used up, the vivid, sparkling, energetic, learned, insatiably
amorous Margot of Navarre, the marvellous portent midway
between the Renaissance and the modern woman, reading
her Plutarch, her Rabelais, her Bible, delighting her father
in her infancy by her gay precocity, and at length surviving
the whole of her family into the seventeenth century; and
Hercule, the youngest son, four years old at the time of the
Dauphin's wedding, healthy for his first eight years and then
ruined physically and psychologically by smallpox.

Those are the children of that long-vanished royal household, and the nature of their establishment, as described by

Williams, was thus: "At the end of the reign it included ten chamberlains, seven *maîtres d'hôtel*, seven butlers, nine cellarers, eight equerries, eight equerries of the stables, thirty-seven pages of honour, eight secretaries, nine ushers of the chambers, twenty-eight *valets de chambres*, four *maréchaux des logis*, four masters of the wardrobe, two comptrollers general, five doctors, three surgeons, four apothecaries, four barbers, four ladies of the bedchamber, five demoiselles of the bedchamber, and ten *femmes de chambre*. What it must have been to feed the royal children and the army of officials and servants who surrounded them may be conjectured from the fact that the kitchen staff numbered fifty-seven persons, and the provisions for a single day comprised twenty-three dozen loaves of bread, eighteen pieces of beef, eight sheep, four calves, twenty capons, one hundred and twenty pullets or pigeons, three kids, six goslings, four leverets, etc. After March, 1533, the Dauphin had an establishment of his own, which numbered over three hundred persons, whose salaries amounted to 68,000 *livres*."

In this luxurious atmosphere Mary of Scotland learned the lessons proper to a Queen. Ronsard was her literary tutor, Amyot, who made Plutarch a Frenchman, taught her Latin, and Danés of the Collège de France taught her Greek. French, Italian and Spanish she acquired at the same time. She had her lessons with the other children, but she speedily outshone them all, rivalling her illustrious contemporaries in this golden age of feminine education. Lady Jane Grey, at the age of thirteen, read Plato in the original; Queen Elizabeth of England at fourteen translated a work by Margaret of Valois; the little Italian girls, pupils of Olympia Morata, acted a comedy of Terence in the presence of the Pope. And thirteen-year-old Mary Stuart recited in the Louvre before King Henry and his Court a Latin discourse which she had herself composed. At that age she was very much occupied with these Latin compositions, high-flown sentiments on set themes of the duty of princes and the eternity of the cardinal virtues. She had a new theme every day, but in spite of the somewhat priggish flavour of these elegant disquisitions she remained gay and delightful and sufficiently human. From a Latin eulogy on the quality of temperance we may turn to a letter to her mother from the vigilant Cardinal of Lorraine: "she has always a very good appetite, and if she were allowed to eat and drink as much as she asks for her stomach would often be the sufferer."

In all other requisite accomplishments Mary showed herself equally apt. We have Brantôme's picture of the white hands that were so freely praised, wandering over the strings of the lute, and they were no less gracefully busy upon the tapestry-frame. She danced and hunted and became an excellent horsewoman. Many years later, when she was detained, though with a semblance of freedom, at Carlisle, we have the following testimony to her interest in sport and her good horsemanship. It is from a report to Elizabeth from Sir Francis Knolles:

"Yesterday her Grace went out at a postern to walk on a playing green toward Scotland, and we, with 24 halberdiers of Master Read's band with divers gentlemen and other servants, waited on her, where about twenty of her retinue played football before her the space of two hours very strongly, nimble and skilfully, without any foul play offered, the smallness of their balls occasioning their fair play. And before yesterday since our coming she went but twice out of the town, once to the like play of football in the same place, and once rode out a-hunting the hare, she galloping so fast upon every occasion, and her whole retinue being so well horsed, that we upon experience thereof, doubted that upon a set course some of her friends out of Scotland might invade and assault us upon the sudden to rescue and take her from us."

It is a vivid glimpse of the wild, fleet creature and her nervous captors.

Politically, Mary accepted unquestionably the tutelage of the Guises, and more especially of the Cardinal of Lorraine. A rumour that she accepted more than this from her zealous guardian owes its origin to Bothwell's later reference to her as "the Cardinal's whore," but it is entirely without foundation. She was as adept a student of politics as of everything else, and there is a remarkable account of her meeting at Rouen with her mother, who had come over to see her in 1550. The eight-year-old Queen is said to have asked: "What factions continued to subsist in the noble families of Scotland, at the same time enquiring by name for those who had evinced most attachment to the ancient faith. She then proceeded to ask, with all the usual expressions of royal benevolence, whether the English still harassed her native country, whether worship remained pure, and the prelates and clergy did their duty."

The schemes of the Guises did not always run smoothly, and in 1557 Montmorency scored a great success by marrying his son to Diane de France, illegitimate daughter of Henry and Diane de Poitiers, and now a widow. The Guises trembled, and for a moment it seemed as if the great project of union between Mary and the Dauphin might fall to the ground. But then came the crushing defeat of Saint-Quentin, at which Montmorency was taken prisoner; and that was swiftly followed by the most brilliant Guise exploit of all, the recapture of Calais. The Guises were uppermost again, and the royal wedding was hurried on.

It was at this juncture that the fourteen-year-old Queen of Scots signed that secret document which was the first weapon that she gave to her calumniators. The Guises, over-reaching themselves in this moment of the fulfilment of their ambition, easily persuaded Henry towards a scheme which would ensure the subjection of Scotland to the French crown, but we shall never be quite certain how Mary was won over, or what her real sentiments were in regard to the treacherous step that was being taken. She declared by this document, that in default of heirs of her body she "gives in pure and free donation to the kings of France, present and to come, all her realm of Scotland, and all her rights and claims to the crown of England," and at the same time she relinquished the right and power of ever retracting the gift. Thereto was added a clause providing for a payment of a million crowns in gold, through the Scottish revenue, in return for the French King's services in defending the country. She must have understood perfectly what she was signing, though, as Martin Hume adds, "with such a nation as the Scots the undertakings signed by Mary would have been in any case impossible of fulfilment." Perhaps her confidence in her body was such that she deemed it a safe chance. We cannot here linger any longer over a case that must remain a matter for learned dispute.

The secret document had been signed on April 4, and now on the 19th Francis and Mary plighted their troth. Thereafter followed feasting and dancing in the Louvre, and five days later came the marriage ceremony at Notre-Dame. Stands had been erected in front of the west door of the cathedral for all the notables of France, both temporal and spiritual, and for the musicians who were to enliven every stage of the day's business. Duke Francis of Guise, casting his arrogant eye over the sumptuous preparations while the crowd was still assembling, had followed the family policy of pleasing the mob by making the courtiers stand back so that the common people should have a clear view.

From the cathedral portal, hung with red curtains embroidered with the silver lilies of France, a covered passage extended to the residence of the Bishop of Paris, and down this passage came at length the bridal procession, led by a hundred gentlemen of the royal household. Then came the princes of the blood and the lords ecclesiastical, together with the Papal legate, and after them the bridegroom, escorted by two of his brothers and the King of Navarre. There, in front of the noble west door, the glittering company took up its position, waiting for the fair-haired northern bride.

In the April of her life, with the King of France at her side, Mary of Scotland walked to her wedding, clad "in a white robe, like unto a lily, fashioned so richly and beautifully that none could imagine it. The train thereof, of marvellous length, was borne by two young damsels. About her neck hung a circlet of untold worth, formed of blazing jewels, and on her head she wore a golden crown studded with pearls, diamonds, rubies, sapphires, emeralds and other precious gems, but above all there was set in the midst of a great carbuncle of the value of five hundred thousand crowns or more." Behind her followed Catherine de' Medici, concealing beneath her smiling mask her feelings on this day of triumph for her enemies. And with Catherine were the other princesses and ladies of the Court, "clothed with such splendour that it could not be set in fewer words than those of a lengthy discourse."

Outside the cathedral, but yet within sanctuary, the Dauphin placed the ring on the finger of his bride, and the Cardinal de Bourbon blessed them. Then they passed through the doors to complete the ritual within the building. While they are there, let us listen once more to Brantôme, who had his place among the enraptured onlookers:

"She seemed a hundred times lovelier than a goddess from the sky, in the morning as she went with brave majesty to her wedding, and in the afternoon as she danced, and in the evening as she walked with modest step and proud mien to offer her vow to the hymeneal deity and to consummate it; in such sort that the general saying echoed through the Court and through the city that the prince who was being united to this princess was beyond all measure fortunate. For if the realm of Scotland were a thing of value, the queen surpassed it therein: since even had she lacked sceptre and crown her very person and her divine beauty would have been worth a kingdom, but being queen she brought to France and to her husband a twofold blessing."

Silver trumpets announced to the crowd outside that the union of France and Scotland had been accomplished in the persons of Francis and Mary, and the heralds cried "Largesse!" Gold and silver coin was therewith flung in profusion to the multitude, who flung themselves upon it with such violence that many were gravely injured, and at last the beggars themselves entreated the heralds to desist. In the nave of Notre-Dame the cry was repeated, and here it was the pages and attendants who fought for the money.

Mass having been celebrated, the whole company repaired to the episcopal palace for the wedding-banquet, after which the dancing began, King Henry leading off with Mary and the Dauphin with his mother Catherine. Till five in the afternoon the ball continued, the golden robes of princes and princesses being "so superbly worked that the Elysian Fields could not have been more lovely." Then all repaired on horseback and in litters to the palace of Les Tournelles, where they took supper, a meal so stimulating that "both matrons and maids leaped in the air for joy." It must have been, one way and another, a heady spectacle.

But that was not all. The most exciting festivities, the "mummeries," so dear to sixteenth-century hedonists, were reserved for the evening. The young and slender bride, in a dress six ells long that had to be borne by a courtier, trod a *pavane* with her still younger sister-in-law Elizabeth. Seven beautiful girls, dressed or undressed to represent the planets, advanced to the sound of a sung epithalamion. The royal children, with those of the families of Guise and Aumale, had a glorious time, riding about on hobby-horses caparisoned in cloth of gold, and then attaching their mimic steeds

to tiny coaches wherein sat merrymakers clothed as pilgrims—
though with a richness that no pilgrim would have recognised. These sang "sweet hymns and canticles in praise of
marriage and the married pair." The apotheosis was at length
reached by the entrance into the ballroom of six galleons
with golden sails, rolling and tossing by a hidden device.
Within each vessel sat a prince of the blood royal, masked,
and each in turn sprang out, seized the lady of his choice,
and sailed away with her to an imaginary Cytherea. The
Dauphin, of course, carried off his bride, to the accompaniment of loud rejoicings. But the selection by the King of
Navarre of his own wife as companion of the voyage seems
to have occasioned general astonishment.

That was one side of the Guise triumph. The other was
the poisoning of four of the Scottish commissioners who had
refused their consent to the coronation of the newly wedded
Dauphin as King of Scotland.

But the King wanted the captive Constable back. He still
retained a genuine affection for the old warrior under whom
he had fought his first battles, and the mounting supremacy
of the Guises had an unhealthy look. Diane de Poitiers, who
had shrewdly enough married one of her daughters to a
Guise and another to a Montmorency, was also anxious for
a more balanced situation.

As for Catherine, the sack of Saint-Quentin had given her
an opportunity for self-assertion, and she had taken it
energetically. The fifteen days in which Coligny had held
so heroically a hopeless position were sufficient to arouse
Paris from the panic into which the Flemish news had
thrown it. At once Catherine stepped in, determined to
stop the rioting in the city and find fresh funds to save the
situation. She went to the Parlement in person and asked for
three hundred thousand livres for the raising of an army of
relief. With admirable discretion she withdrew while the
debate was in progress, and so effective had been her words

and this tactful action that Parlement voted a still larger
sum, and was followed by the provincial centres with further
contributions.

It was a great stroke. It is said that from that day Henry
began to spend the evenings with Catherine instead of with
Diane. A new medal was minted. No longer, as in the old
days, was the King shown on horseback with his mistress
behind him on the crupper. This time there is Henry's
head on one side of the medal and that of Catherine on the
other. At last Catherine's consummate patience is beginning
to earn its reward. "She did not," says Miss Sichel, "win
Henry's love, but she had at least gained his respect." She
had been married to him for twenty-four years.

There is no note of triumph in Catherine's correspondence,
but we can guess what she must have been thinking. Henry
was forty years old, grey-haired but vigorous, a king who had
learned to rule and had success to look forward to. Diane
was close on sixty, and her power could not last for ever.
Catherine had come into the open at just the right moment.

The Treaty of Cateau-Cambrésis, though it left France
in possession of Calais, Metz, Toul and Verdun, was not well
received in Paris. They called it "The Prisoners' Peace,"
saying that many of the conquests of their hero, Guise, had
been shamelessly bartered to get Montmorency and Coligny
back. And the Protestants suspected secret clauses between
Henry and Philip of Spain, for the further persecution of
heretics in their dominions.

But the King threw two more royal weddings to the crowd,
and they forgot their grievances as they poured into the
streets to watch the processions and fight for largesse. Both
weddings arose out of the new treaty. One was between
Henry's sister Marguerite (the second of the three Marguerites de Valois, an undistinguished niece of the learned
sister of Francis I) and the Duke of Savoy. The other was
between the little Princess Elizabeth, playmate of Mary

Stuart, and Philip of Spain, the Most Catholic King. Well might the Protestants tremble at such portents.

As a husband Philip II had already had a sufficiently varied experience. First he had married Mary of Portugal, who died. Next he married Mary Tudor, Queen of England, who also died. Then he had sought the slippery hand of Elizabeth of England, and failed. And now he was to marry the daughter of the King of France. In such manner were the fates of nations decided.

Unable to come to France for his wedding, the Spanish King sent the inflexible Duke of Alba as his proxy. He arrived with the two men who were to become the heroes of Dutch independence, Egmont and Orange, and Paris gave its usual expensive welcome to the distinguished foreigners.

Of the festivities staged for the two weddings there is only one feature which need concern us. For three lovely midsummer days was held the last tournament in the history of the French Court. It was a different Catherine who watched the jousting of the knights. Outwardly she was the same as ever, with her magnificent clothes and her slightly austere smile, but inwardly she had a new confidence which was not even shaken by a dream which visited her after the second days of the tourney. She dreamed that Henry had lost one eye, but she paid no attention to it.

On the third day, wearing the black-and-white favours of Diane and riding a splendid horse belonging to the Duke of Savoy, the King entered the lists. It was a moment to move the multitude, and thunderous cheers broke out as Henry rode into the arena. The time-honoured ceremonies were scrupulously performed, and Catherine, surrounded by the ladies of the Court in a special gallery, watched with a quickening pulse the salute of her husband before he engaged himself. There were four queens together in that gallery, which, says an eyewitness, "was a boastful thing to see."

In the opening jousts the King acquitted himself with great prowess. In the true spirit of chivalry he accepted no credit for it, but from his pavilion sent a gentleman to the Duke of Savoy (who was present only as a spectator) to congratulate him on the excellence of his horse. The Duke returned a message in which he complimented the combatant and begged him not to exert himself further but to rest satisfied with the splendid performance he had already given; and the Queen and all her ladies added their persuasions, saying that the victory already belonged to Henry, that the day was very hot and that the usual hour for the conclusion of the tournament had arrived.

"On the faith of a true knight!" cried the King when the message was brought to him, "I have scarcely loosened my limbs. Bring me another lance, for I will break one more before we depart!"

Then he sent for a certain Montgomery, Captain of the Scottish Guard, and bade him prepare for a last joust with his King. At first Montgomery entreated to be excused, but Henry became angry and peremptorily ordered him, if he wished to be accounted a man of honour, to run against him. The Captain was known to be a brave and skilful rider, and he had no choice but to obey.

From her seat in the gallery Catherine saw her husband canter out again into the lists to the loud delight of the crowd. He still wore the colours that had haunted her for twenty-five years, the black and white of his mistress, but to Catherine he had just sent a message which she had scarcely been able to receive without betraying her triumph. He would break, he said, one more lance for the love of his wife. Incredible, but true.

As the two horses gathered speed towards each other a boy shouted from an upper gallery, "Sire, do not fight!" but those about him silenced him instantly. Later he admitted that he had no idea what prompted him to speak those words.

The slight commotion was lost in the thunder of hooves across the sun-baked turf.

On either side of the low barrier, with lance in rest, the two knights came on. With a splintering shock lance met armour, and the weapon of Montgomery, striking the King's gorget below the visor, shivered to pieces in his hand. Both riders reeled with the blow, their steeds plunging and rearing. Both recovered themselves. And then the King, his head bowed forward, was seen to lurch from the saddle. Watchful attendants caught him before he fell, but the crowd saw that he was badly injured, and a cry of dismay went up. He was carried to his pavilion while the onlookers rushed in confusion from their seats and the horrified Montgomery made his way from the lists to kneel beside the wounded King and beg of him to cut off his hand and his head. But Henry, when he had recovered consciousness, told the Captain that there was nothing to pardon, since he had obeyed his sovereign and borne himself like a valiant knight.

A splinter from Montgomery's lance had penetrated the King's eye, and he had lost much blood before he was removed to Les Tournelles for attendance by the royal surgeons. They dressed the wound, purged the patient, bled him, purged him again, and applied all other remedies known to medical science at that time. For ten days he lingered, and there was time for André Vésale, the greatest doctor of his day, to hurry to Paris from Brussels. Paris became a city of mourning, for hope was speedily abandoned, though a great procession was formed to intercede for the dying monarch. Every resource was tried in vain, except trepanning, which might have saved his life. This operation was, indeed, suggested, but no doctor dared take the risk. Instead, they tried experiments with splinters of the broken lance upon the heads of a number of executed criminals, for medical practice in the sixteenth century was for the most part rather inquisitive than curative. An abscess formed, and it was only a matter of days till the inevitable end. At length the King asked for music, a request which is frequently echoed in the death-bed scenes of the time. Then he blessed the Dauphin, received the Sacrament, and died a little after midday on July 10, 1559.

"Never," said Catherine on one occasion, "did a woman who loved her husband succeed in loving his mistress." Did she really love Henry? The matter can never be put beyond doubt, but the probability must seem that her hatred for Diane was a stronger emotion than anything she felt towards her husband. She had never seen Henry before she married him, and from the very beginning he had been indifferent to her. Her character was more intellectual and less emotional than that of Diane, and throughout her life she continues to give an impression of coldness which effectively excludes the notion of a *grande passion*. But jealousy is easy to mistake for love, and it may be that at times she herself more than half believed that the affection of her husband was all that she desired. Soon after his death she wrote to her daughter Elizabeth in Spain: "Place yourself in the mercy of God, for at one time you have seen me as contented as you are now, since I believed that the only trouble I should ever have was that I was not loved in the way that I desired by your father the King, who no doubt had done me too much honour; but I loved him so greatly that I went always in fear of him, as you are well aware. And now God has taken him away from me... therefore let me serve as a warning to you not to trust too much in a husband's love."

Seldom is Catherine so confiding as this in her correspondence, and it is an illuminating letter. A certain amount is to be discounted as mere maternal admonishment, but it is possible to read a good deal between the lines. Henry had died at the very moment when Catherine had at last won his favour, and when he was most necessary to her ambitions. With a strong King on the throne, and Diane fading swiftly into the background and towards the grave, the Queen could at last have taken her right and profitable place as Consort. It is scarcely to be doubted that, once Diane was powerless or dead, Henry would have turned whole-heartedly to Catherine. Beyond a trivial amour or two, there were no other women in his life but these two, and with her fingers on the prize Catherine would have had the skill not to let it go.

But now there was to be a weak little King of sixteen, with a Consort who was the particular protégé of Catherine's avowed enemies, the Guises. The whole of her plans must be changed, a new line of advance found and used with the utmost energy if she were to survive. The reign of Diane, of course, had come to a decisive end with Henry's death, and even before her husband had breathed his last Catherine had sent a messenger to her rival demanding the return of the crown jewels which the King had given her. That is scarcely the action of a woman consumed with no other emotions than love for her husband and grief at his death. It is said that Diane received the messenger with the words: "Is the King dead?"

"No, Madame," was the reply, "but it is not thought that he will live through the night."

"Then," said Diane, her pride showing through her grief, "as yet there is none who can command me!"

But a little later Catherine received the jewels which had gleamed so temptingly in her imagination at the bedside of the dying King. She also forced Diane to give up the lovely castle of Chenonceaux, built upon arches across the bubbling waters of the little river Cher, and gave her in exchange that of Chaumont on the banks of the Loire. Perhaps Mary Stuart had not been unjustified in calling her the daughter of merchants. She did not touch Anet, which meant nothing to her. Diane was allowed to retire thither, to end her days in the surroundings that had seen her greatness.

Meanwhile the walls of Catherine's chamber were hung

with deepest black, and she adopted for the first time the veiled garb of a widow in which she has invariably appeared to the imagination of later generations. Her weeds are not the sumptuous black and white garments of Diane, almost gay by virtue of their meaning. They are but the outward sign of that veiled cunning which was to carry her to her greatest triumphs. And the tears which she sheds so copiously in the sight of chroniclers are prompted more by annoyance with fate than by affection for the dead. They seem, indeed, like the theatrical grief of the First Player in *Hamlet*—"the mobled queen with bisson rheum."

How would a wife who had loved Henry have acted towards the luckless Montgomery, who was probably more sincerely stricken with grief than any of them? On his deathbed the King had spoken noble and cheerful words to him, refusing even to accept an apology. Driven frantic by distress, the Queen might at that instant have made him suffer for the terrible accident, but afterwards she would surely have repented of such injustice.

Catherine let him go. He was a Protestant, and the suspicion had got about that the King's death had been premeditated by the party of that faith. Wishing to show herself clement towards the Protestants Catherine at first contented herself with banishing him. But she never forgave the man who had been the unwitting cause of this momentary reverse in her fortunes. The wretched Montgomery wandered for many years as a soldier of fortune, but fifteen years after the fatal joust he put himself again in Catherine's power. Fighting for England, he was captured after a courageous defence, having capitulated with ten thousand men on the understanding that his life should be spared. Catherine had him brought to Paris, condemned for high treason, and beheaded and quartered before her eyes in the Place de Grève. She had learned how to wait for vengeance.

# IV

# QUEEN-REGENT

IT was in the gentle countryside of Touraine, the pastoral *pays de vache* that Rabelais had known and loved, that the short summer of Mary Stuart's life as Queen-Consort of France was passed. Long after she had looked back from the boat as it left Calais, repeating over and over again through her tears, *"Adieu, France! Adieu, France!"* she remembered this green valley with its splendid castles and its regal little towns of Blois and Tours and Orleans where she had been so richly received. Back among the mists of her native land she still read Ronsard's poems, and sent him presents, and mourned, with the self-centred grief of a woman who lives on sensuous delights, the early death of her invalid, passionate young husband. The poets vied with each other in glorifying the love of Mary and Francis, and there was no man in France who did not gladly yield to the fair-haired Scottish Queen the right to be as happy as rank and riches could make her. The valley of the Loire, the pleasure-garden of kings, had been chosen for the beneficial effect which its mild climate might have upon the precarious health of the new sovereign, but perhaps there was a thought for Mary also when the question of the royal residences came to be debated.

First the Court was at Blois, then ten miles down the river at Amboise. And at Amboise we see the other side of the picture, the side which all poets, except polemicals, tactfully avoided. For throughout the month of March, 1560, the great round tower that had been hung with precious cloths forty years before for the marriage of Catherine de' Medici's parents, was surmounted by the spiked heads of murdered men. Corpses hung in ropes and chains from the Italianate machicolations, and the Loire ran red with the blood of headless Huguenots. We do not hear much of Mary in the accounts of these Amboise executions which made the names of her Guise uncles and even of her husband—guilty only from lack of resolution—hated and feared throughout France. But we are told that the whole Court assembled each day on a balcony whence a view of the butchery could be obtained, for the Guises "had ordered these things purposely to afford a distraction for the ladies, whom they observed to be showing signs of boredom through remaining so long in one place." This appalling glimpse of the sadism of a cultured sixteenth-century aristocracy has simply to be accepted and remembered. It defies comment.

It was about this time that the term *Huguenots*—derived probably from the Swiss *Eidgenossen*—came into general use to designate the French Protestants. The Reformation, which began among the poorer classes (among the weavers of Lyons, for example, who had suffered in the bloody Vaudois repression shortly before the death of Francis I), had now found among the titled and landed people a formidable following. In his imprisonment after the fall of St. Quentin Gaspard de Coligny had asked for a French Bible to beguile the long hours of idleness and to defeat despair. His open adoption of Protestantism, which dates from this period, has long been the subject of debate, but must be regarded rather as a sincere religious conversion than as a move prompted by political expediency. His liberal-minded brothers, Cardinal Odet and Andelot, also avowed the new faith, and Coligny influence on Condé helped to range the Bourbon princes of the blood on the side of the Reformers. Besides Condé, to whom Coligny looked as a popular leader for the Huguenots, there was the Bourbon Antoine of Navarre, who was generally regarded as a more suitable figure-head. Both the Prince de Condé and the King of Navarre were married to spiritual descendants of Margaret of Valois, ladies of a genuine devotion in whom the love of learning and humanity had bred allegiance to the new ideas. Jeanne of Navarre and Eléonore de Roye, Princesse de Condé, were leading types of the Renaissance woman born into a period when religion had added itself to art and literature as a subject of passionate interest and had usurped the place of all other causes as a political motive. Over against the fierce Catholic tradition of the Guises, Protestantism had raised up its own aristocracy.

Between them stands Catherine de' Medici, cold and passionless, putting every move to the touchstone of common sense. Her son, at sixteen, was legally of age, and she could not be Regent in name. But in his edicts and documents of state the phrase recurs: "Such being the good pleasure of my Lady-Mother, whose every opinion I also hold." Skilfully used, her power could make her position the equivalent of a Regency.

This end, however, could not have been obtained without the consent of the Guises.—till now, with the fallen Diane, her arch-enemies. Francis was still completely dazzled by his lovely young wife, and Mary was still the tool of her uncles. Catherine was a good enough judge of character to realise that her best course lay in allying herself with the Guises and waiting for the mistakes to which their unbounded self-satisfaction would lead them.

One of the first steps which Francis took on coming to the throne—and it is incontestable that his mother was behind him in this—was to disgrace Montmorency once more. The aged Constable must by this time have realised the justice of the text, "Put not thy trust in princes." Relief from his offices, which were handed to the Guises, was offered him as a gesture of honourable ease to his old age, but he was not in the least deceived. Declaring that his sword would always be ready to serve the King if it were needed, he retired to his magnificent castle of Chantilly with a train of such splendour that even in adversity he succeeded in arousing the jealousy of the Guises. If any further evidence were needed that Catherine had never loved her husband, this treatment of his oldest friend might provide it.

There was soon no doubt of the side Catherine had chosen. The Prince de Condé was given a foreign embassy to keep him out of the way for a while, and the King of Navarre was openly snubbed. We have already seen this amiable cavalier honouring his wife at the nuptial drolleries of Mary and Francis. History has not dealt kindly with him, and indeed his character was in marked contrast with the Gascon vigour of his son—that other King of Navarre who was to fight his way to the throne of France. Antoine of Navarre was an irresolute temporiser, too fond of talking and listening, as ready to make specious promises as he was to accept ill-intentioned advice. But he was in an awkward position. His kingdom was an uncomfortable buffer-state between France and Spain, and the close interest which Philip of Spain was now taking in the French political situation placed poor Antoine in a quandary. Was the Huguenot opposition in France strong enough to support him after choosing him as a leader, or would the Guises, backed up by Philip in their Catholic campaign, be more suitable as friends than as enemies? His scholarly and pious wife was a strong influence towards the Huguenot cause, and when on the accession of the new King there came the invitation to proceed to Court, Antoine began to prepare a rich retinue that should suitably impress Catherine de' Medici and gain a powerful ally. But two of his advisers, in the pay of the Guises, persuaded him that Philip was watching him closely from over the border, and that humility would be his best card. He hesitated, and then decided to follow their counsel. And by that time Catherine's mind was made up. Antoine would get no comfort from her. When at last he reached the French Court his reception was a freezing one. Helplessly he swallowed all indignities, flattered the all-powerful Guises, and then trailed back to Navarre, leaving his Huguenot followers disappointed and resentful.

But the Huguenots were neither leaderless nor impotent. There were other Bourbon Princes, there were the three Colignys, and now there was Montmorency, thrown for a time into this camp by the disgrace which left him without office, but not without influence. The insensate Guise pride was leading to the inevitable reaction. Their ambitious Scottish plans had now no less an opponent than Elizabeth of England to face. Their friendship with Spain aroused suspicion and resentment. The plurality of offices collected by the family was an excellent topic for lampoons, and much of the glory of the recapture of Calais was discounted by the growing belief—probably well founded—that that exploit had owed its success in large measure to the plans of Coligny prepared beforehand.

As the new religion spread upwards through the social scale, the burnings and beheadings and imprisonments increased. And by an invariable law the converse process also went on apace. Every savage punitive measure brought more converts into the Huguenot camp. Hatred of the Guises reached at length the stage of a widespread conspiracy. The precise aims of the movement at this instant can never be known, for most of the evidence was obtained under the stress of torture. It was said that a Republic was planned, that the King and the Cardinal of Lorraine were to be killed, and the State administered by a Protestant directorate. Perhaps some of the conspirators were ready to go as far as this; others, probably, would have liked to see Condé on the throne as a Huguenot Louis XIII. But it is doubtful whether such extremist views were shared by the general body of conspirators, who would have been content if they had succeeded in penetrating through the Guise guard to the presence of the young King and in laying their grievances before him.

And there were grievances in plenty to justify the more violent revolutionaries. Sick with fear of the effect of his own misdeeds, the Cardinal of Lorraine went from one enormity to another to stamp out the rising opposition, so that he was deserted even by men of his own party who dreaded the popular vengeance that the gaoler and the headsman were fanning into flame. An astrologer had foretold death for the Cardinal in this year 1560, and he doubled his guard. He even made an arbitrary change in the Court fashion of dress, causing to be abandoned the wide cloaks and tall boots which were dangerous hiding-places for daggers. And he and Catherine decided to move the Court from Blois to Amboise, the stately stronghold which in spite of its Italianate renovation had sufficient of the feudal fortress remaining about it to provide more security than Blois.

There is a letter from Calvin to Coligny, written after the Amboise executions, which shows not only that the anti-Pope of Geneva was aware of the plot, but that projects of definite violence had been communicated to him. Calvin was in correspondence with all the most prominent Huguenots, and the inexorable logic of his lucid mind emerges clearly from the background of hatred and hysteria which made the wars of religion. The scheme, he told Coligny, had seemed to him unjustifiable on spiritual, and imprudent on material grounds. And he had warned the conspirators "that if one drop of blood were shed, all the rivers of Europe would overflow therewith." Events were to bring his grim prophecy to pass.

Impatience and lack of co-ordination sealed the fate of the plot. Scattered bodies of armed men were found in the forests about Amboise and brought to the castle. The King was standing at a window. His mother had told him what to do. With expansive graciousness he gave them all money and asked them what they intended by banding together. Heartened by the royal favour and the chink of coin they

related that forty thousand troops were ready to assemble
a given day to force their way to his Majesty. A sortie wa
made and further parties were rounded up. Spies brought
in fresh reports, and in the dungeons of Amboise the instruments of the torturers succeeded in implicating those whom
the Guises had most reason to fear. The Cardinal, slinking
about the castle with a steel jacket beneath his vestments and
a bodyguard in attendance, concealed with difficulty the panic
of an evil conscience. But his brother the Duke went light-
heartedly about the business of butchery, hanging men from
the battlements, throwing them in sacks into the Loire in
batches of twenty, lopping limbs and heads in the courtyard
as a spectacle for the ladies and gentlemen of his suite. The
King and his brother princes were forced to witness these
displays, not only to add authority to the executions but also
with the definite purpose of still further debasing the degenerate royal stock. Weak sovereigns were going to be necessary to Guise policy, and Catherine too was quite ready to
see the feeble nerves of her own children racked by the
daily spectacle of hideous cruelties. She herself could look
on with impassive face, if not with the perverse gloating of
Francis of Guise. In the only letter in which she gives any
sign of emotion in regard to the slaughter of Huguenots it is
the emotion not of pity but of wonder. The fortitude in the
bearing of certain victims has astonished her. With the cold
eye of a politician she examines such symptoms in order to
determine the possibilities of success for the Protestant cause.

The Prince de Condé, who had now returned to Amboise,
was not unnaturally regarded with grave suspicion by the
Guises. They could not be certain that he had had anything
to do with the plot, but they made several attempts to trap
him into a revelation of his sympathies. One day they sent
for him to join them in a room where a party of men was
being put to death one by one. He refused the summons
but he was compelled by force to stand outside on a balcony

and look in through one of the windows. "I am astonished," he cried, "that the King allows himself to be persuaded to kill so many honest lords and gentlemen."

But the King could do nothing. "Why do my people so hate me?" he asked the Cardinal. "It is because of you. Would to God you would take yourself elsewhere!" And later, carried from place to place in search of health, the wretched youth covered his face with his hands and sobbed when he saw the villagers chasing their screaming children indoors. Rumour had it that Francis II's physical weakness received the treatment of a daily bath of infants' blood.

And Catherine herself, waiting for the Guises to take enough rope to hang themselves, was still in subjection. She appears, says a chronicler at this time, "a tall and powerful woman, with a face full and rubicund . . . her speech is unfeminine, almost that of a rough country woman. She wears a dark robe of fine texture. Her bust is well formed." This is the woman who walks with silent tread through the rooms and corridors of Amboise, descending to the dungeons to hear confessions extracted from some tormented wretch; pondering upon the evidence as she makes her way back to the courtyard where executions are taking place in the thin March sunshine, stealing by night to the chambers of the Guises to learn their secrets as she caresses them, or to persuade them by feminine arts to spare the life of some prisoner whose gratitude may one day be useful to her.

Deferring of necessity to the Guise power, she did not fail to look ahead to the day when the death of her son would remove one important source of that power. There was no likelihood that Francis would live long, for his early marriage and his pitiful anxiety to distinguish himself on horseback had greatly overtaxed his scanty strength. If Catherine were now to associate herself openly with the Guise persecutions she would find herself friendless when the reaction gained

CHARLES DE GUISE, CARDINAL OF LORRAINE
PORTRAIT IN ENAMEL BY LEONARD LIMOUSIN
(Victoria and Albert Museum)

ground. She accordingly sought a middle way, and sent for Gaspard de Coligny to advise her.

The Admiral knew exactly what he wanted, and he was well prepared to give all his support to Catherine if she would commit herself to a tolerant and progressive policy. He urged the removal of the Guises, the transference of power into Catherine's hands as Queen-Mother and the issue of solemn and binding edicts permitting the Catholic and Protestant Churches to exist side by side in France and re-nouncing the use of coercion in religious matters. The honest reasonableness of Coligny's attitude is so striking, and the part assigned to Catherine so attractive, that at this distance from events it seems almost incredible that she should have rejected his proposals. But he asked too much, and the Guises were too strong. If her own power had been assured, Cath-erine might have preferred a policy of toleration towards the Protestant religion, which appealed to her unemotional com-mon sense. But her own power was not assured. She dared not take risks.

On this moment of the meeting of Catherine and Coligny hung the history of France for the next thirty years, and the lives of thousands of its inhabitants. They were both of an age—forty-one—and both were looking to the future. Coligny was sincere and altruistic in his religious attitude, while Catherine had no religious motives at all. But the career of each was inextricably bound up with the religious struggle, and they could have found mutual interests to serve. Their association was indeed to be a close one, but it was to end in the crowning tragedy by which, more than by anything else in their lives, both were to be remembered.

The Amboise terror was nevertheless succeeded by a short period of moderation. Catherine was anxious to gain time, to postpone the coming conflict if possible until after her son's death, which now, it seemed, could not be long delayed. It was not difficult to persuade the Cardinal of Lorraine that a gentler policy might serve him at this moment. "The Tiger of France," as he was called in a violent pamphlet of the day, had outraged even some of his own following by his ferocity, and there is a story of one of his associates—a man who had not previously given noticeable signs of squeamishness—crying in horror on his deathbed: "Go, you have damned us all!" Twelve picked arquebusiers guarded the person of the Guise prelate, and in default of his inaccessible body his effigy was hanged publicly in Paris. Catherine represented to him that the popular hatred which could not be extinguished by violence, might yield to softer measures. She carried her point, and for a while the smile was on the face of the Tiger. Huguenots were allowed to assemble for worship without fear of violence, and a conference was called at Fontainebleau to discuss the situation of the two religions. Coligny's proposal at this meeting that freedom of conscience should be granted to both creeds was received with astonishment, and the King sharply bade him sit down and not waste the time of the assembly with facetious suggestions. But the Fontainebleau Congress was important, for herein Coligny at last emerged publicly and unequivocally as the champion of Protestantism. At the same time he voiced his strong disapproval of the conspiracy of Amboise and of any sectional attempt to interfere with the constitution and order of the State. Coligny was much too reasonable for his century.

Meanwhile Catherine played such a game as Clement ought to have lived to see. When her son came to die she would need the support of the Bourbon Princes, and with this in her mind she was flirting once more with the Protestant cause, encouraging Coligny just as far as she thought prudent, letting it be known that it was her influence that had temporarily stopped the executions, and spreading her net for that deceptive bird the King of Navarre. In her long black gown she paced the polished floors of Amboise, and beside her, his arm linked affectionately in hers, strolled the ineffective Antoine, dressed like a dandy, his beard curled, his ears adorned with tinkling rings. Her conversation, a skilfully baited confection of vivacious pleasantries, intriguing hints, and leading questions heavily disguised, drew from him smooth promises and elegant compliments. It was always so with the King of Navarre. But Catherine was gaining ground, and Antoine was impressed with the idea that she might be no mean ally in face of the terrible Guises.

He had, however, one or two awkward questions to put to her, and one of them concerned his gallant younger brother, the Prince de Condé, who was at that moment securely locked up some way below their feet. Having put him there herself, and personally supervised the addition of bars and gratings to his quarters, Catherine was ready for the question. It was the King, she said suavely, who had insisted upon Condé's arrest and now refused him a trial or a hearing. The notion of Francis insisting upon anything which Catherine and the Guises had not first put into his head was a fantastic one, but the Medici knew well how to embroider the least convincing of statements.

The fact was that while Catherine wanted the uncompromising Condé out of the way so that she could bribe his weaker brother, the Guises were anxious to see both Bourbons kept safely at heel. They had been suspected of complicity in the Amboise conspiracy, and King Francis had been instructed to command their presence. To the royal summons Catherine had added her honeyed persuasions: "I promise you," she had written, "that the King and I will give you the best possible welcome, so that you will have no cause to regret joining a company where you will be so dearly loved and esteemed." Their astute and loyal consorts, the Princesse de Condé and the Queen of Navarre, had begged their husbands not to risk their lives in the nest of the Guises. For these ladies knew well the price that was likely to be exacted at this time for progressive thought. Had not Margaret of Valois herself, in days less troubled and with a brother on the throne of France to protect her, been obliged to receive the Sacrament privately in her chamber because of the intention of a cardinal to give her poison in the chalice? Navarre, indeed, would have yielded to the counsel of his wife, for he had already had experience of a royal reception. But the chivalrous Condé had regarded the invitation as a challenge, and had persuaded his brother to answer it with him. Condé had been arested, Navarre allowed to have these interesting conversations with the Queen-Mother.

The conversations went rather too far for the Guises, and it was decided that Navarre must be killed. The young King himself was to be the principal assassin of his brother monarch. The wretched Francis was flattered and bullied and given his instructions. He was to invite the victim to come alone to his chamber for an interview. There he was to provoke a quarrel and strike him with his dagger as if overcome by one of his sudden hysterical rages. It was not supposed that the debilitated youth could himself dispatch Antoine with a single blow, and the Guises would therefore be in attendance, ready to finish the work as if defending their King.

But Navarre got wind of the plot. Perhaps it was Catherine herself (as she later declared) who warned him, after vainly begging her son to refuse the order of the Guises. For the death of Antoine, though removing a candidate for the Regency when Francis should die, would not really help her plans. It would confirm the balance of power with the Guises and reduce the number of possible allies in her own project. Navarre, at any rate, though he answered a second summons after refusing the first, knew what was prepared for him and faced it bravely. He told a faithful servant of what might be expected, and made him promise, if the plot took effect, to carry his bloodstained shirt like a fiery cross through France and lay it at the feet of his wife in distant

Navarre. Perhaps he was inspired by the example of the mettlesome brother who now languished in the dungeon below him, for this was a moment of real nobility in a life which was too often a record of hesitations and timid betrayals.

Unarmed, Antoine kept his appointment. He saw the dagger in the King's girdle and he saw the ominous figures of the Cardinal and the Duke of Guise in the background. In petulant tones Francis began to upbraid him for his adherence to the new ideas which threatened the disruption of the State. Navarre made a humble reply on which no quarrel could be fastened. Try how he might the young King could raise no cause for violent dispute, and though his hand clutched the hilt of his dagger convulsively from time to time his nerves were unequal to the strain imposed upon them. He broke down and dismissed his intended victim without laying a finger upon him. As the door closed behind the man who was not to have left the room alive, the Cardinal strode forward and poured his contempt on the head of the impotent Francis. But it made no difference. The plot had failed completely.

One Bourbon Prince had escaped, but it seemed that the other was doomed. Condé's devoted wife, Eléonore, set out in person the moment she heard of his arrest, and after great hardships reached his prison. But she was not even allowed to see him or to send him a message. She went on her knees to the implacable Cardinal, she schemed and entreated till at last she obtained an interview with the King. But Francis had been told what to say, and though she only asked for a permit to visit her hubsand and encourage him in his adversity it was coldly denied her. She wrote to foreign powers, to the Protestant Princes of Germany and to Elizabeth of England, begging that pressure might be used to release the royal captive who represented the hope of the Reformed

Religion in France. But the Cardinal had his way. Condé was condemned to death for treason.

Meanwhile Catherine had not finished with the King of Navarre. With all the arts at her command she wooed his favour. His brother was under sentence of death. His own safety was by no means assured. The Guises, she told him, were using all their persuasion to enlist her support in a policy of Bourbon extermination. The King's health was failing rapidly, and when he died she herself would be the key to power in the struggle between Guise and Bourbon. If Antoine would formally renounce in her favour his claim as a Prince of the royal blood to be Regent during the minority of the next king, she would reward him with a share in the government as Lieutenant-General. If he refused, she would be reluctantly forced, for the good of the realm, to take the side of the Guises. Antoine knew well enough what that would mean. He was in a cleft stick. He did as he was asked. Immediately Catherine warned the veteran Montmorency, whose disgrace she herself had twice arranged, that he would shortly be needed again. Then, her plans well laid, she sat back to wait for her son to die.

In November a swelling behind the young King's ear became serious. The doctors could do nothing for him, and the Guises had helplessly to watch the swift decline of the boy who was their instrument of power. Francis of Guise roundly abused the physicians, and swore that the King had been poisoned by Protestants. The Cardinal sat at his bedside, even dictating to him his last prayer. On December 6. 1560, died Francis II of France after a reign of fourteen months. He was not quite eighteen years old.

The execution of Condé had been fixed for December 10. He was saved by a margin of four days.

# CHENONCEAUX

CHENONCEAUX had been a sort of Naboth's vineyard to Catherine. Indifferent to Anet, she had always coveted this less magnificent but no less beautiful retreat that Henry had made over to Diane de Poitiers on his accession. When he lay dying from Montgomery's spear-thrust, Catherine had thought of Chenonceaux, and the messenger who had been sent off to Diane had included the estate in his demands.

That Catherine was morally justified in taking over the château from the rival from whom she had suffered so much will scarcely be disputed. But the legal aspect is a curious one. The mill beside the narrow Cher had been transformed into a charming little villa by Thomas Bohier, Treasurer-General to Francis I. In the manner of the time this Treasurer amassed considerable wealth, lent money to his sovereign, and became involved in a legal action of which the rights and wrongs can never now be known. It appears, at all events, that he himself had incurred debts with the Crown which he was unable to meet. Francis, who had long had his eye on Chenonceaux, took it over on this pretext, and he and the Duchesse d'Étampes, with Henry and Diane, spent at one time and another many happy weeks in this secluded little paradise. Diane fell in love with it, and desired to add it to the chain of sumptuous arbours of pleasure with which she kept Henry's romantic affections bound to herself. When Francis died she had only to ask for it. But her acute head for business told her that legal considerations might arise. The son of Thomas Bohier was living, and the family might one day lay claim to their ancient patrimony. So the original case was examined, and it was found, or at all events announced, that some 90,000 livres of the Bohier debt remained outstanding. Henry promptly demanded a settlement with the Crown, and since the money could not immediately be found he ordered that Chenonceaux should be put up for sale. Agents were sent to the auction to make fictitious bids, but instructed to yield the property at length at Diane's price. Diane bought it for a sum of 50,000 livres, a matter which was easily settled without loss to her, since the payment had to be made to the King. Henry then struck this amount off the Bohier debt, and Chenonceaux was safe for ever from any claim by its original owners. It was therefore private, and not Crown property, that Catherine sequestered from Diane at Henry's death. The digression may be considered worth while for the light which it throws on sixteenth-century litigation.

Both Francis I and Diane had made notable extensions to the castellated mill. Diane constructed a wooden bridge across the Cher, for which Henry sent her fifty trees from the forest of Montrichard, and many notables of the kingdom, as the custom was, contributed gifts for the spacious Italianate gardens which are still preserved in their original geometric form. Cuttings came from all over France, currants, musk roses, apples, aubergines, hazels, elms, strawberry plants, violets, and mulberries for silk, and the surrounding vineyards, not very much esteemed to-day, were greatly enlarged and improved. For the embellishment of the building itself, the indefatigable Philibert de l'Orme was responsible.

But it was under Catherine that Chenonceaux attained that aspect which makes it unique amongst royal residences. For some time she must have had in mind the idea which she was able, on the death of Henry, to put into effect. This was the construction on stone piers of a gallery running right across the stream as on a bridge, with another story above it. For this she sent to Italy not only for artists, but for statues and marble medallions ready made. It is curious to think of this solitary queen, so busily preoccupied with politics, and with no very genuine appreciation of art, working her scheme for Chenonceaux into such perfection that when the estate became hers it only remained to order the prearranged items. By the end of 1560, when Francis II was succeeded by the minor Charles IX, everything was ready!

The celebrated gallery over the river, with its pleasant prospect of cool water from both rows of windows, was intended, we are told, for "banquets à la chasseresse, dancing by torchlight, and other festivities now in fashion." And when Catherine came to take formal possession of her new *pavilion de luxe* every resource was used to demonstrate that she too could play the magnificent Renaissance lady when she chose to do so.

She arrived on horseback, accompanied by the *Petite Bande* which she had copied from that of Francis I. But the new name for these mounted charmers was the *Escadron Volant*, the Flying Squad. Their mission was to hasten at the bidding of their mistress to the side of any man whose secrets she might desire to know or whose power was ripe for a fall. Their weapons were nimble minds, cold hearts and desirable bodies. Already Catherine was wondering which one would best fit the case of the Prince de Condé, whom she had just released from his captivity of Amboise. For Condé was known to be devoted to his wise and charming wife.

"Two cardinals mounted on mules" were also of the company. These were the Cardinal of Lorraine and the Italian Cardinal d'Este. D'Este had brought with him the poet Torquato Tasso, and the inauguration of the new Chenonceaux was thus to be honoured by the presence of the two greatest poets of their time. For Ronsard still accompanied the Court in all its wanderings.

Catherine was now Regent in name as well as in fact. All had gone according to plan. Antoine of Navarre had allowed her claim to the Regency and had been rewarded, as he had been promised, with the office of Lieutenant-General. The Queen-Regent had chosen the Bourbons instead of the Guises, and her colour at this time was openly Protestant. If Antoine had been a man of stronger character the opening of the new reign might have meant victory for the Huguenots and an avoidance of civil war. For the ten-year-old Charles IX, though he had a childish hatred of Huguenots, frankly admired the nobility of the great Coligny, and Catherine herself was strangely attracted by the adventurous, soldierly spirit of Condé, whom she had both imprisoned and released for political purposes. But the guiding principle of her policy was the maintenance of her own power and that of the Valois. By ancient law the nearest Bourbon would succeed the last Valois, and it seemed that the House of Bourbon was by no means unwilling to anticipate the march of events. Though she courted them now, playing them off against the Guises and searching for grounds of reconciliation which might postpone open warfare long enough for her to consolidate her position, Catherine had no intention of letting the Bourbons become as powerful as the Guises had been. As for Coligny, that honest and earnest statesman who would have been the last to attempt usurpation or the break-up of the constitution, Catherine knew him for what he was: the strongest personality, next to herself, in France. She had had enough of rivals during her husband's life, and nothing that Coligny could have done would have averted his fate.

The boy-King was at Chenonceaux, jealously guarded by his mother. Neither Guise nor Bourbon nor Coligny was to be allowed to influence him. "He is endowed," says an observer, "with a quick and lively intelligence, he bears himself soberly and modestly, and in his speech he is courteous and kind." And the chronicler, a Protestant, ends on an optimistic note: "One may reasonably expect great things of him if Heaven be pleased to watch over him." Optimism, however, was liable to be misplaced with Catherine in power, whether the optimist were Catholic or Huguenot.

The bright eyes in the pallid face of the neurotic youth were for nobody but his mother—and one other. Already he was precociously attracted by his brother's lovely young widow, and the Guises, following with approval the direction of his gaze, wondered whether the Scottish question might not still be kept open by a second marriage of Mary with the new King. There was also an alternative scheme hatching in the minds of these overbearing politicians who cared for nothing but the advancement of their own house. Philip of Spain had an available son, Don Carlos, and a firm Spanish connection would not only strengthen the Catholic party, but provide a redoubtable bulwark against the ascendancy of Catherine. But they had two cunning women against them. Neither Catherine de' Medici nor Elizabeth of England was going to allow Mary another powerful marriage.

There are several portraits, in pen and in paint of the eighteen-year-old Mary Stuart in her widowhood. Her famous white mourning garments set off her pale beauty to perfection, and doubtless helped to captivate the doting young Charles. "The whiteness of her complexion," says Brantôme, "strove for mastery with the whiteness of her veil; but at length the artifice of her veil yielded, and the snow of her white countenance overcame its rival."

But Catherine had not forgiven Mary for calling her a daughter of merchants. Representatives from Scotland had arrived in France to solicit the return of the Queen to her distracted native land, and the Regent was determined that she should go. First as the favourite of Diane, then as the instrument of the Guises, Mary had been for too long a thorn in her side. Knox was waiting for her with a rich vocabulary of abuse, Elizabeth with a net of policy. Mary had to go.

Fortunately for us, Brantôme went with her, and has left a splendid account of that sorrowful voyage from Calais. It has been quoted too often to be repeated here, but some other passages are interesting. He is speaking of the project of return:

"Alas, she had no desire nor will to it. I have often heard her say so, and that she dreaded the voyage like death. For she would a hundred times rather have remained as a simple dowager in France, contenting herself with her dowry of Touraine and Poitou, than have gone back to reign in her wild country; but her uncles (some if not all of them), advised her to do so, and even compelled her (though I will not state the means they used). But later they repented of their mistake.

"Nor is it to be doubted that, if the late King Charles had been of age at the time of her departure (he was very small and young), and if he were so much in love with her as I have seen him to be, he would never have let her go but would resolutely have married her; for I have seen him so amorous of her that he never gazed at her portrait without having his eyes so held and ravished that he could neither tear himself away nor resume his seat; and often he said that she was the loveliest princess that had ever been born into the world. He esteemed the late King his brother far too happy to have enjoyed so beautiful a princess, and said that he ought never in the tomb to regret his death, since on earth he had possessed this beauty and this delight, though the possession had been of so short duration. For such enjoyment was of greater worth than his kingdom."

Growing yet more lyrical, Brantôme records that the weather was in sympathy with the grief of Mary's departure: "It is to be observed that this spring in which she was to leave came so late, and was so deceptive and chilly, that in the month of April the season showed no sign of clothing herself with her fair green robe, nor with her fair flowers. Insomuch that the gallants of the Court made auguries thereof, and gave it out that this spring had changed her fair and pleasant clime to a foul and treacherous winter, and was reluctant to clothe herself in her hues of beauty and her verdure for the grief which she must bear at the parting of this lovely queen who was a shining ornament to her. M. de Maison-Fleur, a gentle knight of letters as well as of arms, made a very fine elegy on this subject."

Mary was evidently the only one whose grief at the death of her pitiful young husband was profound. She has left poems on the subject, and if it inevitably strikes us that her sorrow is rather for her own misfortune and loss of youth and pleasure than for the fate of Francis, her attitude is at any rate more human than that attributed by the Scottish Sir James Melville to Catherine: "The Queen was blyeth of the death of King Francis hir sone, because she had no guiding of him." Some other opinions are also worth noting. It is said that Coligny had exclaimed "The King is dead, this means life for us." And the Protestant Théodore de Bèze wrote with the vigour of a psalmist: "Behold the Lord God has awakened and removed that boy." Condé, with his hand on his poniard and declaring that he would never again be seen at Mass, went back to a touching reunion with his family, but Antoine of Navarre maintained a discreet silence, watching the weathercock.

Catherine was the weathercock, veering with every wind. Coligny took his cue from her. Instinctively loyal to the Crown, and fully aware of the immense importance of royalty in France, he determined that the hope of Protestantism lay not in the shifty and irresolute King of Navarre, but in Catherine and her young son. In this view he was by no means generally supported by the Huguenots, who still reposed a misplaced trust in Antoine as a Prince of the Blood. Calvin, for one, had no faith in the showy Protestantism of the Queen-Regent, and it is scarcely surprising that many were chary of accepting a leader so manifestly motivated by the volatile issue of political expediency. But still Coligny made his choice, the choice that killed him. One brief period of frankness and confidence on Catherine's part might have saved France much bloodshed. But she was a true kinswoman of Clement, and she never had such a period.

In the black dress and white collar which she had adopted in her widowhood, a costume so suggestive of Huguenot sympathies, she led the ball at Chenonceaux, her face a smiling mask. If she cast her eyes to the richly carved ceiling she saw her own monogram in arrogant isolation, replacing the galling device of H and D which had previously adorned the roof-beams. Nostradamus, summoned to Blois to read the horoscopes of the royal children, had prophesied the prolonging of the Valois power beyond the most sanguine hopes, though the waxen figures of Catherine's sons stumbled and fell, suggesting early deaths. He had seen lilies flourishing in dung, the lilies of France and Florence, Valois and Medici. Catherine was following her star, and as she moved among the dancers at Chenonceaux she felt within her the thrill of a power that had so long been denied her. For this she would make any sacrifice that policy demanded. Her own star was to rise above the lesser lights of Coligny and Guise and Bourbon, and as long as she lived the Valois would hold their own. Decadent, sickly, hovering between genuis and insanity, they would keep under Catherine's guidance the throne of the only man who had won and kept her friendship, the dead King Francis I.

It is to be remarked, since Nostradamus has been mentioned, that it was Henry II who had called upon him to foretell the fate of his house. Yet the fact continues to be used as a whip for Catherine's back. Balsac, who certainly summed up her character to some effect, gave doubtful authority for later delvers in the occult by his intriguing description of the magic mirror, the philosophic egg, the spilled blood of cock-pigeons and he-goats, in Catherine's mysterious chamber at Blois. That Catherine dabbled in

necromancy is beyond question; but so did everybody at
that time. There were reputed to be three thousand private
astrologers making comfortable livings in Paris alone. An
observatory, since destroyed, was erected for Catherine by
Ruggieri. It contained an astrolabe and an intricately
oriented pillar.

Now Ruggieri is described, even by the Huguenot
chroniclers who sought to blacken Catherine by reference to
forbidden arts, as a mathematician. And that gives the temper
of the whole business. Astrology was a recognised science,
the astrolabe a scientific instrument, just as it had been to
the wisest of the Egyptians. We have since rejected the
attitude, and yet otherwise clear-headed people continue
to throw salt over their left shoulders and to avoid walking
under ladders without attracting to themselves a whole
mythology of sinister legends. There is in the British Museum
Library a single-sheet pamphlet of the eighteenth century
(the superstition-ridden Age of Reason) with a sketch of
the "magic talisman" worn constantly by Catherine de'
Medici. It is engraved with diabolic figures and the names
of occult powers. It is possible, probable even, that the
Queen-Mother did wear such an object. To adjust the perspective one has only to imagine a historian of three centuries
hence coming upon a press photograph of Mrs. Amy Mollison
accepting a large toy black cat at the start of a pioneer flight.
"Satanism and the Early Aeronauts" will at that date make
just as good a title for an article as "Catherine de' Medici
and the Black Arts" does now. And the same sort of people
will read the article.

When she had so badly wanted a child, Catherine may
well have performed propitiatory practices, though there is
equal evidence for the belief that her eccentricities at that
time were undertaken on the advice of a physician. And the
recommendation of a qualified and even famous Court doctor that she should sleep with Henry during her menstrual

periods ought to be at least as horrifying as any meddling with necromancy. There were people who later attributed the sicknesses of the Valois children to this manner of conception. It was not an age in which one ought to attach grave importance to irrational or impious exercises.

Catherine was a monument of heartless common sense, but she liked her amusement. She accepted the ministrations of Nostradamus and Ruggieri because they sustained her belief in herself, in her own character and cunning on which every issue must at last rest. And at Chenonceaux she dallied and danced and listened to the music of lutes floating over the water because such aimless distraction was necessary to her intellectual health. Torches were lit at twilight and a thousand tiny lights sprang up among the trees that Diane had planted, and in the gondolas that Catherine had launched upon the Cher to delight her guests and remind her of Italy. She, the mobled Queen, the sleeping fury, the calculating stateswoman in whom the flame of purpose burned so steadily, could afford to be wistful on such evenings as this. She looked at Mary Stuart in her pale, white-robed loveliness, and thought of her own loveless youth. She looked at the radiant delicate child who was Charles IX and thought of the power that was hers to grasp. It was to be her revenge upon fate, her challenge to a friendless world which she had never intended to placate.

# POISSY

A DOZEN miles below Paris the Seine winds round a wooded plateau which is famous for its spacious views and for the *Fête des Loges* held every summer in the forest, a favourite river resort for the citizens of the capital. On one side is Saint-Germain, with the meagre remains of the château of Henry II; on the other, distant some twenty minutes by a modern motor coach, is Poissy, looking north over the widening river. At Poissy you can see a thirteenth-century bridge, the church in which Saint Louis the King was baptised, and the ruined porch of a Dominican Abbey. Without inconvenience you can do both Saint-Germain and Poissy in a day, omitting neither the statue of the nineteenth-century painter Meissonier at Poissy nor that of James II of England ("erected, *Mesdames et Messieurs,* by your great Queen Victoria") at Saint-Germain.

There is little about that ruined abbey doorway to excite the curiosity of a seasoned sightseer, and he might well be excused for considering that the local liqueur, *crème de noyaux de Poissy,* gives the town a greater title to fame than its ancient monastery. Yet within this monastery, from September 9 to October 20, 1561, was held the Council of Poissy, the early days of which Miss Sichel considers to form the finest chapters of the life of Catherine de' Medici.

Coligny was in reality the prime mover in the attempt at Poissy to find a way out of the religious impasse. "The Admiral," wrote the Venetian Ambassador, "who shows himself more concerned than the rest—not because he loves strife but because he is convinced that the faith which he believes is the true one—desires the holding of a colloquy of a certain number of learned men of either party, whereby it might be

seen which opinions be the better." Coligny, whose whole
life and energy had now been placed at the service of the
new Religion, was confident that in an honest and well-
conducted discussion the Huguenot idea would triumph over
every objection that could be raised by the Papal party.
Théodore de Bèze, an earnest and learned disputant, was to
be the principal spokesman for the Reformers. His master
Calvin might have been more devastating in his logical eloquence, and it had at first been intended that he should be
present. But both Coligny and Catherine feared his power
of making enemies, and persuaded him to delegate the task
to his lieutenant de Bèze. Even in the Huguenot ranks, moreover, there was division between Lutherans and Calvinists,
and for the sake of the pacific object of the Poissy assembly it
was really better that Calvin should remain in Geneva. But
the mistake that Coligny made was in imagining that the
struggle between Catholic and Huguenot could be decided
in a committee-room.

Thus for Coligny—the great professional soldier who (at
all events after St. Quentin) hated war—the Council of Poissy
was intended to usher in the peaceful victory of Protestantism.
For Catherine it was intended to prevent a violent struggle
in which the Bourbons, on whom she counted for the support of her Regency, might be annihilated by the Guises. To
give her her due she would also have been glad to see France
in a state of liberal concord in which advanced intellectual
opinions might flourish unchecked. But she was never an
altruist. The Regency and the survival of the Valois came
first, now as ever. The failure of the Conference, after a hopeful opening, was due partly to general causes but partly also
to the ineffective mixture of Coligny's idealism and Catherine's realism.

Catherine was in a tight corner. The foreign powers were
watching her closely, and she was surrounded by Spanish
spies almost a match for her in cunning. Elizabeth was wait-

ing for a chance to drop on Calais, the Pope for a definite declaration of religious policy which should decide his attitude. At home her subjects hated her where they did not merely mistrust her. By means of her Protestant Chancellor l'Hôpital, another idealist whose perorations were models of tolerance and nobility of temper, she sought to persuade Frenchmen that she could rule equitably. Edicts of amnesty, convocations of the Estates were thrown down to tempt them out of their surliness, but they refused to be cajoled. Protestantism was a Court fashion, and the Regent and her suite attended the *Prêches*—openly heretical assemblies at which celebrated Huguenot preachers allowed free rein to their eloquence. But Paris, though it had a Protestant Governor, remained staunchly Catholic, and not only Catholic but quarrelsome, as Paris had always been. The city that was to see the Fronde, the Revolution and the Barricades, the metropolis of street-fighting, was not to be placated by fair words. Insults and blows were exchanged in the streets between high-born adherents of the rival factions, Huguenot funerals were attacked by angry mobs, and with every fresh outrage the Huguenots cried louder yet for vengeance on the enemies of the God of Battles. In the provinces, in Normandy and Touraine and Anjou and Poitou, where the Reformers had a greater following, it was the Catholics who suffered violence. The country might have been saved by a resolute occupant of the throne who would choose his faction and fight for it with all the force of authority. It could not be saved by a conference, however well-intentioned. But those of us who in the face of every reactionary tendency still prefer talking things over to fighting them out must yield sympathy to Catherine and l'Hôpital and Coligny. They chose the civilised way, and opened the gates to barbarism.

By the time that the Poissy idea became fact the Guises had regained nearly all their lost ground. Montmorency, back once more in the arena, had returned to them as to the party that would preserve the ancient sovereigty of the State against heretical revolutionaries. The Guises did not care a rap for the State if it was to pass out of their hands, but Montmorency believed in them in spite of his own experience, and he had never liked the Italian woman. His move meant the abandonment of strong family ties with the Admiral and his brothers, and with his own son, but of his two great loyalties State came before Family.

A more serious defection, though one that might have been expected, was that of Antoine of Navarre. On April 6 of this year, 1561, in the chapel of Fontainebleau, three men had solemnly taken the sacrament together. They were the Duke of Guise, the Marshal St. André, and Montmorency, and their alliance was called the Triumvirate. Not many months later a fourth member joined the league and badly upset the balance of power in so doing. It was Antoine himself, the popular leader of the Huguenot hopes (though he had never been leader in anything but name) who thus crossed the floor. He loved ease and luxury, he disliked the ascetic aspect of Calvinism, and he badly wanted friendship with the Most Catholic King of Spain. The Guises laid a bait for him and he swallowed it, hook and all.

There had been one strong influence which had hitherto guided the feet of the wire-walking King of Navarre, and that was his wife Jeanne. With all the attachment of which a nervous and fickle temperament was capable he loved his pious wife and her happy Huguenot household. To be drawn into the Guise camp he must be weaned of this bond of affection, and there was only one way to do that. The Guises asked Catherine to lend them one of her Flying Squad, and Catherine considered that this was a moment at which a concession to the Guises might be prudent.

La Belle Rouet was the name of the charmer selected for the job—La Belle Rouet, or Mademoiselle de la Limaudière, which you will. How much Catherine knew of the Guise

ANTOINE DE BOURBON, KING OF NAVARRE
PORTRAIT IN ENAMEL BY LEONARD LIMOUSIN
(Victoria and Albert Museum)

intentions is uncertain, but she was more than willing for
Antoine to lose his good name with the Huguenots, for although he had consented to her Regency he had not lost his
Bourbon blood and was still a potential claimant to her
position. As usual, the Guise scheme was a wildly ambitious
one. First, they wanted to see Antoine divorced from his
staunch and powerful wife. This could be arranged ( Cardinal
d'Este promised them as much in the Pope's name) on the
grounds of Jeanne's heresy. Then, said they to La Belle
Rouet, the seductress herself should marry him and be Queen
of Navarre as a reward for her services. But amongst themselves they said that Antoine should marry the widowed
Mary Stuart and be theirs for ever, with a Catholic Scotland
in his pocket to flaunt before Protestant England. For in such
manner could the religions of nations, it was supposed, be
decided. The Guises were not wont to err on the side of
diffidence.

La Belle Rouet was not the only member of the *Escadron
Volant* to be requisitioned at this time. A use was also found
for Isabelle de Limeuil, a lady of whom it may almost be
said that nothing in her life became her like the leaving of
it. For her deathbed is famous, while little is known of her
life, except the part which she now played as a tool of Catherine and the Guises. It was Isabelle who, when she felt death
approaching, called for her page Julien, and bade him take
his lute and play that fine old melody, "The Defeat of the
Swiss," poignantly suggestive of the springtime of the reign
of Francis I. When he came to the words "All is lost!" she
asked for the phrase to be repeated four or five times, and
at last "All is lost with that chord," said she, and thus she
died. The story is given at greater length in a large number
of works dealing with the social and artistic aspects of the
French Renaissance.

The task appointed to this musically-minded Delilah was
to alienate the affections of the other Bourbon Prince, Condé,

from his wife Eléonore. Just as at Amboise the attempt had been made to kill both these princes, so now they were coupled as the quarry of a new kind of hunt. Condé was no weak and dallying Navarre, and Isabelle had a more difficult mission than that of La Belle Rouet. But the armour of this gallant soldier was not invulnerable. His letters to the lady whom he must have known to be a decoy are not the letters that a married man is supposed to write, except to his wife. If read out in a modern divorce court they would make front-page news for the evening papers. For a time Isabelle certainly possessed him. She had a merry tongue and wanton ways that must have made a strong appeal to a vigorous man weary with the strain of political intrigue; and the reaction of Condé to this sudden temptation is plainly perceived from the fact that he extended his lapses beyond his relations with Isabelle. It must have seemed to him that he was missing something; that life was passing him by in a succession of futile struggles with implacable enemies; that the cause for which he had endangered himself was not only hopeless but ignobly conducted. When Isabelle looked at him with the laughing invitation of her eyes he must have thought that after all there was a suspicion of priggishness in his wife's steadfast loyalty to a faith that offered very little except the likelihood of a violent death. There were sweeter things than a martyr's crown, and Isabelle's light-hearted love was one of them. Having tasted, he drank deeply. He even mixed his drinks.

The mysterious attraction which Condé retained for Catherine de' Medici would be worth a fuller study in the light of this incident of Isabelle de Limeuil, for the Regent was certainly aware of the purpose for which Isabelle had been borrowed. She never liked either Jeanne of Navarre or Eléonore de Condé. They represented a feminine type antithetical to her own, and when it came to argument they showed they were not afraid of her. The merely wilful med-

dlesomeness of a Medici must have been in itself a spur to
this attack on the married bliss of the two Bourbons, and
in the case of Condé a psychiatrist might conclude that
Catherine experienced something akin to the erethism of a
*voyeur* in the contemplation of his seduction. Profligate she
was not, but she continually used for her own ends the
profligacy of others, and it may well be that the satisfaction
she derived from the practice was not exclusively political.
Her love of backstairs methods was not confined to affairs
of State, and while eyewitnesses testify to the strict outward
decorum which she demanded of her following, they testify
also to her unfailing private enjoyment of jest and scandal.
She is said to have laughed good-humouredly at the gross
pleasantry of the artillerymen who gave her name to their
cannon of largest calibre, and Brantôme's account of her
spying on the pleasures of Henry and Diane, though doubtless embroidered, is difficult to regard as pure invention.

It was during the Council of Poissy that the virtue of
Condé and Navarre was encompassed, a fact which should
temper our praise of Catherine's conciliatory move. For even
while the deliberations for peace were going forward she
could not abandon her habits of subterfuge. Let us for a
moment leave the morals of the Bourbons in the balance and
take note of the proceedings in the refectory of the Abbey
of Poissy.

Saint-Germain was the residential centre for the Council,
and the château was filled with the delegates of both parties
and their equipages, who overflowed into the homes of neigh-
bouring nobles. As soon as Théodore de Bèze arrived he
began to hold *Prêches,* which were attended by Catherine
and her son, by Condé and by many others. Private conferences also went on in the château, and de Bèze and the
Cardinal of Lorraine met in a vigorous informal debate on
the general principles of the two religions. Many of the
Catholic representatives were preparing for the Council

which was shortly to be held at Trent—that Council which the greatest of intellectual reformers, Erasmus and Rabelais among them, would have preferred to any schism in the Church; that Council which it had been the life-long effort of Pope Clement to avoid. The disputants were therefore well primed for doctrinaire discussion, so well primed, in fact, that Catholic was ready to argue hotly against Catholic, and men of the same party more than once came to blows over such questions as Baptism, Economy, the Corporeal Presence, and the Laying on of Hands.

Six Cardinals and thirty-six Archbishops were among the dignitaries who thronged the Poissy refectory for the opening session on September 9. Their scarlet robes and the be-jewelled splendour of the Guises and their followers contrasted sharply with the sober black of the Huguenot delegates, and in particular with that of the austere de Bèze who led them. In the highest places sat Catherine and her children —the eleven-year-old King Charles, the ten-year-old Henry of Anjou, the eight-year-old Princesse Margot and the seven-year-old Duc d'Alençon. These nursery politicians were by no means of one mind on the matters at issue, and Margot was later to describe the violent quarrels which the religious clash bred at this time between her immature self and her still younger brother of Alençon. She had a Catholic governess and remained faithful to that creed in spite of her brother, who, she said, "in his childhood had not been able to escape the influence of this wretched Huguenotism. He was continually haranguing me to make me change my faith, often hurling my prayer-book into the fire and making me carry psalms and Huguenot books in my hand." The Prince's youthful companions, it seems, joined in the baiting of Margot, telling her that "it was plain to see I had no intellect; for all intelligent people, without distinction of age or sex, who had but once heard the preaching of Christian charity, had renounced all these bigoted malpractices." When

Alençon threatened that he would have his sister whipped by order of Catherine, she burst into tears, declaring that "he might have me whipped or killed if he wished, but that I would endure the worst punishment rather than damn my soul." When the very children behaved like this, it is scarcely surprising that men who had grown up in the belief that their religion was worth fighting for, or in the belief that fighting was worth the excuse of a religion, should fail to come to terms around the council table.

The boy-King opened the Conference in person, rising from his seat to read in a breaking treble a laborious peroration. The Chancellor de l'Hôpital spoke first for the Reformers, then the Cardinal de Tournon for the Papal party, and then de Bèze, the chief Huguenot spokesman. The only full account which we have of his lengthy address is his own, but there is no need to disbelieve him when he describes it as eloquent. Towards the end, however, he appears to have broken down under furious cross-examination, though he made one sharp retort which deserves to be remembered. The Guise Cardinal, like the Pharisees of old, had demanded a sign to prove the divine inspiration of the new faith. "It is a sufficient miracle," returned de Bèze, "that we, who a month ago were being burned and driven into banishment, are now preaching, not only at the Court, but throughout the country."

From first to last the discussions were conducted with an acrimony that paid little heed to relevance and none at all to reverence. It was in vain for Michel de l'Hôpital to plead for the introduction of a more conciliatory spirit. Neither side was prepared to give way, though at one point, de Bèze, exhausted by debate, was induced to sign an equivocally-worded document of surrender on certain details. "Gentlemen," said the Cardinal de Tournon in one of his speeches, "this Assembly will profit us little or nothing. For the men with whom we have to do are brute beasts, pig-headed in their opinions." The remark illustrates the tone of the whole Council, which we need not follow into its theological convolutions.

Meanwhile Jeanne of Navarre arrived at Saint-Germain with her little son Henry, the boy who was later to marry Margot, and to be known to history as Henry of Navarre. Catherine received her with all the hypocritical warmth of which she was capable, made the first suggestion of the match between Margot and Henry, and at the same time wrote to a friend that she wished Jeanne were dead so that Antoine could marry again. It was on account of Antoine, of course, that Jeanne had hurried north from her kingdom, though as one of the leading spirits of the Huguenot cause and a close intimate of Calvin she would naturally wish to attend the Council of Poissy.

The rumours that had reached her had been correct. Her husband was surrounded by spies, helplessly entangled in the net of the Guises, and bewitched by La Belle Rouet. Through his ambassador, Philip of Spain played with the deluded Antoine in perfect ease, with no intention of yielding him Spanish Navarre, the hope of which had been as tempting a bait for him as the charms of his Circe. To Jeanne the husband with whom she had been so happy, who for many years had so tenderly returned her affection and that of her children, presented a pitiful spectacle. All his better qualities had disappeared under the tutelage of the Guises, and his insidious vices—his vanity, his love of luxury, his selfishness and insincerity—had been allowed to take possession of him. He received her coldly, and at once found occasions for quarrelling with her. So completely had the Guises convinced him that only the heretical influence of his wife stood between himself and fortune that all the love in his small heart had died.

Enervated by debauchery, cruel from covetousness, absurdly exalted by flattery, Antoine did not stop at harsh words. In the presence of his wife, he savagely struck his little son when Henry, brought up in the faith that his father had treacherously abandoned, refused to attend Mass. This was the boy who was one day himself to renounce Protestantism with the memorable phrase, *Paris vaut bien une messe;* but now he was as staunch a chip of the Huguenot block as young Margot was of the Catholic. With tragic dignity Jeanne begged her husband to reconsider his harsh attitude. He had told her that there was a scheme to effect their divorce, and that Spanish Navarre was almost within his grasp. She did not remind him, as she might have done, that the titular right to their kingdom was hers by inheritance and his only by marriage. She simply declared with unshakeable courage that she would not sell her soul for worldly possessions—and by her soul she meant her love of liberty and her hatred of superstition, casuistry and dogma. If he divorced her, she said, it would be their children who would suffer most.

But after Jeanne's arrival at Saint-Germain it seems that for a time the Guises put aside their plot of repudiation and the declaration of the Navarre children as illegitimate, and adopted instead a resolution typical of their house in its audacity. Cardinal d'Este, the Papal Legate, was at Poissy, and had made some impression by his skilful promotion of the Roman cause. It was decided that he should try his hand at winning over the redoubtable Jeanne herself. But Jeanne was a true daughter of the great Margaret of Valois (though it is related that when she was a little girl she had mischievously cut out the heads of the saints from her mother's tapestry-frame, and woven in their place the heads of foxes). She had known what it was like to be thrashed regularly every day because, at the age of twelve, she had publicly refused the hand of the bridegroom selected for her by Francis I. "Had the princess been beaten black and blue," says Miss Sichel, "she would still have been the leader of the Protes-

tants in France, all the more so because of opposition."
D'Este's threats and promises spent their force on this rock
and could not overthrow it. Antoine forcibly prevented his
wife from attending the *Prêches,* but wild horses would not
have drawn her to Mass. A Jesuit teacher was found for her
son. She wept, but she held her head high. And at length,
when she had seen her husband for the last time and was
returning alone to her kingdom, a desperate attempt was
made to capture her and convey her to a prison. Antoine
actually connived at this dastardly plot, which was very nearly
successful. With less than an hour to spare she crossed her
own frontier, saved by an escort that had come out to protect
her from the pursuing force. The Guises had shown their
hand. This was warfare.

La Belle Rouet had done her work well, though needless
to say she did not get her reward. But Isabelle de Limeuil,
who had Condé to deal with, had not the same success. She
brought out the hedonist in the Prince, and the rumours that
he was spending a great deal of his time in the pleasures of
irregular love brought him anxious letters from Calvin and
de Bèze, who rightly feared that such conduct would en-
danger his authority with the Huguenots.

But Eléonore stood by him, refusing to believe that this
was anything but a temporary phase. Her letters to him
during this bitterest period of her life are touching in their
devotion and trust. And at last he came back to her, in time
only to be present at her death and to say to his little daughter: "Try, my darling, to be like her, so that God may help
you as He helped her . . . and so that I may love you more
and more, as I surely shall do if you are as she was." "I am
dead," he wrote in a poem composed at the moment of his
loss, "it is she who is alive."

The utter callousness of the plots against the two Bourbons
—conceived and largely carried out in the name of religion,
and by the princes of the Church—reveals vividly the atmos-

phere in which the abortive Council of Poissy was undertaken. The Guises, with Catherine's assistance, had not
hesitated to strike at the happiness of two women by the most
insidious and despicable means. Well might Catherine
wonder what designs they had upon herself.

But she was not accustomed to wonder for long about such
things. She had ways of satisfying her doubts. In this case the
device employed was the simple one of a tube concealed
behind the hangings, and leading to her own room from
that in which the Triumvirate discussed their plans. Listening at this tube she heard a proposal that she should be
thrown into the Seine.

Again she must change her course. She swung once more
from the Guises to the Bourbons, and in letters to Condé she
confessed with unusual frankness the dangers of her position,
imploring him to stand by her. The one thing that was necessary to each faction was to gain ascendancy over the Regent
and possession of the King, to guide the hand that signed the
edicts. And to that end there was now only one thing left
to do. Intrigues, alliances, conferences, acts of scattered
violence and reprisals, all had served merely to aggravate the
position. The next step was civil war.

# DREUX

IN a little plain of southern Normandy, traversed by an ancient Roman road and by the newer highway from Rouen to Chartres, surrounded by sloping fields crowned with villages and farms, was set the first great battlefield of the armed struggle between Catholic and Huguenot. Only a few miles away, at Anet, the sixty-three-year-old Diane de Poitiers was living in retirement, venturing no more amongst the storms which beat against the walls of her beautiful home, those storms of which she had long ago heard the first mutterings.

The flames of battle which were to cast their glare over France for the remainder of the century—divided by brief truces into seven "Wars of Religion"—had seemed to spring up simultaneously all over the country. The fuel was there, dry and ready for the brand, and the spark kindled by the Massacre of Vassy in Champagne on the first day of March, 1562, raised answering fires in Normandy and Provence, on the sandy shores of the Loire, and in the gorges of the Rhône. Holocausts of priests, slaughter of prisoners, treachery and broken faith, individual assassinations and wholesale butchery, pillage, rape, torture and starvation were common to both parties and all quarters of France. The armies were fighting for possession of Paris and the King; the one that had temporarily obtained such possession gave itself out as the official force of his Majesty and the State, while the other claimed with at least equal justice to be engaged in the sacred task of rescuing the sovereign from his ungodly captors. Meanwhile the helpless peasantry and the inhabitants of widely scattered provincial towns suffered the violence of each faction in turn.

It is obviously impossible here to follow in detail the countless subsidiary campaigns, nor would such an examination assist an understanding of the shifting situation and attitude of Catherine. We can only distinguish certain events which the perspective of time shows to have had a bearing on the course of the wars at large and on the part which the Queen-Mother played in them.

When hostilities grew serious she had retired to Fontainebleau with the King, but very shortly she allowed Antoine of Navarre to induce her to return to Paris, the hub about which the whole disorderly system of civil warfare revolved. To the east, to the north, to the west and to the south of the capital occurred the salient events of the First War; to the east the Massacre of Vassy, to the north the siege of Rouen, to the west the battle of Dreux, to the south the siege of Orleans.

It was perhaps appropriate that the massacre which heralded the long years of much more serious bloodshed known as the Wars of Religion should have taken place on a Sunday. The Duke of Guise, who had a residence in the neighbourhood, went on March 1 with a numerous following of armed men to take dinner in the little town of Vassy. A Huguenot service was in progress in a large granary, in pursuance of the liberties granted a few weeks earlier in the Edict of January—Catherine's last sop to the Protestants. Guise allowed his men to force their way into the granary, where their interference was met with abuse and resistance. Stones were thrown, and one of them hit the Duke. He gave orders to his men to open fire. Sixty of the six hundred worshippers were killed and many more wounded.

It was the signal. A cry of vengeance went up from the Huguenots, while the Catholics praised Guise for his decisive action, comparing him to Moses. Orleans was seized by Condé, Coligny and Andelot, and made the headquarters of the Huguenot resistance. From Orleans began the campaign which, skirting Paris, entered upon its most im-

portant engagements in Normandy. The Catholics called in
Spanish soldiers, the Huguenots obtained help from Germany and England, and on both sides the presence of foreign
mercenaries undoubtedly increased the savagery of the fighting. Coligny, who made strenuous endeavours to maintain
order and honour in his army, soon began to find that to
allow pillage was often the only alternative to mutiny. For
the troops which both parties had summoned to France were
the sons of the unruly mob that had sacked Rome nearly
forty years before.

Between Guise and Coligny, between Paris and Rouen,
Catherine travelled back and forth, seeking a footing for
peace which should both preserve a nominal balance of power
and yet show her clearly which side she must secretly support.
First she forbade Guise to bring an army into Paris. When
he disobeyed her she persuaded Condé to leave the city. She
treated with both parties equally, now warning the Huguenots of an impending attack, now advising the Catholics of
a pregnable point. She summoned each in turn to discuss
terms of settlement, but always the negotiations broke down,
for on one point she would not yield. She and she only was
to administer the Regency and control her son, and since
this was what each of the combatants desired to do, only
the sword could settle the matter. At this distance from events
it is plain to see that on such a basis as this the wars must
be indefinitely prolonged. Both parties wanted the same
thing and Catherine was determined that neither should
have it.

At Rouen Catherine looked her last upon Antoine of
Navarre. Rouen was one of a comfortable number of Protestant strongholds in the north, and English soldiers were as-
sisting in its defence on condition that Le Havre should be
ceded to Elizabeth. For that was the manner in which this
miserable war was being conducted. To do Coligny justice,
he was less to blame in this matter of the cession of Le Havre

than many historians have allowed, and Whitehead shows
clearly that the true import of the terms accorded to Elizabeth had been withheld from himself and Condé when the
agreement was undertaken.

Besieging Rouen for the Papal party, the turncoat King
of Navarre was seriously wounded, but at first no anxiety
was felt for him. Catherine, on frequent visits of inspection,
found him lying on a silken couch as a convalescent, with
Le Belle Rouet at his side and the merriest of his companions
gathered about him. Rouen at last fell to the Catholics and
Antoine was borne through the city in triumph in a litter.
Plucking up spirit he began to partake in pleasures such as
a sick man could scarcely enjoy in safety. Dancers and musicians entertained him, rich food was served him, La Belle
Rouet seldom left his bed. When Catherine came to visit
him for the last time he had been told that his end was near,
and seemed so melancholy that the Regent advised him to
get somebody to read to him. He replied that the people
around him were now for the most part tainted with Huguenotism—a noteworthy observation when one reflects that
he was in the military camp of the Papal party. Catherine
had her answer, an equivocal answer which was the last that
she addressed to him. "They are no less your servants for
that," she said, and we may still wonder what was in her
mind.

Then followed a series of confessions, recantations and
contradictory declarations which showed how incomplete had
been the fickle Antoine's conversion. Catholic priests and
Huguenot ministers visited him alternately, and when at
length he died each party claimed that he had passed to its
own heaven in the spirit of its own creed. He was only thirty-
four years of age.

The autumn ran into a hard and bitter winter with no
cessation of fighting and no decisive victory on either side.
The Huguenots recaptured Rouen and marched southwards

through a land disfigured by bloodshed and famine. The capital was their natural objective, that capital in which the bitter weather filled the hospitals to overflowing. The miseries of war found their way everywhere, and though as yet there had been no fighting in Paris the city was racked by want and pestilence. Catherine herself, who was famous for her vitality and her abundant appetite, was, according to one chronicler, suffering from whooping-cough.

But she was well enough to go out alone to parley with Condé beyond the walls of Paris. The Guises, who at the moment represented authority as against the revolutionary Huguenots, were expecting help from Spain, and the Regent wished to temporise until the foreign troops should arrive. She talked with Condé for five hours and returned by torchlight, having been unable to reach any agreement. Two further interviews followed with no more success. Then came the reinforcements from Philip of Spain. The Huguenot army was encamped near Dreux, on the border of Normandy, beside the road between Rouen and Chartres. And here, in that gently rolling countryside with its alternate woods and meadowland, Catholic and Protestant joined battle.

It was December 19, 1562. The sleep of Condé, who was with the main body of his troops, had been troubled by dreams. He had seen armies contending in the sky in a rain of blood, he had been hag-ridden and witnessed the baleful assembly of witches. Such portents as these were popularly held, by Catholics and Protestants alike, to foretell the loss of crowns and the alteration of the kingdoms of the world. One is tempted to wonder whether one of the sinister female figures that had appeared to him had borne the outward seeming of Catherine de' Medici, with whom, in his tent at Chantilly, he had so recently been engaged in a grim battle of wits. Catherine had walked the flagstones above his prison at Amboise, spinning fair promises to his shifty brother. She had sent him the miraculous message of release after the death of Francis II. She had detached Isabelle de Limeuil from her company of official sirens to sing to him, weary of journeys and tumult, the perilously seductive songs of lotus-land. On the eve of the first open engagement of the war in which his beliefs and fortunes were inextricably bound up, the shape of Catherine might well haunt the dreams of Condé. For it is more than likely that she herself suffered occasional insomnia on his account. And Catherine has been given worse names than that of witch, both during and since her lifetime. One ambitious commentator, indeed, has gone so far as to identify her with the Third Witch in *Macbeth*—to which one can only reply that Hecate, who is the arch-witch in the play, is another name for Diane.

It wanted two hours to daylight when Condé rose and donned his armour, eager for battle and well knowing that the issue must be forced on that day. Coligny was more difficult to convince of the imminence of the clash, but by eight o'clock the army was on the move and at midday they came within earshot of the enemy, drawn up across the plain on a line north-east of them. Condé, Coligny and Andelot at once went forward to take stock of the position.

From a little-known source Whitehead has derived a quotation setting forth the characteristics of Condé and Coligny as they were observed at this time by one who cannot be accused of bias in their favour, for he was the Papal Nuncio, Santa Croce. The passage is worth repeating at this point, while the two leaders reconnoitre the ground before the battle of Dreux:

"The pursuits and talents of each are different. The Admiral excels in counsel, the Prince in action. The strength of the latter lies in a certain impetuosity of mind, that of the former in a steady constancy. The one is shrewd, the other still shrewder. Just as the Prince has a more pleasing character, the Admiral has one more austere. The Prince, too, is a lover of racing, jumping, exhibitions of wrestling, hunting, public shows, every kind of armed contest, horses, sports, jests, the dancing of girls, and the singing of women. But with the Admiral there always seems to be a certain seriousness of thought and action. Then, again, the Prince is a most graceful speaker, while the eloquence of the Admiral is of a graver kind, since he has become familiar with the Latin tongue, and devotes himself earnestly to theological pursuits. The latter, also, is zealous in State affairs and swift to punish wrongs, the former being more easy-going. And while the Admiral consults as to what must needs be done, the Prince does it. Then, too, the former gives audience to ambassadors, busies himself with supplies and finance, decides points of law, fortifies positions, draws up the line of battle, pitches the camp, reviews the army, chooses the place and time of battle, and superintends religious affairs. The Prince, on the other hand, asks for dangers and the fight; and while he is small and of elegant figure, the former uses a toothpick and has it in his mouth day and night. Yet both, by their graciousness and generosity, are a power with all."

The Catholic position was a strong one. Their flanks (Guise on the right and the veteran Constable on the left) were protected by villages. In the centre, on slightly rising ground, were Swiss pikemen, this body and the left wing being reinforced with artillery, while the cavalry were scattered in small bodies along the whole line. Their total forces were of a formidable number, between seventeen and eighteen thousand. The Huguenots, though better supplied with cavalry, were in the main slightly outnumbered, nor had they any tactical advantage of ground. But there could be no more manœuvring. Battle was unavoidable.

Théodore de Béze was with the Huguenot army, and it was he that led the service before the battle. Each regiment had its own chant, selected from Marot's psalms, and while these attempts to propitiate the God of Battles were going forward in the one army, the other was staking its claim on divine assistance by the singing of Mass and the pronunciation of a general Absolution. The custom, confusing enough to a celestial arbiter, is one which dies hard.

The flower of the Huguenot nobility was among the white-scarfed cavalry in the centre, under Condé. Coligny led the right flank, opposite the Constable. When battle was delivered the fiercest fighting was between Condé and the Swiss centre of the Catholics. Again and again each side charged, inflicting and suffering heavy losses, but re-forming always for a fresh attack. On the right, however, the fierce onslaught of Coligny had broken the Catholic left, and Montmorency, fighting as was his wont in the ranks of his men, was taken prisoner. His flank collapsed completely and horsemen galloped desperately to Paris to spread a woeful report that the Catholics were defeated and the Constable slain.

With this flank turned, it looked indeed like victory for the Huguenots. But Guise, probably the best soldier on the field, had kept his wing intact behind the village of Épinay, and at the critical moment, with a confident cry of, "Now, my friends, the day is ours!" he bore down with overwhelming impetus upon the Huguenot left and the exhausted centre. Coligny rallied his men and made a gallant reply from the other wing, but in vain. His centre was routed and Condé taken prisoner. The Admiral himself, just as darkness closed in on the short winter day, was forced to cut his way out and make an orderly retirement. Losses on both sides were about equal, but Guise remained in possession of the field. The victory was with the Catholics.

It is stated in one account that the Huguenots slew their prisoners after the fight, sparing only the Constable de Montmorency. As in so many other incidents in a period that has found more than its share of grossly biassed historians, the truth will probably never be known. It seems likely that on both sides the fighting was savage in the extreme, for the mixed incentives of religion and pillage are not conducive to gentleness. But among the higher orders the conventional practices of chivalry were still popular where they could be followed without disadvantage, and we may believe the witness who testifies that on that night the Duke of Guise "slept in the same bed with his prisoner Condé, as if they had been the best friends in the world." Condé had an impressionable heart, which was the reason why Catherine at this time made her successive overtures to him rather than to Coligny, whom she feared as a match for herself in resolution of purpose. And Sir Thomas Smith, who was with the English troops in the campaign, wrote to Elizabeth that on account of Guise's courteous conduct, "the prince weeps, and says that he never meant but quietness."

Condé was sent to meditate upon quietness at Chartres, while the Constable was held at Orleans, the capital of Huguenot France. Coligny, who had always been the virtual leader of the Protestants, was naturally—though against his will—elected to the command of the army in Condé's place. By a succession of minor manœuvres he had now to prevent himself being cut off from Orleans. In Paris, meanwhile, the full story of the battle of Dreux had been circulated. Guise made a triumphal return, and the King and Catherine rode in a glittering procession to a service of thanksgiving for this deliverance from their enemies. But Catherine knew well enough that her enemies were not all outside Paris.

The Guise victory was not complete. At all costs peace must be made before either side had gained complete ascendancy. The English had taken full advantage of their invitation and were extending their power alarmingly in Normandy. Calais might very soon be theirs again, and France thrown back to the Hundred Years' War. There could scarcely be a better excuse than this for seeking peace, and it was still possible to move Condé by an appeal to the interests of the country at large. Negotiations, which of course included terms for the exchange of the two distinguished captives, went tortuously forward. "If things had been worse than they are after all this war," wrote Catherine to an intimate friend, "blame might have fallen on the government of a woman; but honest folk should blame only the government of the men who desire to play the part of kings. If I am not further hindered, I hope it will henceforth be seen that women have a more genuine regard for their country than those who have reduced it to its present state."

The Regent was sincere enough in her desire for peace, but that desire did not spring from any love for France. Nor was she in a very good position to throw stones at those who wished to play the part of kings.

## ORLEANS

FEBRUARY, 1563. Catherine and Charles were at Blois, awaiting some sign of decision in the desultory warfare which still went on over the territory between Blois and Paris. In this fantastic war it was scarcely necessary for the King to have the bodyguard which had protected his brother Francis II after the Amboise executions, and he came and went with his mother in comparative security through the theatre of hostilities, while thousands of his innocent subjects suffered the most barbarous deaths at the hands of those who sought to obtain power over him. And at Blois, in the little panelled chamber which has excited so much speculation, Catherine wielded her own weapons. The poison-phial was doubtless among them, though the number of poisonings attributed to the Queen-Mother must certainly be in excess of those she actually committed. The concealed cabinets, sliding partitions and so forth, which the guide will nowadays point out with sinister satisfaction, are as much a tribute to the craftsman's love of meticulous detail as to Catherine's own predilections to secrecy, and if every masked drawer in sixteenth-century cabinet-making be held to constitute a receptacle for insidious means of murder, it becomes difficult to see how any Frenchman of the time could have died a natural death.

Higher up the Loire the Duke of Guise was laying siege to Orleans, the city which Charles V had called the finest in France, the city once sanctified by Joan of Arc and now, in the Catholic view, defiled by the occupation of the Huguenots. Andelot was in charge of the defence, Coligny having just left the city on an attempt to re-establish communication with the English forces in the north.

On the north bank of the Loire some suburbs of Orleans
had been invested by Guise, and on the evening of February
18 he paid a visit of inspection to certain islands on which
artillery had been established to command the bridge and
its approaches. On his way back to his quarters he was shot
in the back by a Huguenot spy named Poltrot, who had
concealed himself behind a hedge. Three bullets entered the
Duke's body. Poltrot, mounted upon a horse purchased with
Coligny's money, rode swiftly from the scene of the crime,
but, having lost his way, he found to his terror that, when
morning came, he was still close to the Catholic camp. Again
he tried to get away, but two days later a soldier earned the
sum of four thousand crowns which Catherine had instantly
offered for the capture of the miscreant alive. At the same
time she had had surgeons sent to the bedside of Guise and
had expressed in a letter her hope of his recovery, her de-
testation of the deed, and her desire for vengeance. But the
Duke did not recover. After lingering in great pain (there
were some who said that the bullets had been poisoned)
for nearly a week, he died on the 24th.

Here are comments on his death by two Englishmen:

"He was not only the greatest soldier in France, but in all
Christendom. Inured to fatigue, experienced in warfare,
courteous, amiable and generous, he was equally beloved by
officers and men. . . . Some are so cankered that they would
say it was the Queen's doing, and now she had her desire. . . .
A day will come when Coligny in his turn will be assassinated
in expiation of this murder." (*Sir Thomas Smith.*)

"The death of the Guisian Pharaoh . . . has, believe me, affected my inmost heart and soul. It was so sudden, so op-
portune, so fortunate, and so far exceeding all our hopes
and expectations." (*Bishop Jewel.*)

Sudden and generally unforeseen it certainly was, and
there were many to whom it seemed a gracious act of Providence, for since Dreux, the Huguenots had been openly pray-

ing for Guise's death. But the testimony of Smith opens questions which will doubtless still receive divergent answers, though all the available material must now have been collected and sifted a hundred times over. How nearly were Catherine and Coligny connected with this deed for which, as the Englishman prophesied, the Admiral would at length have to pay with his life?

Without any reference to direct evidence, it can be seen that both Catherine and Coligny might have desired the death of Guise. The horror which Catherine made public, her offer of a reward for the capture of Poltrot, and her assent (after delay) to his execution, can scarcely be allowed to have any bearing on the case, and only six weeks after the event she told Condé that Guise's murder "had no less redeemed her out of prison than the same had set him, the Prince, at liberty." To us, as to her contemporaries, her words are deceptive and contradictory. It is to her actions that we must look, and the fearlessness with which she laid herself open to a denunciation by Poltrot during the many examinations of the prisoner is a weighty argument in her favour. Had she been guilty, the risks which she took after the deed would appear entirely foreign to her character. The death of the man whom she had overheard plotting to throw her into the Seine cannot possibly have grieved her. But any widespread suspicion that she was the instigator of the crime would have ruined her. To Paris the dead man was a martyr, and a formal charge against the Regent would have meant revolution.

It would have been a very different matter, however, if Catherine, after contriving the assassination of Guise, had been able to clear herself and implicate Coligny. She might thus have rid herself at one blow of two powerful rivals, and it is this idea, so suitable to be applied to the Medici Queen, which has chiefly sustained those historians who are inclined to read into the surviving documents a proof of her guilt.

The accusation against Coligny is much more definite, and his position on the whole clearer. During nine separate examinations the prisoner affirmed six times that the deed had been done by order of Coligny, and three times that Coligny had had nothing to do with it. There was evidence that money had passed between the Admiral and Poltrot, but since Poltrot was admittedly in the Huguenot service, and since the money had been expressly given him for the purpose of buying a horse, the circumstance was hardly a damning one. Of all the principal figures of French history at this period, Coligny was probably the least ignoble. And yet the murder of Guise would have been by no means impossible to his nature. Nobility was a slippery commodity in these wars, and Coligny cannot be freed of responsibility for all the acts of brutality committed by the men under his command, while the fact that he held out the sack of Paris as an inducement to the German mercenaries is established by a letter in his own hand.

His best defence before history is the frankness with which he met Poltrot's denunciation. He at once admitted that, although he had never instigated the deed, he was heartily glad that it had occurred. He had made it clear, he said, that while he would not himself take a hand in such an attempt, he would do nothing to oppose it, and on the field of battle he would have no hesitation in training his finest marksmen and his heaviest pieces on the person of the Duke. And he added that his attitude has been influenced by the discovery that the Guises, on their side, had set on foot definite plots against his own life. That is surely not the confession of a guilty man endeavouring to exculpate himself.

The bulk of the evidence on every side points to the belief that Poltrot, though acting on his own initiative, had reason to expect a reward for the murder from the Huguenot leaders, and assistance in escaping the consequences of the act. It really mattered little whether Coligny or Catherine or neither was responsible, and it matters still less to-day. But it mattered a great deal that Coligny was held to be responsible, and for the purposes of history that is all that need be remembered.

For the Guises believed sincerely, and continued to believe, that the Admiral's hands were red with the blood of the head of their house. If they had thought, and if Paris had thought, that Catherine had inspired the crime, history would have been very different. As it was, those three shots at Orleans made inevitable the hideous expiations of St. Bartholomew's Day. A new motive now dominates the internecine struggle. The wars of Religion have become a bloodfeud and Coligny's fate is sealed.

# V

## QUEEN-MOTHER

## ROUEN

"I AM an Englishwoman," cried the wrathful Gloriana, "and the Queen of France is a Florentine, but it shall be seen which of us two shall outwit the other!"

Elizabeth had reason to be incensed. The English were being expelled from Normandy without ceremony, and the French Court was at Rouen, the ancient English stronghold where Joan the Witch had been burned. For Catherine had seized her opportunity to patch up a peace and free the country of the foreigners who, invited over to rescue Charles from the grip of the Catholics, had very naturally outstayed their welcome. As for Condé, once more released from captivity by the death of Guise and promptly won over in an emotional interview to the task of removing his English allies, Elizabeth declared roundly that he was "good for nothing but to be thrown to the dogs." Not very long ago she had with equal spirit called him the "Joshua of the people of God."

It was indeed a golden opportunity that had been presented to the Regent, for the number of men with whom she had to treat had been opportunely reduced. On the Catholic side, Guise and Antoine of Navarre were dead, and the Cardinal of Lorraine was at Trent for the General Council. Of the Huguenots, Coligny was far enough from Blois at Caen, and Condé, as well as the Catholic Constable, was in the subordinate position of having to be released from prison for the settlement. All had gone according to plan, and a treaty grimly labelled the Peace of Amboise had been signed within a few weeks of the Orleans assassination. Wasted by disease, the remnants of the English had not proved troublesome, and at last there was a breathing-space.

The first thing that Catherine did with this respite was to call an Assembly at Rouen to declare Charles fit to rule, although he was only in his fourteenth year. This was not a mark of special maternal indulgence for her son, for whom she had far less affection than for his twelve-year-old brother, Henry, Duke of Orleans. The tutors that were found for Charles had been instructed that their charge was not to become morally or physically strong. He was to be, as far as possible, a replica of the pitiful Francis II, with no possibility of independence and with a hopeful tendency to an early death, which should place his younger brother on the throne. Catherine, determined to have her line of Valois, was equally determined to regulate it according to her own ambitions. And while the fitful passions of Charles came yearly to look more like insanity, his mother's eyes dwelt with tender hopes upon the delicate features and long Medici hands of Henry.

Not love, than, but policy had dictated the official emergence of Charles from his minority. For now that the King of Navarre was dead, Condé was the senior Bourbon Prince, equipped with an inconvenient claim to the Regency. Condé had never signed away his rights, and seemed inclined at this moment to revive them. The remedy was simple. There was to be no Regent. Charles would become King in his own title, and Catherine, as Queen-Mother, would actually lose none of her power.

It was time, thought Catherine, that the people of France were treated to an outward and visible sign of this power. The King, about whose person the storm of civil war had raged, must be shown to his subjects, who must at the same time take note of the rank and authority of the Queen-Mother. A royal progress would be more effective than many edicts, and in this interval of peace it would be politic to distract aggrieved and bewildered Frenchmen with those dazzling side-shows to which the most oppressed populace was always delighted to flock. She therefore threw herself vigorously into the organisation, advance publicity and stage-management of a magnificent tour through her son's dominions. It was to take place in the following year, and would afford opportunities also for certain diplomatic conversations on which she had set her heart. She feared Philip of Spain and she thought herself a match for Elizabeth of England. Both attitudes pointed to the conclusion of a pact or two, and pacts and pageants went very well together. It was not long before Catherine, laying her plans in Rouen, had everything cut and dried.

Bayonne, where the Pyrenees meet the Bay of Biscay, was to be the ultimate goal of her worldly pilgrimage, for there, besides conducting negotiations with Spain, she would have the chance of meeting again someone of whom she was genuinely fond—her daughter Elizabeth, whom she had not seen since her marriage to Philip five years before.

In the spring of 1564 the calvacade set out from Rouen. We cannot follow it from town to town and join the audience at the sports and processions, the masques and allegories at every stopping-place. Nymphs emerged from artificial grottoes and recited the verses which Ronsard had dashed off for the occasion, tournaments were held on land and river, rich and curious objects were given and received—orders and collars of gold, coffers decorated with coloured enamels of the sieges of Troy or Jericho, clocks in which the Holy Ghost and Peter's Cock came out and addressed each other at the hour, silver comfit-boxes, fashioned like nautilus-shells, drawn by dolphins and driven by mermaids. Nor can we pause to watch the daily life of the moving Court, to listen to Catherine's jests and ponder on their hidden meaning, to discover whom she attracts and whom she repels, to observe the careful coaching of the impressionable Charles as a possible suitor for Elizabeth of England, to keep touch with innumerable amorous intrigues and to wonder whether those precocious children, the Princess Margot and the Prince Henry of Navarre are really lovers or only licentious little chatterboxes.

But at Saintes, which lies near the mouth of the Charente at the south-west corner of the Rabelais country, we may conveniently linger for a moment to forget politics and meet a potter, who here had the good fortune to be presented to the royal visitors. For politics, after all, are not the sole, nor always the most enduring material of history. In this spring of 1564, for example, there were born two men who will be remembered when Catherine de' Medici is forgotten. One was born at Pisa and became an astronomer. The other was born at Stratford-on-Avon and became a poet.

# SAINTES

MASTER BERNARD PALISSY, the most celebrated craftsman in Saintes, had had to wait a long time for the meeting with Catherine and Charles that was to bring him fortune. For he was nearly sixty years old when the Court arrived at this venerable city of lawyers, the magisterial metropolis of a considerable district. The usual festivities were arranged and the townspeople were presented with a Roman holiday to compensate them for previous acts of butchery and disarm them for future ones. Prominent citizens were presented to the King and the Queen-Mother, and each brought with him a suitable gift. When the turn of Bernard Palissy came, he put into Catherine's hands some choice specimens of his work in enamelled earthenware. Curious in detail and marvellously lifelike, his was the type of art which had always appealed to the bourgeois patron. Mary Stuart had been right—Catherine was the daughter of merchants. She was interested in Palissy's work, and when he followed up his advantage by designing a grotto for her, she promised to find use for his services when she should return to Paris. She kept her promise, and two years later the potter of Saintes had his own studio and ovens in the rising palace of the Tuileries.

Life had always been a struggle for Palissy, and this was a great day for him. He came of simple artisan stock, the stock that had produced the first Huguenots. He had sung Marot's psalms with his fellow craftsmen, and had been involved in the fierce revolt against the salt-tax in his native province in 1546. The ill wind in that case had blown him into the favour of the Constable de Montmorency, who had been sent to suppress the rising and had chanced to meet the potter. Montmorency was a great patron, and in his service Palissy had at last been able to conclude his twelve years' arduous search for a pure white paste which would enable him to produce faithfully-coloured enamels of everything in nature. But a living that depended on the fluctuating fortunes of the Constable was naturally an unstable business, and only with the meeting with Catherine does Bernard Palissy become a name to quicken the pulse of art collectors.

Palissy was undoubtedly a genius, but he was not an artistic genïus. He was a Leonardo *manqué*, a universal scientist, inquisitive, laborious, brilliantly speculative, but entirely without Leonardo's æsthetic sensibility. Anatole France says that he had never seen Leonardo's notebooks, but in his intensive study of fossils he reached the same epoch-making conclusion on which the science of geology was later based—the perception of the time-factor in the formation of strata. He busied himself with an almost eighteenth-century enthusiasm with the "nature of things," he held that agriculture should be a science and not a fortuitous acceptance of divine bounty, and he anticipated developments in chemistry and physics with some astounding discoveries. But his first, last and dearest love was his faïence. To find the secret that he sought he endured all that a man may endure, and he made his family suffer, too; for when they were half-starving and without a piece of money in the world, he hurled his miserable sticks of furniture into his kilns.

What he did with his secret when at last it had been found may be studied to-day in private collections and in the art museums of the world. A dish of Palissy ware is manifestly designed for admiration rather than for service. The ferns, the leaves, the shells and the snake coiled in the centre are raised above the surface and gleam in all the variety of their natural colours. The birds that pecked at the fruit in Apelles' picture would certainly test their beaks on these snail-shells— or no, perhaps they would be scared away by the snake. It is

all so amazingly done that we catch our breath at the artifice of it. And there are scores of other wonders—fishes that
seem still wet from the sea, toads that one is astonished not
to find slimy to the touch, lizards basking in the sun, fronds
and plantains with the dew still on them.

But it remains artifice and not art. Well might the craft
of Palissy appeal to Catherine de' Medici, for it bears the
unmistakable stamp of her period. "A time of decadence,"
says Miss Sichel at the very outset of her study of Catherine,
"is a time of over-attention to detail"—which is about as
true as a generalisation can be, and certainly better than
Lecky's "sensuality is the vice of young men and old nations."

In this latter half of the sixteenth century broad tendencies
are hard to discover. Following the fortunes of Catherine
step by step, we can no more foresee the results of any particular action than she could foresee them herself. She had
purpose without policy, and it was far too individualistic a
purpose to carry the nation with her. Across the Channel
Elizabeth was identifying herself with her country, so that
now our view of Elizabethan England is a pattern of wide
and resolute development into which the brightly coloured
details fit themselves as we probe further; while our view
of France under Catherine de' Medici is a confusion of lurid
detail, a succession of close-ups, a film with vivid shots but
a thin plot. Living for herself and in the present, Catherine
took colour from her age and gave it back again. Living
for a national idea and facing both ways at once, Elizabeth
became the lens of a different glimpse of history.

The decadence which is apparent in the arts of the period
is no less apparent in other facets of life. For this is the morning after the Thousand and One Nights before—bright nights
of Renaissance revelry when sensuality had at least been
open and unashamed. The splendid thirst is gone and only
the craving for stimulation remains. Then the expense of
spirit, now the waste of shame. But the retribution brings

no sense of repentance with it, for of all times this is the most deficient in morals, good or bad. Subterfuge and expedient are the only devices of conduct, individual whim the only incentive. There are Huguenots and Catholics who have persuaded themselves that they are accomplishing a noble purpose, and the battle-cry of the indomitable Jeanne of Navarre is "Either Peace Assured, or Victory Completed, or Death with Honour." But it is by such isolated exceptions that the rule of lack of conscience is proved.

The canker eats its way to the roots of social life. Religion is elaborate and cynical, politics are little more than opportunism, vices are cold and curious, art is meticulous and perverted, amusements are fantastic and passionless. Clothing reaches at this time its highest point of ridiculous extravagance, and the description of a Court function is never complete without a catalogue of the money spent on jewels and "new fangles." There are few more illuminating guides to the temper of an age than a study of its costume, and one may frequently find oneself in sympathy with the moralists and satirists of this period who found in contemporary fashion their favourite targets. In England there is Stubbes' *Anatomie of Abuses,* in France the *Remonstrance charitable aux dames et damoyselles de France sur leurs ornemens dissolus,* by A. E (stienne) . And now it is no longer the Mediæval Church fighting the menace of feminism; it is a desperate body of reasonable men trembling for the sanity of Europe. Continuous abuse, mocking or incensed, is poured upon the "trunk sleeves of wyre, and whalebone bodies, backs of lathes and stiff bumbasted verdugals," the roses on the gentlemen's shoes "big enough to hide the cloven foot," the ruffs "smeared and starched in the devils' liquor," the "wide saucy sleeves that would be in every dish before their master," the bosoms raised to open view and the waists unnaturally contracted. The costume of the early Renaissance had been magnificent, but now it was not enough to be magnificent; eccentricity was the important thing.

We can see it all in those plates that Palissy made—invention without creative impulse, art debased by the universal desire to deceive, to dazzle the eye and leave the heart unmoved. They are the epitome of a soulless and cunning and superficial age, reminding us whenever we look at them that Leonardo died when Catherine was born.

Much ill-considered praise has been lavished upon this "High Renaissance," and Catherine has even been extolled as a patroness of the arts. She collected extensively, it is true, but it was the competitive spirit which urged her to do so. Nowhere is her bourgeois origin more strikingly revealed than in her attitude to artists. She drove hard bargains with them, dealt with them as with tradespeople, and liked their work to be turned out as from a factory. By doubtful means she obtained the celebrated Strozzi Library, and when she coveted a piece of furniture belonging to one of her Ministers, she arranged to have the owner executed on a charge of malversation. Of portraits she was particularly fond, for to her the only realities were men and women. Three hundred and forty-one portraits are mentioned in the inventory of her possessions, and letters remain concerning the commission of several of them. It is to be gathered from these letters that in a later age Catherine would have collected three hundred and forty-one photographs.

For Catherine was far too mundane, far too preoccupied with the material difficulties which others made for her and which she made for herself, to become a leisurely and fastidious patroness. Her own nature and the circumstances of her life forbade it. She followed the prevailing taste for architecture, added to Chenonceaux, continued the Louvre, and built the Tuileries, but these were as much measures of policy as anything else. She had time for science, for science fortified her rationalistic attitude. But she had neither time nor inclination for art. And it was really as a scientist, an amusing inventor, that she employed Bernard Palissy. Indeed, it is as a scientist that Palissy deserves to be remembered.

The halt that we have made at Saintes before proceeding with Charles and Catherine to Bayonne is not an unreasonable one. For at this time Catherine was standing between two phases of her long life. She had engineered a temporary peace and she had time to look about her before entering on the crowning period of her career. She had had fourteen years of stormy childhood, fourteen years of initiation at the Court of Francis, eleven years of bitter humiliation as Queen-Consort, six years of unremitting struggle for power as Regent. She had carved out her place in history and must keep it, and with this year, 1564, we meet face to face at last the mobled queen. In the very midst of the period of sinister fulfilment that is to follow falls the day that gave us Catherine the legend, the day but for which Catherine might have remained an unregarded figure in an age of confusion, and St. Bartholomew the forgotten patron of a London hospital.

# BAYONNE

LONG before Biarritz and Saint-Jean-de-Luz had been discovered by millionaire trippers, the luxury of Catherine's Court came to spread itself for a few weeks between the mountains and the sea. After leaving Saintes, a halt had been made at Bordeaux, where the English Ambassador was interviewed with the object of arranging a match between Charles and the Virgin Queen. Elizabeth was thirty-one years old at the time, Charles not quite fifteen. "I should be very glad," said Charles, carefully instructed by his mother, to the Ambassador, "if your mistress would be as well pleased with my age as I am with hers." But Elizabeth was not well pleased with the idea of living in France, as she would have had to do as the consort of Charles. This was only one of many objections which prevented Catherine's remarkable project. And once again, as we read of the negotiations for a royal marriage, we tremble at the thought of what such marriages could mean to history. A peace had been arranged with England and Catherine had to be content with that.

The winter was passed in the south, where Catherine was careful to make conciliatory gestures in various strongly Protestant centres. It was a hard and bitter winter, but a short one. Spring came to Bayonne, and it was so hot that several soldiers in Catherine's following collapsed and died in their heavy armour. Philip of Spain had at last given permission for his wife Elizabeth to proceed to Bayonne to meet her mother. The reunion took place in the month of May, at Saint-Jean-de-Luz, with the picturesque accompaniment of a river-pageant and "a cannonade as furious as 'twas possible to hear." Delighted to see her daughter once more, Catherine gave her a very honourable entry into Bayonne. Charles loaded his sister with presents, and to the usual Court festivals of banquet and tournament were added the traditional entertainments of a southern spring. It is worth noticing that the tournaments had changed in character since the accidental death of Henry II and were now more formal and less dangerous. Montgomery's spear-thrust had been one more blow at the moribund feudal chivalry.

With a somewhat feminine petulance Philip had refused to come himself to meet his neighbour-sovereign Charles of France and his mother-in-law Catherine. At first he had likewise refused to allow his young Queen to make the journey, and although he at length conceded the point he took the opportunity of insulting Catherine by sending shabby and ill-equipped horsemen in her train. He sent also the strongest man in his kingdom, the Duke of Alba, whose hands were soon to be stained with the Council of Blood in the Netherlands.

The tall, gaunt figure of the Toledan was the skeleton at the feast of gaiety arranged to mask the diplomacy of Bayonne. Alba was fifty-five years old, nine years older than Catherine. We have his portrait in paint by Antonio Moro, in black armour and wearing about his neck the collar of the Golden Fleece, that emblem of nobility which could not save his gallant opponent, Egmont, from the scaffold; and we have his portrait in memorable words in Schiller's *Don Carlos* and Goethe's *Egmont*. He was of immense height, made yet more impressive by the emaciation brought on by hard campaigning. His straggling beard was now touched with white, but his dark eyes had still the metallic glitter which had made him feared both as soldier and diplomat, and his thin mouth was set in a firm and cruel line. There was no room for pity in this man, and Catherine would not find here those emotional weaknesses which she lacked herself and which in other men she had been accustomed to turn to her advantage.

There were preliminary skirmishes, many of them, between the spare Toledan and the plump and formidable
Queen-Mother, each with a young apprentice in attendance,
Charles upon Catherine and Elizabeth of Spain upon Alba.
Catherine had two further marriages on her programme, that
of Princess Margot (already promised to young Henry of
Navarre) to the Infante Don Carlos, and that of her second
surviving son, Henry of Anjou, to the middle-aged and widowed sister of Philip. Neither of these schemes fared better
than her crafty suit for the hand of the still craftier Elizabeth
of England; nor were her general diplomatic overtures to
Alba very successful. For she had the initial disadvantage of
being the soliciting party. It was she that was afraid, not
Alba, and with all his subtlety he played upon her fear. At
all costs she must ward off the danger of a Catholic League
of Spain and the Papacy and the Duchy of Savoy against
France. She had already come to terms with Protestant
England, and the Peace of Amboise, though it had cunningly
robbed the French Huguenots of nearly everything that they
had gained, could be interpreted by an orthodox observer as
a further sop to Protestantism. Iconoclasm in his Provinces
of the Netherlands was rousing the moody Philip to such fury
that he was in no mind to be tolerant towards the new religion. He was, after all, the Most Catholic King, and in
Alba he had the sharpest sword in Europe for the defence
of Holy Church.

Catherine wanted the impossible—security without concessions. When Alba taunted her with her shifty favours
towards the heretics, she grew angry. "Your Chancellor,
l'Hôpital, is a confessed Huguenot," said the Duke. "He is
*not* a Huguenot!" retorted Catherine. "You, Madam," said
Alba smoothly, "are the only person in France who believes
that." Elizabeth now broke in to support Alba's contention
and refute her mother, and the Duke followed this up by demanding coldly a straight answer to the only question that

had brought them to Bayonne. Was the Queen-Mother, guid-ing her son, prepared to take immediate steps to suppress the opponents of the older faith in France? Needless to say, he did not get a straight answer.

And so it went on, each party endeavouring to head the other off, each party changing the subject with consummate skill whenever the ground looked dangerous. "These are not matters of divine law but of political expediency," ob-served Catherine drily when Alba raised the embarrassing point of the Council of Poissy. It summed up her attitude, it almost summed up her career. Alba was outraged by such a statement, for divine law was what he had been enforcing all his life at the point of his sword.

It came at last to the private meeting which has ever since invited speculation. It was in the middle of June, and the ladies and gentlemen of the Court, in clothes which the modern visitor to the Azure Coast would regard as intoler-able, lay listlessly beside the fountains in the gardens of Bayonne. In the dim gallery of Catherine's palace the two black-robed actors in this brief drama paced slowly up and down, talking with lowered voices. To this day nobody knows exactly what they said to each other, though that bold little Gascon, Prince Henry of Navarre, had concealed him-self behind some hangings and overheard one phrase as the whispering shadows passed him. "The head of one salmon," Alba was saying, "is worth the heads of a thousand frogs." This, at all events, is what Henry repeated to his mother some years later.

The salmon was Coligny. In the light of later corre-spondence, and in particular of a letter written by Alba just after the Massacre of St. Bartholomew, it is practically certain that Catherine promised him at Bayonne that Coligny should die. Perhaps she promised too that Coligny's brothers, Odet and Andelot, and Condé as well, should share his fate; for that is what the Duke must have demanded. But one may

imagine that any undertaking to kill Condé was made with
a mental reservation. The matter, at any rate, was soon to be
taken out of Catherine's hands by the Prince's death on the
battlefield.

The larger question, still vigorously disputed, is this: did
Catherine pledge herself to organise a general massacre of
Huguenots such as that which took place seven years later?
Some have held that a selected list of necessary victims was
drawn up as the price of peace with Philip, others that the
terms included wholesale extermination. The ink that has
been poured out through succeeding centuries on this point
is a testimony to the diplomacy of the two masters of guile
who trod that shady corridor in Bayonne in midsummer 1565.
Every document bearing on the matter has been examined
by scholars as minutely as though it had been a codex of the
scriptures, and difference of opinion hangs in some cases upon
a *le* instead of a *la,* or upon the distribution of emphasis in
an ambiguous phrase. Whatever Catherine promised, she took
good care that nothing could ever be finally proved against
her. We may guess and deduce, and we may make very strong
presumptions. But as the great Karl Breul used to say, mac-
aronically, when he reached a disputed passage in an Old
High German text: *Ignoramus, vielleicht ignorabimus.*

So the memorable meeting was concluded and the parties
left Bayonne; Alba to take council with his sovereign for
the suppression of the disturbances in the Netherlands attributed to the too tolerant rule of Margaret of Parma (whom
we met so long ago in Florence with the youthful Catherine) ; Elizabeth like some childish vision of Velasquez, cum-
bered by an enormous skirt and the stifling formality of a
great Court, to die in Madrid at the age of twenty-three without seeing her mother again; Charles in floods of tears which
the aged Constable vainly endeavoured to abate, telling him
gently that a king must not cry and that his sister would be
well and happy in Spain, and glad to get back to her royal

husband; Catherine with grim foreboding to face a situation which now could only have one end—renewed and bloodier war.

For here again, as in the case of the Orleans assassination, importance lies less in what had happened than in what was believed to have happened. Whether Coligny were guilty or innocent of instigating the murder of Guise, the Catholics believed him guilty and acted accordingly. Whether Catherine were guilty or innocent of pledging herself to slaughter the Huguenots, the Huguenots believed her guilty and hastened to forestall her by reopening the war.

They had good reason to be suspicious. Without the added fear of a secret pact of Bayonne they had already suffered, during these years of nominal peace, by oppressing interpretations of the equivocal Peace of Amboise. Coligny, though he was shortly absolved in Council from any complicity in the Guise murder, knew well that this was not the end. Five hundred Huguenots, he declared in public, had been killed by separate acts of violence since the Peace of Amboise. Catholics too had been struck down in broad daylight in the streets of Paris. It was indeed an uneasy kind of peace.

And then came the news that the King (or Catherine) had armed six thousand Swiss Guards as a measure of safety while the King of Spain was passing north with Alba to the suppression of the Netherlands. The motive for assembling these troops was doubted, and the Huguenots, with Condé once more eager for the fray, determined to strike first. They struck boldly with a well-planned attempt to kidnap the King from Meaux. Having been foiled in this *coup d'état* they proceeded to blockade Paris. The rivers of blood that Calvin had prophesied were beginning to flow freely.

# MONTAIGNE

IN the first days of the year 1571, when the oak and beech woods of Périgord were bare and the ground rang like iron at every hoof-beat, a man approaching forty years of age returned contemplatively to the Périgueux estate of Montaigne which by the death of his father had passed into his possession. His name was Michel Eyquem, now Sieur de Montaigne, and we know a great deal about his appearance, just as we know each detail of his habits of thought and action, communicated in the self-revelatory pages of the "Essays" which he was shortly to begin.

"As for me," he writes, "I am of a strong and well compacted stature, my face is not fat but full, my complexion between joviall and melancholy, indifferently sanguine and hot. . . . I have found few, that have not outgone me, except it were in running, wherein I was of the middle sort. As for musicke, were it either in voice, which I have most harsh, and very unapt, or in instruments, I could never be taught any part of it. As for dancing, playing at tennis, or wrestling; I could never attaine to any indifferent sufficiencie; but none at all in swimming, in fencing, in vaulting, or in leaping. My hands are so stiffe and nummie, that I can hardly write for my selfe, so that what I have once scribbled, I had rather frame it a new, then take the paines to correct it; and I reade but little better. . . . I was never good carver at the table. I could never make readie nor arme a Horse: Nor handsomely carry a Hawke upon my fist, nor cast her off, or let her flie, nor could I ever speake to Dogges, to Birds, or to Horses. The Conditions of my body are, in fine, very well agreeing with those of my minde, wherein is nothing lively; but only a compleate and constant vigor."

It will be seen that this man, who has been called the wisest Frenchman of his day, was something of a misfit. He wore breeches and jerkin of a sober black and white and condemned the fantastic costumes of the Court and the Swiss Guards, and the ladies who " (as dainty-nice as they be) are many times seene to goe open-breasted, as low as their navill." He prided himself (for there is more than a hint of self-satisfaction in the apparent modesty of his confession) on his lack of address in Court games and dancing. He preached a gospel of moderation in all things, at a time when the worst excesses were being committed. And the quality which he recognised in his mind was the quality of which France stood most sorely in need—"a compleate and constant vigor."

Yet in many respects Montaigne approached the type of his age, and in some he recalls Catherine herself. Like her he was sceptical, rationalistic, fond of the middle way, and like her he had little or no interest in art. Compromise was natural to him, and beside his frank scepticism we find an equally frank regard for authority in religious as well as temporal matters. On kingship he has the folowing significant remarks:

"It hath hapned to simple women, to weake children, and to mad men, to command great states, as well as the most sufficient Princes. And the gullish or shallow-pated (saith *Thucidides*) doe more ordinarily come unto them, than the wisest and subtilest. We ascribe their good fortunes effects, unto their prudence. . . . We need but looke upon a man advanced to dignity; had we but three daies before knowne him to bee of little or no worth at all: an image of greatnesse, and an Idea of sufficiency, doth insensibly glide and creepe into our opinions; and we perswade our selves, that increasing in state, and credit, and followers, hee is also increased in merit."

Only a few months before, Montaigne had journeyed full of hope to Paris, the city which he had loved since his early days at college there, and of which he was to write: "This great matchlesse Citie, great in people, great in regard of the felicitie of her situation; but above all, great and incomparable in varietie and diversitie of commodities: the glory of *France,* and one of the noblest and chiefe ornaments of the world. God of his mercy free hir, and chase away all our divisions from hir. . . . I forewarne hir, that of all factions, that shall be the worst, which shall breed discord in hir. And for hir sake, I onely feare hir selfe."

But he had found the city a prey to the divisions he dreaded, and abandoning all ambitions to diplomatic power he had escaped from this atmosphere of hatred and suspicion and daily treachery and ridden back to Périgord, through the wasted countryside of Touraine and Poitou, resolved henceforth to live as a private gentleman upon his secluded estate.

To understand the situation which disillusioned this eager and gifted man we shall have to recapitulate. Four and a half years had passed since the presageful meeting at Bayonne, years of violent fighting broken by two temporary treaties. Threatened by the Huguenot enterprise, the King and Court had been safely escorted by the Constable from Meaux to Paris. In the drawn battle of Saint-Denis, just outside the northern walls of the capital, the Constable de Montmorency was slain and one of the last links with the vanished age of Francis I thus broken. The amazing charge of Condé's handful of cavalry against the Catholic line in this battle had deserved to make it a brilliant victory for the Huguenots. But in the ensuing confusion, when Coligny was twice carried by a frightened horse into the press of Catholic fugitives, it was impossible to force home the advantage. The issue remained undecided, and trouble among the German allies of the Huguenots compelled them to accept another truce before they had reached a position to dictate terms. The Peace of Longjumeau, signed on March 23, 1568, was little more than a slightly extended Peace of Amboise, with Protestant worship permitted in certain provincial towns. "This bloody and unfaithful peace," Coligny called it, for up and down the country the Huguenots were still being slaughtered without mercy. It was no peace, but unofficial guerilla warfare, and where the Huguenots were strong enough to exact reprisals they took their revenge with no unsteady hand.

Meanwhile Coligny and Condé made bitter complaints in writing to the King and the Queen-Mother. Charles's instinctive hatred of the Huguenots, which in spite of his early schooling in their faith and his friendship for individuals among them, had never disappeared, had been strengthened by the attempt on his person at Meaux and also by certain things which he had seen during his southern tour. For this wayward and nervous youth had an æsthetic sensibility rare in his time, and the sight of desecrated mediæval churches and rifled tombs—the work of the iconoclastic element in the Huguenot Béarnais—had roused in him the anti-Puritan feeling of the artist. He did not want religious warfare, but he was convinced that the Huguenots were the troublesome party and that their suppression was the only cure for the present evils.

As for Catherine, she sought as usual to put off the plaintiffs with fair words. "Your sentiments may be sincere," retorted Coligny impatiently, "but there is no power behind them." He and Condé had gone so far as to draw up an exhaustive catalogue of the wrongs inflicted upon them, with the names of persons assassinated and the details of every such injury. They demanded the removal from power of the Cardinal of Lorraine, "the source, root and origin of the ruin and subversion which threaten the Crown"; and the fiery Condé exclaimed that "God will not leave unpunished the shedding of so much innocent blood, which continually cries to Him for vengeance!"

Catherine disliked the mention of God in diplomatic con-

versations. She disliked the whole tone of this business.
She felt that she had sufficient difficulties in her path without
complicating them by displays of hysteria. Alba was watching her closely from the Netherlands endeavouring, she suspected, to prolong the internal unrest of France until he
should have leisure to reckon with her. A couple of months
before, on June 5, 1568, he had given her a notable example
by the execution of Horn and Egmont in Brussels. It was an
obvious hint that the heads of Coligny and Condé would
look better upon spikes, and Catherine could not fail to
recognise the suggestion. Peace with Alba, peace in France,
leisure for her ambitions, an end to Huguenot complaints by
putting an end to the complainants—this is what she saw.
The protests of Condé and Coligny (which had all been
made in correspondence) had rendered the Queen-Mother
desperate. She may not have intended the immediate deaths
of the burdensome pair, for we may still doubt whether
she would ever have killed Condé if she could have avoided
it. But she certainly plotted their capture. Guise was dead,
Montmorency was dead, Antoine of Navarre was dead.
Catherine desired further reductions in the ranks of the
potentates.

She laid her plans carefully, but they were betrayed to
her intended victims. Fully aware now of what they had to
face, Condé and Coligny prepared to retire with the army
to the Protestant stronghold of La Rochelle, a well-defended
city which had the great advantage of an outlet to the sea
and thus to communication with foreign allies and sources
of supply for a hard-pressed garrison. The sanguinary peace
had now become the Third War of Religion, and it was
only with great difficulty that the two Huguenots found a
way with their troops to La Rochelle. At the fording of the
Loire, indeed, they were saved from destruction only by a
piece of fortune suggesting a parallel with the crossing of
the Red Sea by the Israelites—a parallel which was naturally

put to pious use in a psalm of deliverance on the opposite bank.

From La Rochelle began an autumn campaign against odds so heavy that Coligny quoted the splendid words of Themistocles: "Our destruction had been certain had our danger been less." In this moment of gravest peril the finer side of the Huguenots was revealed. By strenuous regulations the leaders managed for a time to secure better order amongst their men. There was more bravery and less cruelty, and the fighting was undertaken in the spirit expressed by de Bèze years before in a retort to the King of Navarre: "It is for the Church of God, in whose name I speak, to endure blows and not to give them. But may it please you to remember that it is an anvil which has worn out many hammers." For the Huguenot cause at this time appeared so hopeless that such as attached themselves to it must have done so from conviction rather than from any hope of gain.

After months of fighting throughout the west it came at last, in March of the following year, to the battle of Jarnac, on the Charente. The Huguenot forces were not strong enough to sustain an engagement on so wide a front as was offered them. Condé was cut off from Coligny, and Andelot, whose cavalry, tired out by a day's marching and fighting, made a last and quite ineffectual charge and then rode off the field. Forced back to the river, heavily outnumbered, Condé pointed to the motto on his standard and crying aloud "For Christ and Country!" charged with his little band into the main Catholic army. With desperate valour he and his men fought their way almost through the Royalists, but at last he was completely surrounded. Borne down by sheer numbers he surrendered, and in the act of giving up his sword was shot dead by an enemy who has never been identified. Six years before, at Dreux, he had shared as an honourable prisoner the bed of his captor. Now his body was strapped to the back of an ass and carried amidst jeering and triumph through Jarnac. And that helps to show why Montaigne retired to his castle.

The Court was at Metz when the news of Jarnac arrived. Catherine had been ill—dangerously ill, said the doctors—of a fever, and in her dreams she had cried aloud that the Huguenots were in flight and Condé dead in a hedge. Then came the messenger to tell her of the victory and receive the customary reward. "Why wake me for that?" asked the invalid irritably when she had heard him. "I knew it already. Did I not see it all myself?" One is reminded of that earlier dream which had warned her of the death of her husband, and of several other visions and prophecies which have engaged the attention of magicians but ought rather to engage that of psychologists.

Charles also was in bed, for it was late at night. "My greatest enemy is dead!" he exclaimed when the news was brought to him. On his bare knees he offered a grateful prayer, than threw on a dressing-gown and hurried eagerly to his mother's bedside. Her fever must have left her suddenly on this eventful night, or perhaps she took a risk. At any rate she suffered herself to be dragged off by her impulsive son to hear a *Te Deum* in Metz Cathedral.

It was the seventeen-year-old Henry of Anjou who had commanded the main Catholic body at Jarnac and had thus won his spurs, a circumstance which delighted his mother, Catherine, but robbed the jealous King of some of his pleasure in the victory. The younger generation was now taking up the struggle with enthusiasm, while the men who had seen its birth were one by one leaving the stormy scene. Henry, Duke of Guise, had succeeded his murdered father, Francis, as titular head of the house, though it was still the grim Cardinal of Lorraine who directed the Guise policy. And that remarkable woman Jeanne of Navarre, who had snapped her fingers at a Papal excommunication and resolutely held the South for the Protestants, now hastened to

the Huguenot camp and presented to the disconsolate soldiers her young son Henry and the son of Condé. The effect
was electrifying. Moved by the staunch bearing and eloquence of the wronged and widowed Queen the men accepted
the two Princes with a great shout of loyalty. It was a scene
familiar to history. And while Coligny naturally remained
the leader of the party in all but name, the perpetual desire
for a royal connection was satisfied in the persons of the two
high-born youths—"the Admiral's pages" as they were affectionately called.

Coligny had no son to succeed him if death in battle or
by treachery should overtake him. Within the space of a few
months he had lost his wife, his son and Condé, and hard
upon Condé's death came that of the Admiral's gallant
brother Andelot, whom the Huguenots called the *chevalier
sans peur*. Andelot died at Saintes, suddenly and in his bed.
No proof of poisoning was ever brought, but the suspicion
was natural then and it is not difficult to share it. If Andelot
were poisoned it was probably the result of a Spanish plot,
winked at, but not directly instigated by Catherine. For she
had been having more trouble with Spain, and the Spanish
Ambassador had so far forgotten diplomatic etiquette as to lay
hold on her robe and demand the assassination of Coligny
and several other prominent Huguenots. "Never dare to
speak so again!" exclaimed Catherine, but she was nervous.
The Huguenots still held Rochelle securely and she feared
that they might bring the English once more into France
by that route. She tried to bluff the Spanish envoy into believing that the power had passed from her hands into those
of her growing sons, but he was not to be put off. "When
open force fails," he told her meaningly, "there remain
Italian weapons of which a Florentine should be aware."
And an Italian in her service was overheard to say that these
wars would be won not by captains but by cooks.

Robbed of his dearest relatives and friends, Coligny knew

that his own life was the chief target of the plotters. Several
attempts had already been made, and the death of Coligny
at this moment would have been the death of the cause
he served, for only he could lead the Huguenots out of their
present desperate straits. The measures against him were
not all secret. A price of fifty thousand crowns was set upon
his head, and the Parlement of Paris publicly sentenced him
in his absence "to be hanged and strangled on a gallows to
be erected for the purpose in the Place de Grève before the
Hôtel de Ville of Paris, his dead body there to remain hanging for the space of twenty-four hours, and thence to be
carried and hanged upon the gibbet of Montfaucon in the
most high and exalted place."

With the cooks mixing their poisons for him and the
carpenters busy with his scaffold, his comrades dead and his
cause at its lowest ebb, Coligny turned cruel. The previous
charges against him of excessive severity are scattered and
sometimes refutable. But now for a little he went berserk.
Huguenots had been butchered in Provence, and Coligny
took barbarous vengeance in Périgord. It was a grim business, the bloody struggle of a lonely man against his own
despair, and it left him weak and ill and his purpose but
little advanced. Anjou and his Catholics still held the Loire,
and the struggle raged up and down Poitou with a fury that
brought no decisive result. Niort, Parthenay, Lusignan,
Poitiers—those pleasant names that are scattered through
the rich pages of Rabelais occur now as the battlefields of
a fierce campaign, and one is reminded of the destructive
advance of Picrochole and his troops through the Poitevin
landscape:

"Then immediately in all disorder, without keeping either
rank or file, they took the fields one amongst another, wast-
ing, spoiling, destroying and making havock of all wherever
they went, not sparing poor nor rich, privileged nor un-
privileged places, Church nor laity, drove away oxen and

cows, bulls, calves, heifers, wethers, ewes, lambs, goats, kids, hens, capons, chickens, geese, ganders, goslings, hogs, swine, pigs and such like. Beating down the walnuts, plucking the grapes, tearing the hedges, shaking the fruit-trees, and committing such incomparable abuses, that the like abomination was never heard of."

A crushing defeat at Moncontour, with wholesale slaughter of his German mercenaries, only served to rouse Coligny to fresh efforts, and while the Catholics were celebrating the extinction of the Huguenot cause he was making swift journeys with his two noble "pages" to establish connection with the Protestant strongholds of the south. Charles and Catherine sent an envoy to Jeanne of Navarre at La Rochelle offering terms of peace. A condition was that Protestantism might be carried on in private, but not in public. Jeanne proudly refused the offer, and when at length the Peace of Saint-Germain brought hostilities once more to a nominal standstill its clauses were much more favourable to the Huguenots. By his uncompromising energy, and with the brave support of Jeanne, Coligny had turned the tide.

This was the peace that had brought Montaigne to Paris to seek his fortune. He found a Queen-Mother involved in plots and projects that no man could with certainty fathom; a jealous, frivolous, hysterical King, turning first to one side and then to the other in intermittent efforts to assert himself; a city in which murder lurked at every corner, intrigue behind every curtain, and poison, as it was said, in the most innocent places—in books and gloves and rings and the saddles of horses. He found neither valour nor dignity nor wisdom, but only the nervous fear and hatred of man for man and the shifty councils of ambitious factions.

His château in Périgord lay in the centre of the theatre of war, but marauding troops had never disturbed its peace. Its door stood open to friend and stranger, and within its walls, in a round tower lined with books, a man might sit and occupy himself with more permanent affairs than those of Guise and Huguenot. On February 28, 1571, which was his thirty-eighth birthday, Michel de Montaigne inscribed upon his library wall a legend to commemorate the beginning of his work upon those Essays which he intended for "the corner of a library, and to amuse a neighbour, a kinsman, or a friend of mine withall, who, by this image, may happily take pleasure to renew acquaintance and to reconverse with me." But he did not close the windows of his round tower while he examined himself and his thoughts at such prodigious and fascinating length. He kept them open upon the troubled landscape of France, and several of the titles of his Essays conjure up visions of the forced marches of Catholic and Protestant, of sieges and battles and the degenerating arts of warfare, of cruelty and chicanery and irresolute government, of pale-mouthed vice and immoderate fashions, of portents and prognostications and the trembling fortunes of nations and men. He discourses, for instance, "Of the Battell of Dreux," "Of Steeds Called Destriers," "Of Vanitie," "Of the Use of Apparell," 'To Avoid Voluptuousnesse in Regard to Life," "Of Cowardize the Mother of Crueltie," "Of Vaine Subtilties," and "Of the Libertie of Conscience."

And with one more quotation from Montaigne we may leave him and pursue once more the path to St. Bartholomew:

"In these dismembrings or havocks of *France,* and divisions whereinto we are miserably falne, I perceive every man travell and busie himself to defend his owne cause, and the better sort with much dissembling and falsehood. Hee that should plainely and roundly write of it, should write rashly and viciously. Take the best and justest part, what is it else but the member of a crased, worme-eaten and corrupted body?"

Try as we may, it is impossible to make the Wars of Religion heroic.

## BLOIS

THE lordly castle of Blois, sprawling above the narrow streets of the town, between the broad Loire and the mild sky of Touraine, had now become Catherine's favourite residence. Here Charles d'Orléans had found some relief from his melancholy, and had paced the court-yard, a graceful figure in black, composing his exquisite rondeaux. Hither Louis XII had ridden back from his Milanese exploits, bearing the first of the Italian treasures which were to flood France until the salamander King had exclaimed "I am stifled in gold!" The noble equestrian figure of Louis was carved at Blois, and his symbol of the porcupine, and Francis I's symbol of the salamander, and the drooping Claude's symbol of the ermine. Here the *Petite Bande* of Francis had climbed the famous spiral stair like a rainbow vision of Jacob, and here in the great Renaissance wing overlooking the wide gardens, Catherine had her bedroom and her little chamber with its neatly-fitted cupboards, the panels covered with the excessive decoration that enervated taste decreed.

To this Court of Blois came Coligny on September 12, 1571. The Peace of Saint-Germain had at last given Protestantism a status, and La Rochelle was virtually a state within a state, where Jeanne and Coligny could treat with ambassadors and whence the Huguenot sailors could rove the seas on the track of Philip's galleons. It was not without demanding security that Coligny ventured out of his stronghold at the invitation of King Charles. To the mysterious deaths of well-known men had now been added that of Odet, the Admiral's Cardinal brother and long ago the patron of Rabelais. Odet had died in England, again it was said by poison, and his ghost is still believed to walk in Canterbury

Cathedral. Only Coligny and Jeanne were left, and the Admiral knew well enough that a declared peace did not mean safety from assassination. Friends warned him of the dangers lurking at Court, but Brantôme tells us that he answered: "Better to die by a bold thrust than live a hundred years in fear!" The safeguards for which he asked were accorded him. and with some fifty companions, but without any of the customary display, he rode on that September afternoon up the hill to the gate of the castle.

Catherine was again confined to her bed with a feverish attack, but it was not a serious one. The reception took place at her bedside, in the presence of the King, the Queen (Charles had lately married Elizabeth of Austria), the Princess Margot, the Cardinal de Bourbon and the Duc de Montpensier. A single attendant entered the room with the Admiral, who twice made obeisance to the King and then seemed about to cast himself at his feet. But the impulsive Charles intercepted the movement, took Coligny by the shoulders, embraced him thrice and said: "Good father, now that we have you here we shall not let you go again!" But he had no thought of the sinister meaning which now we might read into the words. Through all the vicissitudes of civil war and through his own shifting allegiances he had continued to regard the Admiral as his hero.

Coligny then advanced towards Catherine, who greeted him warmly, "but without the usual kiss." She thought that he had greatly aged since she had last seen him, and indeed they had all aged. She herself had passed her fifty-second year, and all around her she saw the younger generation growing in importance and ambition. The sons of her former enemies and confederates now trod the galleries of Blois, their swords kept bright for the struggle that was not dead, but only dormant. Her own sons were bearded, and the invitation to Coligny had to some extent been a gesture of self-assertion on the part of Charles.

The pleasure of Charles at the return of the warrior was quite unfeigned. He at once took Coligny into his confidence, and an observer recounts that the Admiral "is to be found each day at the rising of the King, as well as when he dines and sups. At all hours he is close to his chair, and with the same freedom as those who never left the Court. And the King reasons and discourses with him as he does with the rest, so that it truly seems as though the past were buried in perpetual oblivion." Such familiarity by no means decreased the eagerness of Coligny's enemies to be rid of him, and the young Duke of Guise was overheard to declare that if he were once left alone with the Huguenot with a sword in his hand he would settle the matter.

It was the soldier in Coligny that appealed to the neurotic Charles. As we read the reports of the Venetian Ambassadors on the subject of this freak of nature who sat on the throne of Saint Louis we are inevitably reminded of Peter III of Russia. Like Peter, Charles had been given an upbringing that deliberately encouraged his worst features. Like Peter, he had an insensate passion for soldiers and feats of arms. Where Peter ranged his toy soldiers about his cardboard castle and drilled his lackeys in the palace corridors, Charles betook himself to his portable forge and hammered out greaves and cuirasses with a fury that left him weak and trembling. Like Peter, too, Charles delighted to exhaust his suite at the chase or in other violent exercises. Like Peter he was foul-mouthed and clumsy in deceit. Like Peter he was immensely to be pitied.

Unlike Peter, however, Charles was able to make love. His amours were not many, but they were more effectual than those of the impotent Czar. He had not chosen Elizabeth of Austria, that staunch little Catholic, for himself, but he did not treat her badly. He rather liked her, for she was quiet and amiable and faithful to him. For himself he chose Marie Touchet, the daughter of a provincial judge, who was for a time a Huguenot, but later changed sides. Marie her-self may have been a Huguenot, though this has never been finally settled. But she had complete power over him, and he loved her devotedly. It was for his mistress that he called in the terrible remorse of his deathbed. It is said, too, that he had had an earlier mistress whose existence he had man-aged to keep secret from his mother, but if Catherine did not find out about her it is not surprising that little evidence of the affair remains.

Charles may well have been attractive to women, for never did King stand more sorely in need of right and steady in-fluence and of rescue from his perverse tutors. His portraits, too, show him as a slender and rather handsome figure, though the descriptions of those who knew him do not al-ways bear this out. On one feature contemporaries seem agreed. His golden-brown eyes, the eyes of his father, were extraordinarily beautiful. He would not willingly meet the glance of another, but when the long lashes rose for an in-stant the effect was strangely compulsive. And he had in-herited more than his eyes from Henry. He had Henry's passion for music, and though he was eager to hunt whenever the weather was fine, the gathering of rainclouds over the towers of Blois was the signal for poets and musicians to congregate in his chamber for his pleasure. Like Henry, too, he turned his own hand to poetry, and left some competent verses of praise for Ronsard, his adored "Prince of Poets"; while his unfinished book on his favourite sport, *De la Vénerie*, must be allowed unusual literary promise which in happier circumstances might have borne rich fruit.

At every turn, indeed, in an examination of the character of Charles IX, one is tempted to wonder what might have been. There was so much that was good in him, so much that was never given a chance to express itself. He had all the weakness of the highly strung æsthete, the restlessness, the moods of morbid brooding and uncontrolled folly, the taste for eccentric pleasures such as nocturnal visits to the bedsides of noblemen to flog them, the shrinking fear of his own excesses. But he had also the sensibility of the æsthete, and if the great Amyot had been allowed as much power over his royal pupil as were the two Italians whom Catherine set to degenerate him, history might have been very different.

Catherine at this time was energetic and vigorous in spite of occasional fevers and the first twinges of the rheumatism which was later to cause her great discomfort. Her appetite remained a by-word, and there are few observers who do not make reference to it. It even came to be used by the bolder ambassadors for the purpose of annoying her when it was convenient to do so. While the Queen-Mother ate heartily and without distinction all that was put before her, her son showed a rather curious tendency to frugality. We find him refusing rich dishes and strong liquors which might accentuate the mental instability which he himself dreaded, and the royal account books show Charles to have been the least personally extravagant of the Valois. The demoniacal violence of his daily exercise was perhaps in some degree another attempt by the mishandled youth to curb his tendency to dangerous passions.

On his hunting expeditions his mother frequently accompanied him, in spite of her fifty odd years. Brantôme tells us that she continued to indulge in the sport regularly until her sixtieth year, recking little of its fatigues and hazards although on one occasion she broke her leg and on another injured her head. "There is no one in the Court who can keep pace with her when walking," says a Venetian, in 1570. "She is benevolent, courteous and affable to all," adds the same enthusiastic witness, "making it her business to see that none leaves her dissatisfied, at least as far as words are concerned, of which she is very liberal." Her gift of persuasion and pleasant conversation, the gift that had been her only standby when she arrived at the French Court nearly

*Courtesy of Archives Photographiques, Paris, and The Studio, London*

## HARLEQUINADE AT THE COURT OF CHARLES IX
## (1572)

(Detail of painting in Bayeux Museum, attributed to Frans Pourbus the elder)

forty years before, showed no signs of deserting her, though
those who were able to learn by experience had come to
attach little importance to her smooth words. Once, she laid
her hand upon the arm of a courtier, calling him "My
friend." "Madame," begged the gentleman, "call me rather
'my enemy'; for when you address me as friend it means
either that you take me for a fool or else that you are angry
with me."

Charles made bad jokes and Catherine laughed at them.
Her laughter was as hearty as her appetite; it was almost
Rabelaisian. "She would split her sides," says Brantôme, "at
the comedies and tragi-comedies which she loved to have
performed, for she was jovial by nature." In the spirit of
liberal princes she could join in the mirth when a jest went
against herself, as we have seen in the gross incident of the
Huguenot cannon. She did not care for tragedies, and after
a performance at Blois of the *Sophonisbe* of Saint-Gelais, in
which her children took part, she resolved to see no more
such gloomy spectacles, saying that they brought ill-luck to
the affairs of the kingdom. Amateur theatricals were a favourite Court pastime of the period, and the professional players
who were summoned to amuse royalty had often to stand
aside and see their parts played by kings and queens. Charles
was particularly addicted to this form of distraction. He had
histrionic gifts and a characteristic fondness for self-dramati-
sation. It was partly a form of exhibitionism allied to his
other peculiarities, and one is reminded that Gilles de Rais,
pattern and paragon of sadists, had done remarkable pioneer
work for the secular theatre in France.

In the case of the Commedia dell' Arte, which with other
features of Italian social life had followed Catherine to
France, the stock members of the cast had necessarily to
appear, for the entertainment was largely of an improvisatory
nature, based on the strictly defined attributes of each per-
former. But there was nothing to prevent the ladies and

gentlemen of the Court joining in the fun in minor or supple-
mentary parts, and so they did. The painting at Bayeux
attributed to Frans Pourbus the elder is regarded by Pierre
Louis Duchartre as "the oldest and most important document in the iconography of the Commedia dell' Arte now
extant," and shows the company of Alberto Ganessa performing at the Court of Charles IX. Brigella, Zanni, Pantaloon and Harlequin are being assisted (though their attitudes
rather suggest that the assistance is none too welcome) by
amateurs who include Charles, Catherine, Henry of Anjou,
Alençon, Princess Margot, Henry of Guise, and Marie
Touchet. In the foreground the sprightly Margot kneels in
mimic supplication before Guise and the King, who appear
to be disputing. Clad in a white doublet, Charles is giving,
as we might expect, a most spirited performance. Directly
behind this group Anjou stands disdainfully aloof, and near
him Alençon is holding the Queen-Mother by the hand,
gazing with some show of anxiety at her inscrutable profile.
In the extreme right background is Charles's mistress. This
scene of stilted frivolity bears the grim date of 1572.

Such was the type of amusement in which Catherine sought
to relieve her own anxieties and to keep others from too close
attention to matters which she desired to maintain under
her own control. She was undoubtedly the busiest person
at the Court. "Scarcely has she time to eat or drink or
sleep, so great are her harassing cares," reports Giovanni
Correro towards the end of the Third War of Religion. "She
runs hither and thither between the armies, doing a man's
work, without a thought of sparing herself. Yet she is beloved by no one in the land—or at least by few. The
Huguenots say that she has given them fine words and feigned
welcomes, while all the time she has been treating with the
Catholic King [of Spain] and scheming their destruction. The
Catholics, on the other hand, declare that if she had not
exalted and favoured the Huguenots, these latter would not

have been able to do what they have done. Moreover, this is an age in France when every man presumes. He thinks of something, then passionately asks for it. If his request is refused, he grumbles and throws the blame on the Queen-Mother. And as she is a stranger, though she were to give all, they would only say that she gave nothing of her own."

It is a charitable view of Catherine and her difficulties that the Venetian takes. Certainly her cares were many, and it is possible to believe in the picture which Correro gives later on, one of the rare close-ups of Catherine from an intimate angle: "I know also that she has been seen weeping in her cabinet more than once. Then forcing herself, she has dried her eyes and appeared in public with a smiling countenance." But we cannot allow a few womanly tears to prejudice us unduly in her favour. Her own selfish and persistent policy of strengthening the throne while weakening its occupant was responsible for many of her troubles, and the pitiless nature of her character does not call for pity in her biographers. By careful selection among her letters and the records of her contemporaries quite a favourable case could be made out for Catherine. Her misdeeds could be transferred to the responsibility of others (she herself spent much thought in so transferring them) and her efforts at pacification emphasised at the expense of her hypocrisy and double-dealing. But when every black is toned to a half-light, and every half-light painted white, when every unconfirmed suspicion is dismissed and every ambiguity favourably interpreted, there remains St. Bartholomew. To declare that Paris was athirst for blood is not to absolve the woman who, from whatever motives, saw to it that the thirst was slaked.

When Coligny arrived at Blois he well knew with whom he had to deal. After the first formal meeting he sought out Catherine alone, and asked her bluntly whether she would really answer for his safety. "I know well enough," she replied, "that you can trust us no more than we can trust you. Have you not offended my son, the King, and taken arms against him? Well, we will overlook that, and I promise you that if you will serve him as a good and loyal subject I will reward you with every kind of favour."

Her assurance was valueless. Coligny recognised her guile in hinting at the affair of Meaux and thereby shifting the responsibility for his life to the shoulders of the King. He knew that as far as Charles was concerned he had nothing to fear. But he knew also that however independent Charles endeavoured to appear, the Queen-Mother could always choose the moment and the methods to goad her son into one of his hysterical fits and subject him completely to her purposes.

Nor was Coligny blinded for long by the blaze of glory which followed on his return to Court. Already famous throughout Europe for his conduct of the Third War, he now found himself publicly exalted among his former enemies, given a State Entry into Paris and favoured as the King's closest, indeed as his only councillor. It was not false security which made him ignore the repeated warnings whispered to him in the galleries and alcoves of Blois and sent to him in anonymous letters. It was the honest conviction that he could use his influence on the King for the country's good, and for Charles's happiness as well; for Coligny returned the youth's hero-worship with a genuine and fatherly affection.

The Admiral lost no time in impressing the King with his ideas of a reconstructed national policy. With Spain, the traditional enemy of France, there must, he declared, be no more compromise. Friendship with England, a campaign in the Netherlands to take advantage of the revolt against Spanish oppression, vigorous colonisation in the West Indies and Florida (whither Coligny at his own expense had previously sent two Huguenot expeditions to combat the Spanish power in the New World—these were to be the steps towards an enlarged and orderly France wherein liberty of religious conscience should be a guiding principle. But it was not quite so simple as it looked. England was very jealous of any interference in the Netherlands except her own, and Spain, with spies everywhere, did not mean to be balked of her hold on French policy, A few weeks after Coligny's arrival at Blois came the news of Lepanto, the great naval engagement, wherein Cervantes was wounded (though that fact, of course, was not sufficiently important to be mentioned in despatches). "There was a man sent from God whose name was John" was the text of the Papal thanksgiving for the defeat of the Turks. For Don John of Austria had struck a great blow for Christendom against the infidels. But Huguenots were heretics, if not infidels, and Lepanto was a Spanish victory as well as a Christian one. The news might well give Coligny pause.

Confident that she could win back her son whenever she needed to do so, Catherine made the Admiral a generous allowance of rope. She too had her schemes, and they were deeply laid. She did not intend to have Coligny as a rival, but to a certain extent she shared his view of foreign policy. Maintaining outward friendship with Spain she yet sought means to strengthen herself against that long-feared aggressor, and the Netherlands were a tempting bait. The death of her daughter Elizabeth in child-bed three years previously had possibly contributed to her growing revulsion from a policy favourable to Spain, and since the Infante Don Carlos had also died there was no more question of a marriage in that quarter. But it was still with marriages that she played. The Virgin Queen had refused Charles, so Catherine had offered Henry of Anjou, whom she also refused after a period of characteristic dalliance. Nothing daunted, Catherine now planned to marry her youngest son, Alençon, to the English sovereign. One of the Fugger News-Letters, dated from Antwerp, June 30, 1571, shows that the project was then known. The writer refers also to the death of Odet de Coligny (Cardinal de Châtillon) :

"About the conspirators who poisoned the Cardinal de Châtillon I have heard nothing more. A man who came from England last week tells me they have been arrested more on suspicion than as being proved guilty of the crime. These people cannot be trusted ... Marshal de Damville, brother of Admiral de Montmorency, is said too to be going to England to negotiate a marriage between this Queen and the brother of his King. But it appears that under this pretext he is to conduct other negotiations. A strange world!"

At the same time the Queen-Mother planned to marry her daughter, Margot, to Henry of Navarre. It was the match that she had proposed to Jeanne ten years ago at the time of the Council of Poissy, but things were very different now. With the young Prince de Condé, Henry of Navarre was now the titular leader of the Huguenots, while Margot had remained all the time at the Court, a Royalist and a Catholic in spite of her free and easy ways. In her stronghold of La Rochelle Jeanne was a more important person than she had been when she came to Poissy after her errant husband, and she was not the one to make compromises. But Catherine had already lured Coligny from the Huguenot fortress, and the same methods could be tried with Jeanne. But for these plans Coligny might have met his fate earlier at the hands of an assassin at Blois. For the moment, however, Catherine needed him as a bait for Jeanne, and she needed him alive. By every means in her power she sought to calm his suspicions, though she knew that he would not trust her for long.

And at last she got Jeanne to Blois and the marriage was arranged. It was perhaps the cleverest thing that Catherine ever did, for it was not given to many to dupe the Queen of Navarre. At this period the Queen-Mother seems to have been at the height of her crafty powers, tireless, ruthless, at times almost oblivious of the very difficulties she was over-coming. Had she ever attached any importance to moral qualities she would have rejected as hopeless the idea of bending two such characters as Coligny and Jeanne to her purposes.

It was a long struggle of wits. Jeanne could see the advantage of uniting France and Navarre against Catholic Spain, but the religious question caused her terrible mis-giving. The order of the marriage ceremony itself, whether Catholic or Protestant, was a point of tremendous importance to the future of her religion. Blunt and outspoken, she had no weapon against Catherine's brilliant attack but her own dogged courage. She did not attempt to conceal her hatred of the Queen-Mother, who on her side hated her with a venom otherwise reserved for Coligny. Catherine's aim in these discussions was to make Jeanne lose her temper first, and well she knew how to accumulate pin-pricks until her victim was almost worn out with distress. Everything was tried, threats, taunts, promises, cynical arguments. And all the time Jeanne saw around her the corruption of the Valois Court, the frivolous pleasures, the extravagant dress, the subterfuges which covered the young King's retirement to the bed of his mistress—everything that could shock a high Huguenot standard of morals was openly displayed before her. Catherine, for her part, was angry that Jeanne had refused to bring her son with her, for she felt that she could have twisted Henry round her finger as she had twisted his father Antoine. But she was confident that once the marriage had been put into effect Henry would prove a second Antoine and renounce his Protestant faith. And with this confidence she fought her slow way to victory. The marriage ceremony should be so arranged as not to offend the bridegroom's Huguenot principles. Each party would have liberty to con-science and action. The union of France and Navarre would be an equable one, ordered for the mutual benefit of the two States. Jeanne gave in; the contract was signed.

At once the triumphant Queen-Mother set about the arrangements for the marriage in Paris, the marriage that was to become known as *Les Noces Vermeilles*—the Scarlet Nuptials. For when once the ring was set on Margot's finger, Catherine could proceed with her work of destroying Coligny.

# PARIS

THERE was a shop close to the Louvre at which the Queen-Mother was a frequent customer when she was in Paris. The shopkeeper, an Italian, sold gloves, necklaces, perfumes and sundry trinkets much in demand at Court. But his speciality was poisoned gloves, which he contrived with unrivalled artistry.

As soon as the marriage between Valois and Bourbon had been agreed upon, Catherine persuaded Jeanne to leave Blois and proceed to Paris so as to ensure that the preparations for the ceremony were such as she should wish. It was towards the end of May when Jeanne reached the capital. On June 4th she was taken ill. Five days later she was dead.

*Ignoramus, ignorabimus.* The autopsy was declared to reveal an advanced stage of consumption, rendered fatal by a chill. Nor was the Queen of Navarre known to have bought or received a pair of perfumed gloves, a vanity which one imagines would not have had a great appeal to her Puritan tastes.

Yet the suspicion still lurks, and it is difficult to dislodge it entirely. Here was one of Catherine's two remaining foes conveniently and suddenly dead just after the signing of the contract on which the Queen-Mother had set her crafty heart. The Catholics rejoiced, the Protestants lamented, Coligny was ill with grief and Catherine went smoothly on her way. If Jeanne had not died, St. Bartholomew's Eve might conceivably have been avoided, but a death would assuredly have been found for Coligny.

In an age when poisoning is a recognised weapon for private and political purposes it is inevitable that the sudden death of any important personage should be attributed to

its use. The practice of medicine was slow in its development in comparison with the other arts which thrived during
the Renaissance. Internal surgery was practically never successful, and internal complaints were wrapped in mystery
and fantastic speculation. It is natural, therefore, that many
natural deaths should have been widely regarded as cases of
poisoning, and it is natural also that many cases of poisoning
should have escaped detection. Catherine certainly used
poisons on several occasions, but it is quite impossible to
give with any confidence a list of her victims. It seems certain also that she was largely responsible for the spread of
the practice in France—it was one of the Italian arts that she
fostered. In that masterpiece of lightly borne scholarship,
*The Lore of the Unicorn,* Mr. Odell Shepard says of
Catherine:

"Her family had been remarkable even in Italy for its
frequent resort to poison and for equally frequent deaths
from poisoning—one reason for the equality being, perhaps,
the fact that the family had a way of practising upon its own
members. The famous 'laboratory' in the palace of Cosimo
I, which none but he ever entered, has often been supposed
to have been devoted to the manufacture of poisons. Cosimo's
son, for whom Andrea Bacci wrote his book on the unicorn,
died in agony of unascertained cause, followed in fifteen
hours by his wife, and it was observed at the time that his
brother, Cardinal Ferdinand de' Medici, made what seemed
undignified haste to divest himself of his robes so as to succeed him."

The enormous value set at the time upon the alicorn, the
horn of the unicorn (narwhal to sceptics), as a sovereign
detector of poison, shows the dread in which the exalted
continually lived of this manner of death. We have seen that
Clement VII presented an alicorn to Francis I on the marriage of Catherine to Henry of Orleans, a gift which Mr.
Shepard suggests "might certainly have been taken as a grace-

ful intimation that Catherine was not expected to practise
her family's talents upon her husband's kin—or that, in case
she did so, they might be prepared." We have seen also
that the Constable de Montmorency added an alicorn to the
medicine cupboard of the royal nursery. As late as 1641
there was a unicorn's horn in the Tower of London valued at
forty thousand pounds, though Mr. Shepard points out that
the rich setting must have played a large part in this estimate,
since by then the alicorn's therapeutic stock had fallen con-
siderably. Perhaps the most celebrated alicorn in Christendom was that preserved at St. Denis and described by John
Evelyn as being seven feet in length. The Italian physician,
Jerome Cardan, who came to France in 1552 and has left
interesting notes on the practice of medicine at the French
Court, was taken "to see the private treasure vaults of the
King of France at the church of St. Denis, a place of no very
great fame, but rather the more noteworthy in my estimation
especially because of the perfect horn of a unicorn preserved
therein." This same Cardan, who wrote well over two hundred books on medicine, astronomy, mathematics, physics,
history, theology, moral philosophy and other subjects, and
claimed to have been extolled in seventy-three works by
his contemporaries, had been called in 1536 to the bedside
of a patrician boy of seven, afflicted with an unknown malady.
Cardan wrote a prescription of "pearls, bone of unicorn and
gems," and the unfortunate patient died after violent vomit-
ing. These isolated evidences of beliefs that were general in
the sixteenth century give some indication of the difficulties
that beset the modern historian anxious to prove or disprove
a charge of poisoning.

Coligny was at his country estate of Châtillon, being
nursed back to health by his second wife, when the news of
the death of Jeanne reached him. His ensuing depression was
only relieved by the peace of his surroundings, the devotion
of his wife and servants, and the quiet home-life which he

was enjoying for the last time. While the expedition to the Netherlands which he had urged was meeting with indifferent fortune (Catherine had countenanced this plan in order to keep him quiet on other subjects), the Admiral passed the summer evenings in the perusal of the Book of Job and the composition of those memoirs which after his death moved even his enemies to admiration by their noble simplicity.

The Court had moved to Paris for the coming wedding, the date of which could not yet be fixed. Coligny was recalled from his retreat. "Alas, my good master," cried one of his tenants as the Admiral mounted his horse, "why do you go to your destruction? If you reach Paris you will die there, you and all your company, and we shall never see you again."

Catherine had been hard at work during his absence, playing with all her skill on the King's sensibilities and minimising the favour which Coligny had won in other quarters. He found a Council of War in session, but it had already been decided that he should not lead an army to the Netherlands in person, as he had wished to do. The Guises and Alba's agents had made up lost ground, and the idea of an open breach with Spain had been dropped.

Still the warning letters poured in to Coligny. "Remember Amboise!" was the cry, or "The hands that were dipped in blood at Vassy are now ready for you!" He brushed them aside with scorn, and quickly recovered the trust and favour of Charles. Catherine and Anjou again found themselves excluded from the Privy Chamber for the sake of Coligny, and Anjou wrote that both he and his mother were convinced that "the Admiral had imprinted evil thoughts concerning us upon the King."

But Charles was nervous. His theatrical declarations on the glory of dying on an honourable battlefield revealed his constant dread of assassination. Desperately he engineered an official reconciliation between Guise and Coligny, but it was a sinister handshake that passed between the two in the royal presence.

Busy as ever, Coligny helped to promote the alliance with England that had long been sought by Catherine herself. But she did not relish the move, for Alba was already sufficiently annoyed by the prospect of the union of France and Navarre. The Admiral was wrecking her policies by his open dealings. She saw all her plans going awry, Elizabeth retreating, Alba threatening, the Pope hesitating to send his consent to the wedding. But the wedding must take place, and at last Catherine fixed it for August 18, sending at the same time secret instructions to the Governor of Lyons to allow no post through from Rome until after the event.

Paris was thronged with Huguenots arrived for the ceremony. But the followers of Guise, reaching the capital first, occupied all the most convenient lodgings and were able to stay together. The Huguenots were forced to find scattered quarters in different parts of the city. The air was alive with rumours. "The wedding favours," said one courtier, "are like to be blood-red."

At six o'clock on the evening of the 18th the wedding took place on a raised dais in the *parvis* of Notre Dame. A platform hung with cloth of gold ran from the cathedral to the Bishop's Palace. The bridegroom and his suite had put off their mourning array and were magnificently dressed. The bride wore a blue mantle with a train four yards long and a cape of ermine. Her diadem was valued at a hundred thousand crowns, and King Charles's dress, cap and dagger at nearly six hundred thousand crowns. Anjou wore thirty-two huge pearls in his hat, and a hundred and twenty ladies were garbed in such splendour that the occasion far outshone all the previous weddings of royal daughters.

The next three days and nights were given over to feasting and elaborate displays, jousting, dancing and the favourite Court charades, all undertaken on the most costly scale.

Catholic and Huguenot, with hatred in their hearts, feasted together, passed each other with laughter in the endless *pavanes,* and played their symbolic parts in fantastic allegories. The sacrifice was being richly dressed before the knife should be raised.

Soon after eleven o'clock on the following morning (Friday, August 22) a messenger came to Charles, who was enjoying a vigorous game in the Louvre tennis courts. "The Admiral has been shot through the arm by an assassin," said the messenger. "God's blood!" cried the King, hurling his racquet to the ground, "will they never let me in peace?" Only a few moments previously the Admiral had been watching the beginning of the game, and the outrage must have been committed close to the Louvre. The messenger hurried into the Palace to give the news to Catherine, who was just sitting down to table. Without a word she returned to her room.

In the meantime angry Huguenots had gathered in the Rue des Poulies where the incident had occurred. With drawn swords they shouted execrations upon the Guises, and a party of them even made their way to the Hôtel de Guise and demonstrated beneath the windows. For there was no possible doubt that the Guises were responsible. The Admiral had been walking slowly along the street on his way to his lodging, reading a petition which had been handed to him. He stopped for a moment with the intention of adjusting his shoes, which were causing him discomfort, and that chance action probably prolonged his life for two days. For the shot which rang out at that instant from an upper window missed its mark, breaking his right forefinger and passing through his left arm at the elbow. With great presence of mind the Admiral at once raised his mutilated right hand towards the barred window about which a wisp of smoke still hung. His bewildered attendants collected themselves and forced the door of the building. But the would-be assassin had got away, and there is still some doubt as to his identity, though there is general agreement that he was an agent selected for the purpose by Catherine, Anjou and the Guises, in a secret council held some days previously.

The King's physician, Ambrose Paré, was despatched with all haste to the injured Admiral's bedside. Amputation of the left arm, which was the first course suggested, was found to be unnecessary, but the treatment decided upon must have been painful in the extreme. The arm was several times lanced and the bullet extracted, while the injured right forefinger was removed with pincers at the third attempt. The patient endured this primitive surgery with exemplary courage, talking calmly to his visitors and declaring his faith in God and his loyalty to the Crown. At length Charles, who like Catherine had retired to his chamber, came to see his wounded friend. The Admiral's nerves must have been like iron, for he seized the opportunity to discuss afresh the expedition to the Netherlands, and to warn the King against Alba. By this time Catherine had sufficiently collected herself to approach the man whose murder she had planned. She was anxious to find out on whom suspicion rested, for it had been her hope that Alba would be implicated and so delivered into her hands. But there was no reference to the Toledan, and she had to be content with the less convenient charge against Guise. Some time was spent in discussing the personnel of the commission of inquiry which Charles was determined to set up. Then the King asked if the bullet had been found. It was brought to him, and Catherine drily remarked: "I am glad that the pellet is out of his flesh, for I very well remember that when Monsieur de Guise was murdered near Orleans the doctors told me that he might have been saved if the shots could have been extracted, even though they were poisoned." We may interpret as we please this reference to the deed that had started the feud. Meanwhile the King was gazing with a reluctant fascination at the bloodstained coat of the Admiral, and muttering strangely under his breath. Catherine looked quickly at him. She saw that his diseased mind was ready for her attentions, and she began to hasten their departure. Before they left, however, Coligny begged to speak with Charles alone, and Catherine had reluctantly to allow them a few moments in private.

But on their way back to the Louvre she bullied the nerve-racked young man, pestering him to tell her what the Admiral had said. At last he could stand it no longer. " 'Sdeath, then, since you *will* have it out of me," he cried, as they reached the Palace, "he told me that all power had collapsed in your hands, and that I should suffer for it in the end!" Then he ran swiftly up the broad staircase and locked himself in his room.

Catherine was joined in her own room by Anjou, who found her in a fury at Coligny's words. She was too angry, in fact, to discuss what was next to be done, and though Anjou tells us that it was resolved "to kill the Admiral by some means or other," the details were postponed until the following day.

At the same time another meeting had been postponed. The Huguenot leaders had assembled in a room below that in which Coligny was lying. Some had urged immediate reprisals, others had suggested that they should all leave Paris, taking the wounded Admiral with them, while others again had declared that the King was to be trusted and would permit no further outrage. At length they dispersed, to meet again on Saturday.

But though Anjou had found his mother unprepared to take counsel with him, that agile brain was not idle. Alone in her chamber Catherine took stock of her position. She had scotched the snake, not killed it. The plot had miscarried, Alba had not been accused, Charles had been filled with ideas of avenging his friend, and her own name was being shouted in the streets by angry Huguenots. If she did not act quickly the Huguenots would either rise and destroy her or else carry her prey safely out of the city. Mentally she made a list of those who must help her to forestall such measures. There were six of them. One was her son, Anjou, a Savoyard, one was a Frenchman (Tavannes of the *Memoirs*), four were Italians—Nemours (Guise's stepfather), Nevers, Birago and Gondi, Count de Retz. These she summoned to meet her next day in the gardens of the Tuileries.

Saturday came, and the Huguenot chiefs conferred again. This time it was determined, on the advice of Navarre and Condé, to remain in Paris, but to find adequate protection for the helpless Coligny. Navarre sent five of his Swiss to the house, and the King was also petitioned to provide a guard. With great readiness Charles ordered fifty Swiss arquebusiers to proceed to the house in the Rue de Béthisy, but Anjou was at hand to arrange that a certain Cosseins, an inveterate enemy of the Admiral, should be put in command of the company.

On the scorched turf of the Tuileries, between high yew hedges, Catherine paced up and down with her sinister confederates. They had had a spy at the Huguenot meeting, and assured her that there was a plot to attack the Louvre and kill herself, the King, the Guises and Anjou. Catherine was ready to believe them, and even without such an incentive she was determined that Coligny must die at once. For the moment she had lost her grip on Charles, but she knew how to regain it.

Dismissing the council of murder she sent de Retz to the King's chamber to prepare him by expatiating on the Huguenot plots against him. Such is the evidence of Margot of Navarre, though other accounts omit this preliminary move. That evening, at all events, Catherine herself approached her son. She was with him for over an hour. Beginning with quiet arguments she catalogued Huguenot offences against the Crown and urged him to rid himself of these troublesome folk before fresh dangers should arise. The death of Coligny would avenge previous murders and satisfy the national conscience. The Admiral had ruined French foreign policy, exasperated Spain, and placed Charles himself in danger of his life. Then, as her victim remained obstinate, she raised her voice to the tones he had been taught to fear from his cradle. Aiming at his most vulnerable spot she played upon his terror of assassination. His weak nerves already frayed, the wretched youth showed signs of breaking down. Choosing her moment, Catherine then summoned her previous advisers and several others. Glancing this way and that Charles must have felt like one of his own hunted stags, and he who could never look anyone in the eye now found himself fixed by a dozen pairs of eyes lit by one terrible purpose. But still he would not answer. Supported by her confederates Catherine tortured him with lurid warnings of the fearful death that was planned for him. He had the birds caged in Paris, she cried, and must destroy them now or never. The deaths of the Admiral and a few others would save himself and the country.

Charles writhed this way and that, the muscles of his face twitching spasmodically, but he did not speak. Then Catherine played her ace. If he would not consent to save himself she would resign all part in the government and leave him to his fate. At another moment the King might have received such an announcement with arrogant pleasure, but now he dreaded above all things to be left alone, at the mercy of friends and enemies who were so hard to distinguish. He interrupted his mother at last. "I cannot break faith!" he cried. "No hand must be raised against the Admiral!" It was the only thought left in his tortured brain, and it had to be removed. With clear-headed precision Catherine continued her merciless third degree. If he thought the Admiral his friend, she insisted, he was woefully mistaken. Coligny was a

traitor and merited a traitor's death. Charles had been duped.
Had he forgotten the assault of Meaux?

Charles had not forgotten. In his weaker moments the
memory of that attempt still rankled, and now his strength
was almost at an end. Catching sight of her triumph Catherine returned with renewed vigour to the assault. She was
working for one of those hysterical fits in which she could
have her will of him. But never before had she known the fit
to be so long in coming.

Desperately Charles turned from his mother's blazing eyes
and asked the advice of the rest of the company. They were
perfectly unanimous. If he would save his own life and those
of his family he must despatch the Huguenots, and at once.
Their answer was a foregone conclusion and the King's
appeal in itself showed that Catherine had won. Suddenly
Charles crumpled up and the fit took him. His eyes blood-
shot, his mouth flecked with foam, he screamed at his tor-
mentors, and his scream was the word they had been awaiting,
the word that was to run through Paris on the morrow. *Kill!*

"Kill the Admiral then if you will! I consent! But kill
every Huguenot in France as well, that none may be left to
reproach me with the deed!"

Then he faced Catherine. "It is your will," he cried. "Kill
them all, kill them all!" And with frenzied imprecations he
rushed from the room, leaving his mother and her councillors
to debate coolly on the methods to be employed.

The debate was a long one, but it was finally decided that
the royal consent to a general massacre should be acted
upon, though Navarre and Condé were to be spared. Catherine had no mind to exterminate the Bourbons and leave
the Guises without rivals. To each of the principal Catholics
a prominent victim was assigned. At dawn on the next day,
the day of St. Bartholomew, the great bell of the Palais de
Justice was to give the signal.

His mind completely turned, Charles was now as eager

as any of the conspirators to put the bloody business into execution. With the lucid attention to detail of the demented, he helped with the arrangements that were going rapidly forward. The Provost of Merchants had audience with him and received his instructions. In every window there was to be a light, at every door an armed man with a torch in his hand and a white handkerchief tied round his left arm.

The hour came for the King's *Coucher,* the formal assembly at his retirement for the night. Huguenots and Catholics stood together in his chamber for the last time. On a sudden impulse of pity he had invited thirty or forty Huguenot gentlemen to pass the night in the Louvre, and when his great friend La Rochefoucauld—also a Huguenot—came to bid him good night the King grasped him by the sleeve. "Do not go, my Foucauld," he begged, "stay here and sleep with my *valets de chambre.*" But La Rochefoucauld laughed the invitation aside and took his leave. The curtains of the King's bed were drawn. All was quiet.

But in Catherine's chamber the murderers still discussed the morrow's work. Princess Margot, the four days' bride, had said good night to her mother, scarcely understanding what all the whispering was about. And at last the whisperers dispersed and Catherine was left alone to await the dawn of St. Bartholomew. Once she had waited twenty years for vengeance upon a rival, but now she could not wait a few hours. Charles's fit might pass, and remorse follow before dawn. Between two and three in the morning she left her room and went to that of the King. On her way through the Louvre she heard a disturbance below. Some of the Huguenots, suspicious of the flitting lights and noise of stealthy feet, had become involved in a controversy with the guards. Waking her son from his uneasy sleep, Catherine told him that the Huguenots were striking the first blow and that the signal for attack must be advanced. Orders were given for the bell of St. Germain l'Auxerrois, close to

CHARLES IX
Bronze by Germain Pilon
(Wallace Collection)

the Palace, to be tolled, and as the first peal floated over the dark city and echoed from its spires and towers, the Duke of Guise set out.

Among the company of Guise were the Duc d'Aumale and the illegitimate son of Henry II, that Bastard of Angoulême whom we were prepared to meet again on this day. In a few moments they were at the house of Coligny. Cosseins, the treacherous captain of the Swiss Guard, was ready for them. He knocked at the gate and one of the Admiral's servants opened to him. "A message from his Majesty!" said Cosseins briefly, and before the man could reply he had seized him by the neck and poniarded him. The murderers poured in over the body of the servant, killing several more before the remainder could bar the inner door against them. The noise aroused Coligny from sleep. He realised at once that his hour had come, but he showed no sign of fear. He was too weak to rise, but he bade his servants lift him to the floor and put a loose robe upon him. Then his pastor Merlin prayed with him, till the cry came: "They are bursting the door! Monseigneur, it is God who calls us now!" "As for me," replied the Admiral calmly, "I have prepared myself unto death aforehand." Then he bade them all save themselves while yet there was a chance, and at last, with tears in their eyes, they consented to do so. Only Nicolas Muss, Coligny's aged German interpreter, refused absolutely to leave his master. The rest climbed through the window and thence to the roof, and though they were sighted and some shot down, there were others who lived to give their account of the Admiral's last moments. Ambrose Paré, the physician, had been summoned to the Louvre a few hours previously, for the King would not have him killed.

The Swiss under Cosseins had now been induced to kill their compatriots, the servants of Navarre, and swarmed over the wreckage of the door into Coligny's chamber. Muss they slaughtered at the threshold. In the first faint streaks of light they saw the Admiral, white-haired though he was only fifty-three, kneeling with a serene countenance beside his bed. They hesitated to kill even a heretic while he was praying, but at length a certain Janovitch, a Bohemian (hence usually called Bême) asked: "Are you the Admiral?" "Yes, young man," was the calm reply, "I am the Admiral. Do what you will, but do not think that such as you can shorten my life." Bême immediately ran him through the body with his sword, and then the whole pack leaped upon him. Swords, daggers, pikes, battle-axes and pistols effected what the bullet of two days before had failed to achieve. From the courtyard below Guise called up to his desperadoes to know if the work were finished. "It is done!" shouted Bême. "Then throw him down that we may see for ourselves!" demanded Guise. As the body, pierced with nearly a dozen wounds, was lifted through the window the hands made one convulsive clutch at the sill and then stiffened. It fell at the feet of Guise, and the Bastard of Angoulême, stooping down, wiped the blood from the almost unrecognisable features. "It is he!" he said, and dealt the corpse a kick.

At that moment a breathless messenger arrived from the Louvre to tell Guise that the Admiral had better be spared for the present. Staring into the darkness from a window of the Palace, Catherine had fancied that the Huguenots were really opening the attack, and had had a sudden access of panic. "Tell the Queen-Mother that it is too late," said Guise.

Throughout that terrible day the body of the Admiral lay in the court-yard. Passers-by spat upon it, kicked it, or hacked pieces from it in their rage. It was dragged to the Seine, thrown in, pulled out again, until finally such as remained was hanged by the heels to the gibbet of Mont-faucon. It is said that the head was sent to Rome as a present to the Pope.

As the day brightened the envoys of the Pope collected joyful news to send to him. "Nothing is to be seen in the streets but white crosses in hats and caps, and it is a beautiful sight," wrote one, and "everywhere," reported another, "we have seen rivers of blood and mountains of corpses." From the murder of Coligny the Bastard of Angoulême rode off with Guise and his friends, rousing their followers to the work. "Kill, kill!" they shouted through the streets, "it is the King's command!" They had eight hundred horse, with artillery and infantry in support, not to mention the hundreds of private assassins who answered the summons. In the three days of slaughter several thousand Huguenots, men, women and children, perished—the exact figure can never be known. Besieged in their houses, struck down in the streets, shot dead as they tried to escape over the roofs, pursued in boats when they leaped into the river to save themselves, stabbed in their beds with their wives, or at table, or in the sanctuary of the churches, they were given no time either to draw a weapon or to prepare themselves for death. A few got clear of the city on horseback, a few found refuge in the British Embassy, and a few contrived to escape by wearing the white favours of the Catholics. But the majority had not the smallest chance of survival. Not for the first, nor for the last time, Paris had tasted blood and gone mad with it, and the opportunities taken to settle private scores form not the least appalling aspect of the massacre. The famous Greek scholar Ramus, a Huguenot, but an entirely inoffensive one, was butchered in a peculiarly revolting manner at the instigation of a rival who was jealous of his University professorship.

But we must return to the Louvre, where we left Catherine standing at her window, anxiously waiting for the dawn to show her which way matters were going. There is no doubt that at this moment she was convinced that the imminent threat of assassination hung over herself and the royal family. That does not excuse her, but it helps to explain her.

Two other women, the one a young bride and the other expecting to become a mother, had been early astir in the Louvre on St. Bartholomew's Day. Margot of Navarre, fearful of what the morning would bring, had lain awake the whole night, her Huguenot husband beside her. As soon as it was light Henry rose, saying that he would go and play tennis until he could speak with the King, whom he was resolved to ask for justice and a new guarantee of safety. Tired out by her long watch, and thinking that the mysterious danger was now past, Margot fell at last into a profound sleep. She was awakened an hour later by a loud knocking at the door of her room, and the cry of "Navarre! Navarre!" Her nurse opened the door, and a gasping fugitive, bleeding from severe wounds in the arm, rushed past her and flung himself upon Margot's bed. He was closely followed by four archers of the guard, who paid no respect for the privacy of the Princess but advanced towards the bed with drawn swords to despatch their wounded victim. The screams of Margot and her nurse brought the Captain of the Guard on the scene, and just in time the archers were ordered out of the room. Laughing heartily, the Captain then granted Margot's request for the life of the hunted man who still clung to her in terror. He was one of Navarre's gentlemen, de Léran by name, and the Princess bathed and bandaged his wounds and left him in charge of her nurse. Then, changing her bloodstained nightgown and throwing on a cloak, she hurried to the room of her sister Claude. On her way thither another Huguenot gentleman fell so close to her that she feared lest the halberd-thrust that killed him should pierce her own body at the same time, and no sooner had she entered her sister's chamber than two more ran to her to beg her protection.

In her own room the Queen, pregnant by the raving Charles, was praying in Spanish, with tears running down her cheeks. They had told her what was afoot, and that her husband had ordered the slaughter. Completely unregarded in this tragic moment she could do nothing but pray for forgiveness for the man who had allowed himself to be led into such a crime.

Meanwhile, in the King's apartment, Navarre and Condé were being put to the test. Charles had summoned them, as he said, to save their lives, but he would not spare their followers. When they arrived in his presence with their gentlemen attending them, the King took them aside and ordered his guard to "turn out all these scoundrels!" Instantly the whole of their suite was conducted downstairs and massacred. Then he gave the two Princes their choice —"the Mass or death!" Navarre, recognisably the son of Antoine, temporised, talking round the subject. Condé heroically stood his ground and refused to recant, though the furious King drew his dagger and held it at his throat. It was the unloved Queen who saved his life. Arriving at a fortunate moment she threw herself at the feet of her husband, weeping bitterly, and implored him to call a halt to the horror within and without the Palace. Charles's madness was passing, leaving him weak again. He listened to her, and spared Condé. At about noon he even tried to stop the massacre, but the blood-lust was easier to release than to control. His frenzy increased by a growing realisation of what he had done, he took an arquebus and went to the window, whence he himself shot down the fugitives in the street below and on the river. Throughout the three days of carnage he insisted upon his own responsibility, acknowledging that he had ordered the massacre. But now and then a whim took him to save certain individuals. A number of Huguenot gentlemen had the wit to proclaim themselves atheists, and were pardoned for having no religion instead of being slain for having the wrong one. But those who had been invited to spend the night in the Louvre were killed almost to a man, and La Rochefoucauld, who had refused the invitation, was one of the first to die after Coligny. The murderers entered his house, masked. One of them was the brother of Chicot the jester, and La Rochefoucauld, who was still in bed and had no suspicion of their real errand, recognised him. He at once concluded that this was one of the nocturnal flagellation parties so popular with the crazy Charles. But even as he turned to the intruders with a jest they stabbed him through and through.

Catherine's first misgivings soon passed with the broadening of the day and the cheerful sounds of Catholic vengeance. The evidence of triumph was before her eyes. Huguenots lay dead in the courtyard of the Louvre and on the staircases. Their bodies were brought in and laid before her where she sat with the ladies of her Flying Squadron. With jests and pleasantry the victims were identified one by one. Did we not know Catherine and her Court and the complete cynicism of the air they breathed, the accounts of this grim scene, even where they are collaborated beyond doubt, would be impossible to believe.

Before the bloodshed was over there were public processions of thanksgiving. Paris had not only been saved but had enjoyed a riotous holiday in the accomplishment of the salvation and had earned the blessing of the Pope for the affair. The Cardinal who was sent from Rome with official congratulations paused in Lyons to receive the homage of all true Catholics, who were at the moment engaged in their own private St. Bartholomew—for the Paris massacre was the signal for similar outbreaks in different parts of the country.

Paris was saved, and so was Catherine. It was her supreme moment. "Never before," she wrote, "was I in so fearful a predicament, and never did I issue therefrom with greater comfort and rejoicing." "Go back to your master," she said proudly to the Spanish envoy, "tell him what you have seen, tell him what you have heard." The Savoyard envoy considered that the Queen-Mother looked ten years younger, as if she had emerged from a severe illness or from great peril.

But while the Cardinal of Lorraine (who was in Rome at the time) wrote to Charles that "this is the best news I ever heard," and while Philip of Spain and Alba hastened to add their applause, Elizabeth of England was so shocked that at first she refused to see the French Ambassador, and there were lively fears of reprisals upon Catholics in London and the provinces. Walsingham, the English Ambassador in Paris, is still remembered for the unqualified attitude that he adopted. Freshly exulting, Catherine showed him some papers that had been taken from Coligny's house when he was killed. Among them were the Admiral's manuscript notes on the projected war in the Netherlands, and with these she hoped to rouse the Ambassador to anger against Coligny and approval of the massacre. "See!" she said, "this is the work of your noble friend! You can read for yourself how he loved England!" "Madam," replied Walsingham quietly, "he loved France!" And later, when Charles tried to excuse himself for the massacre, the Ambassador was equally ready with a reply. "If the Huguenots were guilty," he said, "they ought to have been punished by justice and not by murder."

And that, it must still seem, is an adequate reply to any excuse that can be made, either for Catherine or for Charles, or for any other who had a hand in what de Bèze called "a cruelty so barbarous and inhuman that as long as the world shall be the world, and after the world shall have perished, the authors of the enterprise shall be held in perpetual execration."

But there are always two sides to a question, and it might be fair at this juncture to quote from the address of thanksgiving pronounced by the Pope in the Church of St. Mark in Rome.

"In times so turbulent as these it seems that God is now beginning in His mercy to turn His eyes upon us."

# LUSIGNAN

THE castle of Lusignan in Poitou was "so admirable and so old that one might deem it the fairest example of ancient fortification and the noblest ornament of antiquity in all France." Thus Brantôme, who liked to flatter castles no less than women. But towards the end of 1574 this handsome pile was rased to the ground by Montpensier, who was engaged in reducing the remaining Huguenot strongholds in the interests of the new King, Henry III. It was the period of an armed truce between the Fifth and Sixth Wars of Religion. The Massacre of St. Bartholomew, though it destroyed nearly all the Huguenot leaders, could not destroy the Huguenot impulse, and the disorder of the State had thrown a number of Catholics into the opposite camp.

Active as ever, though she was nearly fifty-six, Catherine followed the army of Montpensier in Poitou. Events had moved quickly since the Massacre, and her difficulties had grown no less with the removal of her successive rivals. In these last two years the younger generation had given her a great deal of trouble. In the Catholic army that laid siege to La Rochelle in 1572 Navarre and Condé had fought against the Huguenots. Now more than ever opportunism was the substitute of conviction, and men changed sides with bewildering rapidity. Only within the stout walls of La Rochelle was faith still an inspiring force, and the appearance on the battlements of a company of Huguenot ladies in shining robes, singing psalms, as well as their defiant planting of a hawthorn tree on the highest tower, were impressive gestures in these times of burnt-out emotion. And the brave defenders might say that the psalms and the hawthorn did not fail of their effect, for the departure of Anjou to be King of Poland had put an end to the siege and the Fifth War.

The election of Henry of Anjou to the Polish throne came as a great relief to his jealous brothers, but Catherine, accompanying him as far as the border of the Palatinate on his way to his new kingdom, told him as she took her leave that she looked to see him again before long. Charles, afflicted in one lung and exhausted in mind, could not last long. But these words of Catherine to her favourite son were dangerous ones.

Henry's journey to Cracow, through the Netherlands and the domains of the German Protestant Princes, must have been a trying one. It was almost exactly a year after the Massacre, and his host for some time was the Elector Palatine, a man with a grim sense of humour. The weak and impressionable young Valois found his apartments decorated with lively paintings of the slaughter in Paris and the provinces. A portrait of Coligny confronted him when he sat down to eat, and on the table broadsheets concerning Huguenot sufferings had been left with studied carelessness. Henry's dreams were haunted by the same terrible visions that now troubled Charles, and when he got to Poland he felt compelled to unburden his guilty conscience with the remarkable account of Saint Bartholomew's Day which has been of such service to historians.

Charles, sinking visibly, had no male heirs. At any moment Catherine looked for the opportunity of recalling Henry to the throne which she had for so long been preparing for him. But the adventurous Alençon was a difficulty. It suited his plans now to show Huguenot sympathies, so that the leaderless party might rally round him and perhaps carve out a throne for him when Charles should die. Navarre also was giving signs of returning to his former allegiance, and Catherine had to watch the two Princes carefully. One bold attempt at escape from her vigilance was betrayed to her by

Margot. She had two accomplices tortured and executed, and tightened her grip on Alençon and Navarre. One of those accomplices had been the lover of Margot, the other of the Duchesse de Nevers, and though Catherine had nipped a revolution in the bud she had added to her enemies.

And then, on May 30, 1574, a month before his twenty-fourth birthday, the haunted and unhappy King died. His last words were these: "Thank God that I leave no male child to wear the crown after me." His feelings can be understood, for no heir would have been allowed by Catherine to contest the claim of Henry.

The journey of Anjou from Poland to France was one of the most theatrical exploits in this false and glittering age. Romantic by nature, he made the most of it. No one in Poland could have prevented his departure, but he chose to "escape" at dead of night, taking the Crown jewels with him. After a series of fantastic adventures the last and most decadent of the Valois reached Italy, where he spent some time enjoying the favours of a variety of women and the extravagant fêtes of which he was deemed worthy. At length he reached Lyons, where he amused himself by joining a party of religious flagellants and flogging himself and his companions till the blood flowed. By good fortune he had the Cardinal of Lorraine with him, and the chill which that unholy churchman caught on this occasion resulted in his death, whereof nobody was more glad than his old accomplice Catherine. Thence by slow stages, pursued by the open execrations of his people, Henry reached Rheims and was crowned as Henry III. One more of Catherine's long-cherished purposes had been put into effect.

The ruins of Lusignan castle presented a grievous spectacle. Montpensier and his army had passed on to spend the night in Poitiers, but Catherine lingered long at the scene of desolation, and was heard to say that her general had exceeded his instructions in laying the huge fortress level with the ground. To her perpetually practical mind it appeared a foolish gesture, a waste of fortifications which might one day have served the besiegers' purpose. Always, it seemed, unnecessary violence was being used in the accomplishment of purposes which she fostered. France was being decimated by these incessant wars. Famine was taking as swift a toll as the sword, and while Catherine had been absent in the east, accompanying Henry on the first stage of his journey to Cracow, three thousand starving Parisians had marched upon Fontainebleau. Precautions had to be taken to prevent serious riots. The Queen-Mother could not be everywhere at once.

There was something that fascinated her about Lusignan, something more than the sight of power laid low, and she stayed so long at the spot that she did not reach Poitiers till after nightfall. The legend of Mélusine, the reputed builder of the castle, was not only the most famous fairy-story in France. Centuries later it was to be described by a learned German anthropologist as the "childhood's dream of world-history," and modern scholars have traced it to Lithuania and Tibet, to Greenland and Hawaii. It was recounted by Jean d'Arras in one of the great prose-romances of the fourteenth century, and Catherine, with her abiding interest in the occult, must often have thought about Mélusine.

Mélusine was originally a Celtic deity, protectress of a well in Poitou. Her association with Lusignan is really due to the ambitions of the great Lusignan family, crusaders and kings of Cyprus and Jerusalem, who made her the foundress of their house. Her own story and that of the Lusignans (which ended only in 1933 with the death in Milan of Guido de Lusignano) cannot be told here. It is sufficient to notice that she had a mermaid's tail every Saturday night and could build or destroy castles in a day. Rabelais, that liberal enthusiast for things Poitevin, tells us to "visit Lusignan. Parthenay, Vovent, Mervent and Pouzauges in Poitou. There you will find a Cloud of Witnesses, not of your Affidavit-Men of the right stamp, but credible, time out of mind, that will take their Corporal Oath, on Rigome's Knuckle-bone, that Mélusine their first Founder, or Foundress, which you please, was Woman from the Head to the Prick-purse, and thence downwards was a Serpentine Chitterling, or, if you'll have it otherwise, a Chitterlingdiz'd Serpent."

According to Brantôme's sketch of the life of Montpensier, Catherine was eager to know more about this woman with the serpent's tail. She therefore questioned "the good old women who wash their clothes in the fountain."

"Some told her that they sometimes saw her coming to the fountain to bathe, in the form of a very beautiful woman and in widow's weeds; others said that they saw her—though very seldom, and on Saturdays only at vespers (for in that condition she would scarce permit herself to be seen)—bathing herself, the one half of her body like that of a fair lady and the other half like a serpent; some said that they saw her completely clothed, walking abroad with great dignity; others, that she appeared on the summit of the largest tower of her castle, in the shape of a beautiful woman and of a serpent; some said that when a grave disaster in the kingdom was about to occur, or a change of reign, or death or mishap to her kin—the most exalted in France and some of them kings—she would be heard three days before the event repeating thrice a bitter and terrible cry: this is held to be very truth . . . and during the siege, but above all when the order was given to lay the castle in ruins, many soldiers and gentlemen-at-arms who were there affirm that she gave forth her loudest cries and lamentations; this is quite true, on the word of honest men."

A grave disaster in the kingdom, a change of reign . . . Catherine had seen four changes in reign and faced innumerable situations of gravity. The disasters that had occurred, she genuinely believed, were fewer and less terrible than those that she had contrived to avoid. But Mélusine had uttered her warning cry when the soldiers of Montpensier were advancing. Catherine could not choose but listen to the washerwomen, and, having listened, keep their sayings in her heart. The powers which she placated with the aid of Ruggieri had often foretold important events to her. She had had a premonition of her husband's death, and of that of the elder Condé. Just before the news reached her of the death of the Cardinal of Lorraine she had been at dinner. Her glass was in her hand, she was about to drink, when suddenly the company was astonished to hear her exclaim: "Jesus, there is the Cardinal! I see him before me!" Then she added in a jocular tone: "I am much deceived if I did not see the good man soaring up to Paradise." It was not entirely a convenient gift, this one of second sight, and there was more than one occasion when Catherine's foreknowledge of a prominent fatality was the natural cause of suspicion.

Of the Cardinal's death, however, she was innocent enough. But that did not prevent her from having strange dreams about him, dreams which caused her to scream wildly in the night, rousing her startled ladies. Of all those who shared the guilt of St. Bartholomew's Eve Catherine suffered the least from qualms of conscience. Yet the death after a perverted prank of him whom she herself called "the wickedest of men," haunted her for many a night. Nerves that had stood the most searching of tests could be upset by a trifling circumstance. It is one of those things that constantly remind us that Catherine was human.

With her mind full of trouble she gazed at the charred beams and scattered blocks of stone that yesterday had been the castle of Lusignan. So easily might the careful labour of years be destroyed, and boundless ambition ground into the dust. The fortunes of some of the greatest names in France had been tossed about in these never-ending feuds, while with ruthless single-mindedness she had kept her own position and kept the house of Valois on the throne. But the fight was not over yet, and she was growing old. Little more than two years after St. Bartholomew she feared the Huguenots more than she had ever done. "Like cats," she had said to a deputation from Aigues-Mortes, "you Huguenots fall many times but always find your feet again. . . . Yet for the Huguenots I will do my best, as I have always done, provided they will trust me and be reasonable." But there was now a general opinion that one could not trust the Queen-Mother and be reasonable at the same time. The Huguenot power was thriving on adversity. The anvil of which de Bèze had spoken was growing the harder with each blow of the hammer. No French sovereign had been insulted and abused as Henry had been on his way to his coronation.

Catherine herself could laugh at insults, and as she thought of Mélusine she must have remembered how often she herself had been compared to a serpent—a subtle, specious serpent like that in the centre of a Palissy dish. They had called her other names, too, and a satire passed from mouth to mouth and at length openly printed in Paris had suggested that the only difference between the Queen-Mother and Jezebel was that no dog would sink so low as to eat the Queen-Mother's flesh. She knew perfectly well that all the evils of the kingdom were laid at her door, and that the books and pamphlets directed against her were as popular with Catholics as with Huguenots. With a fine scorn she sent for a copy of a scurrilous book called the *Life of St. Catherine,* which purported to be a biography of herself. "She has it read aloud to her," says a contemporary, "and laughs till she can scarcely contain herself. She says that if they had only given her notice beforehand she would have told them of many things of which they knew nothing, and of some that they have forgotten, which would greatly have increased the size of their book."

But there were more direct gestures than books printed in the cellars of Lyons. In February, 1573, six months after St. Bartholomew, the Fugger correspondent in Paris wrote the following account of what was by no means an isolated occurrence:

"On the 5th day of February, being the first Sunday in Lent, the Queen-Mother of France drove with her daughter, the Queen of Navarre, and other Princes and Attendants of the Court, about vesper time to the College of Jesuits to hear the reading of vespers. She was escorted by M. de Lorraine, M. de Bourbon and three Cardinals driving on horseback. The students of Paris, who are wont to indulge in scuffles with the servants of the Court, had collected in bands outside the College, where they began quarrelling and brawling with the muleteers. When the courtiers and the Princes came out of the College and were about to bestride their horses and enter their coaches, the students attacked them with rapiers and cudgels, surrounded the carriages with great turbulence, thrust their hands into the bosom of the Queen of Navarre, and mockingly stroked her plumes. The Cardinal de Lorraine they pushed into the deepest hole in the deepest mud. The aged Queen they not only assaulted with unsheathed foils, but also insulted in obscene, foul and lewd terms, which it would be shameful to repeat. The reason thereof has not been imparted to me, neither what devilry drove them into such disorderly conduct."

Unsheathed rapiers at her throat, the Tiger of France pushed into the mud. Such incidents as these must have taxed even Catherine's robust sense of humour, and the story vividly illuminates the atmosphere in which she brought her schemes one by one to fruition. To expect her to be sensitive to public opinion would plainly be absurd, and if she could endure such attacks as this she could likewise meet the soberest and most reasonable appeal without yielding an inch.

Politically it is not in the least important that Catherine

paused at Lusignan to view the ruins and hear the story of Mélusine. Nevertheless it is a piquant moment. Here legend confronts legend and monster considers monster. Portraits have been drawn of Catherine that are no less fantastic than the fifteenth-century woodcuts of the snake-tailed enchantress of Poitou. For the woman fair above and foul below is one of the oldest ideas in the world. It springs to the mind of the hermit assailed by temptation and the profligate smitten with disillusion. There is Milton's portress of Hell-gate, and Lear's bitter cry:

> Down from the waist they are centaurs,
> Though women all above:
> But to the girdle do the gods inherit,
> Beneath is all the fiends'.

About Catherine's romantic metamorphosis there is little or no sexual symbolism; and yet much of the mythology of horror that has gathered round her is due to the fact that she was a woman. Given sufficient love-affairs posterity will excuse a woman almost any crime; without them it is merciless. Catherine never asked mercy of her own world and she would not ask it of posterity, but at least she earned the right to be judged unsentimentally. Denied all the normal channels of feminine self-expression she was given a man's work to do, and she did it like a true disciple of Macchiavelli. Her crimes were not more heinous because she was a woman, though we may legitimately be astonished that a woman could place herself in such a position that those crimes inevitably followed. She both summed up and exaggerated the tendencies of her age, and only by coming to understand that age can we ever understand Catherine.

# CHENONCEAUX

THE King at Plessis-les-Tours gave a banquet for Monsieur le Duc, his brother, and for the lords and captains who had accompanied him at the siege and capture of La Charité, whereat the ladies, dressed in green and in men's clothes, served at table, and all the guests were likewise dressed in green; for this occasion a levy of sixty thousand francs' worth of green silk was made in Paris and elsewhere. The Queen-Mother followed with a banquet of her own at Chenonceaux, which is calculated to have cost more than a hundred thousand pounds, obtained by way of loan from the most well-to-do servants of the King, and even from certain Italians who well knew how to reimburse themselves at a double rate. At this fine banquet the loveliest and most honoured ladies of the Court, half-naked and with their hair unbound like brides, were employed in the service. Madame de Sauve was mistress of the ceremonies, and all was carried out in a magnificent manner."—*From a private letter dated May 15, 1577.*

Chenonceaux, the fairy-palace hung across the Cher, must needs outdo Plessis, with its memories of the thrifty Louis XI. And Catherine must needs outdo Henry in display. The luxurious, effeminate King, to whom "the position of a private person with £10,000 a year was the real idea of happiness," had exclaimed three years before when he was being fabulously entertained in Venice: "If only my Queen-Mother were here she would take her share in these honours which I owe solely to her." And Catherine felt herself under the frequent necessity of reminding her favourite son that his power was hers. If Henry had extorted sixty thousand francs from his people for a feast, she must hasten to borrow a hundred thousand pounds for a greater one. If Plessis had seen a banquet, Chenonceaux must see an orgy.

The guest of honour at both celebrations was Alençon, who now, as the King's younger brother, was commonly given the title of *Monsieur*.[1] Catherine had always neglected him for the sake of Henry, and he in his turn hated his mother and was jealous of his brother. In company, however, all was amity, and never more so than now. For the capture of La Charité was Alençon's first victory for the Court party, to which he had lately returned. In these latter years Catherine spent much of her time in bringing her wayward offspring to heel. Two of them, Alençon and Margot, had recently formed an alliance which astonished and angered their mother. But it was a very natural one. Both the young people were adventurous by disposition, and both were sceptics. They had seen very little of each other during their childhood, and were only thrown together at a time when each had much to gain by intrigue. Margot, the most brilliant member of her family, entered the political arena with the same sparkling gaiety with which she abandoned herself to a succession of lovers. Alençon had more vindictiveness in his make-up, and none of the natural health which made his sister remarkable among Catherine's children. But he too had a characteristic love of the game, and for a time the pair ran well enough together to give the Queen-Mother a deal of trouble.

The natural camp for rebels from the Court was that of the Huguenots. Jeanne and Coligny were dead, and creed now counted for nothing in society. Yet still the Huguenot hankering for princely leaders gave restive members of the

---

[1] In 1576 Alençon also took the title of Anjou, but for the purpose of clarity the name of Alençon is retained throughout this book. Similarly Catherine's daughter Marguerite de Navarre is constantly referred to by her nickname of Margot, to avoid confusion with the two other celebrated bearers of the name.

Court their chance, and Margot and Alençon easily formed themselves, with Henry of Navarre, into an opposition triumvirate. Henry, the bold and carefree young Gascon, occupied himself as pleasantly with his mistresses as his wife did with her lovers, but though a separation was inevitable the pair remained on the whole good friends, both recognising their complete incompatibility as husband and wife.

Catherine watched them closely. Navarre she feared more than Alençon, for the dread of a Bourbon *coup d'état* had always been a decisive factor in her policies. Once before she had surprised a plan of escape, the inevitable preliminary to revolution, and two men had died for it. She did not intend any further plans to succeed.

But they did succeed. Alençon was the first to get away. On one of his customary visits to the house of his mistress at Monceaux he left his coach and guards at the door, walked straight through to find a horse waiting for him at the back of the house, and galloped off to Dreux, a town which belonged to him by royal grant. The king heard the news at the dinner-table and gave himself up to fury. He cross-questioned Margot but could get nothing out of her.

From Dreux Alençon busily wrote letters explaining his action. Attempts, he said, had been made to poison him, and he had no choice but to become a rebel. Catherine tried subtle means to get him back, and vented her anger on Margot, who remained virtually a prisoner in the midst of the Court, a hostage for her brother. The marriage with Elizabeth of England was again hung out as a bait for Alençon, and his mother succeeded in obtaining interviews with him at Blois and Chambord. She took Margot with her for conciliatory purposes, but though a truce was engineered the position remained critical. Alençon was gathering his forces about him and Condé was hurrying to join him.

And then Navarre made his escape. He was more cunning than Alençon, who had narrowly avoided being thrown into the Bastille when a suspicion of his intention got about. Navarre deliberately spread a rumour that he was about to depart to his southern kingdom, and even succeeded in convincing Catherine and the King, whose company he had avoided, that he had already left Paris. Then he suddenly burst in upon them during a service in the Sainte-Chapelle, laughing in the hearty manner for which he was famous. Artfully he lulled their suspicions by this feint, and then carried out his real exploit, with only a handful of attendants, after hunting with Guise at Senlis. It is said that as soon as he had crossed the Loire on his way to Navarre he broke the silence that he had so far preserved on the flight with these words: "God be praised, for that He hath delivered me. *They* were the death of my mother in Paris; *they* murdered the Admiral and all my noblest servants; and *they* would not have done much better by me if God had not preserved me." It was a decisive moment for Henry and for France.

Catherine fell back upon a well-tried expedient. She went to parley with Alençon and Condé and took her Flying Squad with her. With the assistance of these skilful charmers she arrived at an agreement, but it was the most advantageous peace that the Huguenots had yet known. The *Paix de Monsieur,* as it was called, was signed in May, 1576. It is one of the ironies of this faithless period that Alençon, who joined the Huguenots from motives of pure expediency and deserted them again within a few months, gained for them a more favourable recognition than any of his great and devoted predecessors had succeeded in obtaining. As soon as the Peace had been signed the adventurer returned to Court to prosecute his plans for supporting the Catholics in the Netherlands, and the capable Margot, pretending that she must take the waters of Spa on account of erysipelas, went off to Belgium as his spy.

Alençon was not handsome, though romance had gathered

round his name. He was small and ill-formed, and his face
was marked by the ravages of smallpox. But his high forehead, crowned with jet-black hair, gave a certain dignity to
his features, and he could appear princely when he chose.
He appeared princely now at Chenonceaux, playing the victorious soldier with that air so easily assumed by the children
of Valois and Medici. For the moment he was the hero.
Navarre had allowed La Cherité to fall into his hands without
attempting to relieve it, and had thereafter submitted to the
King, though with no intention of returning to Court. This
happy issue for the royal party had been achieved by intrigue
far more than by arms, and Catherine had reason to give
herself up to festivity for a while.

But no two persons in this extravagant assembly trusted
one another. Alençon had exchanged fair words with the
King on his return, but Henry knew of his ambitions in the
Netherlands and had secretly put several awkward spokes in
his wheel. Whether the designs of Alençon would aid or
hinder French policy mattered nothing. Indeed the greater
the success of the younger Prince, and the greater his chance
services to his country, the greater would be the jealous
King's determination to undo him.

He made a fantastic figure at the banquet, this last Valois
King, with his long feminine hands, his curled hair, his ear-
rings, his lustrous dark eyes set in a pale and narrow face.
For the courtiers who fawned upon him the scornful name of
*Mignons* had but lately been coined. As councillors these
ganymedes were about as much use as the lapdogs which
their master collected so assiduously, travelling far in search
of new pets and lavishing tearful embraces on dogs and
courtiers alike. If the dress of King and Court had been extravagant in the last reign it now, under this emasculated
influence, reached the very peak of luxurious absurdity.
"Who can containe the mutable French in one and the

same fashion?" asked the English traveller Moryson, and at Plessis the novelty had been for all the guests to be dressed in green silk, while the ladies who served them were garbed as men. Since the King himself had been known to appear in the streets of Paris wearing a woman's bodice, very low in the neck, with several strings of pearls about his throat, this transvestitism was not very startling. And here at Chenonceaux, by way of a change, the ladies adhered unequivocally to their sex by appearing half-naked. The sight did not greatly interest Henry, but it had not been intended for him. It was the familiar net spread by Catherine to catch others.

Madame de Sauve was now the leader of the *Escadron Volant,* and it was she who was responsible for the various delights offered on this occasion to jaded senses. She had done notable work in the past, running Navarre and Alençon as simultaneous lovers so as to breed between them a quarrel which it took all Margot's cunning to patch up. She distinguished herself shortly afterwards in the negotiations for the *Paix de Monsieur,* and she still had enough power over Alençon to be very useful. Madame de Montpensier, wife of the bigoted Catholic soldier, was another of the scantily clad assistants, and Madame Villequier was here enjoying her last fling. Shortly after the Chenonceaux saturnalia jealousy got the better of her husband, who killed her before the eyes of her innumerable lovers and the rest of the Court.

Catherine knew that as far as Henry was concerned she must rely on her own influence alone, an influence which, as she recognised bitterly, was beginning to fail. The King had certainly a taste in women, and two days after his coronation had astonished Europe by marrying Louise de Vaudemont, cousin of the deceased Cardinal of Lorraine and mistress of a gentleman who had come to Rheims to attend the royal ceremony. Before that, Henry had imagined himself to be passionately in love with the Princesse de Condé, and it was her sudden death that had been given as the reason for his escapade with the Lyons flagellants. After his accession he continued to amuse himself with a series of gallantries, but any sort of emotion so exhausted him that he was never in love long enough for the purposes of political intrigue. Living entirely on his weakened nerves he needed constant stimulation and constant change. Always some fresh buffoonery was invented by his *Mignons,* and his pleasures grew more grotesque from day to day. He was twenty-six now, and already he looked old. In ten years more his hair would be as white as snow and all his teeth would be gone.

Stout and smiling, in swollen sleeves and an enormous skirt, Catherine moved among her guests, now whispering in an attentive ear, now sparring towards one of those duels of repartee which were her favourite diversion, now shaken with great gusts of laughter at some unlooked-for drollery in the evening's festivities.

But the cares of state and of ambition were heavy upon her, and her final grief was to be the disaffection of the son on whom she had centred all her scant affections and all her far-reaching hopes. Eight months earlier the Estates had met in the great hall at Blois, and she had fancied that out of this meeting might come a satisfactory settlement of religious difficulties such as would put an end to the wars and enable her at last to centralise the power as she desired. But Henry had shown plainly enough that he intended to go his own irresponsible way, deciding questions of importance as his mood dictated. The Assembly had angered him by protesting against the follies of his *Mignons,* against the influence of Italians at Court, and against his unconstitutional methods of raising money for his pleasures. While Catherine went beyond her usual cautious procedure and made an open declaration in favour of peace, Henry obstinately insisted upon uniformity of religion. He did more. He joined the newly-formed Catholic League, an alliance of nobles pledged, with the assistance of the Holy Spirit, to crush finally and for ever the Huguenot party.

Only one thing could follow that abortive meeting at Blois, and Catherine knew well that all hopes of a permanent peace had been wrecked. She was never accustomed to look very far ahead, but as she grew older, anxiety for the future came to add to the periodical discomfort of her rheumatism. Gazing about her at the glittering crowd of enervated voluptuaries who thronged the river-gallery of Chenonceaux, she wondered what these creatures would make of a new and fiercer civil war.

## PARIS

TRY as she might, Catherine could not avert the disaster to her life's ambitions. Ageing and heavy as she was, she journeyed across France with astounding resolution, first to the south and then to the north, seeking to pacify the combatants who were sharpening their swords for the final struggle. She travelled through districts so plague-ridden that the birds dropped dead as they flew across the fields; she put herself in constant peril of accident and assault; tortured by sciatica she retained her cheerful diplomatic smile, and gave audience all day and every day, at her rising, during her meals, and far on into the small hours. But the discord which she had years ago fostered for her own purposes was now to have its revenge upon her. Only a formal excuse was needed for war, and the most farcical excuse was found. Determined to pick a quarrel with Navarre, the King insulted Margot. Henry was ready for the challenge, and the *Guerre des Amoureux* was the romantic title bestowed upon the hostilities, which lasted only for a few months.

The death of Alençon in 1584 was the next severe blow for Catherine, not as a mother, but as a politician. For Henry of Navarre was now the nearest in succession to the throne. The House of Valois had dwindled to one foppish degenerate, playing with his lapdogs and his *Mignons* while the Bourbon star rose ominously in the south.

Into his thirty years of life Alençon had contrived to crowd a remarkable series of exploits. He had won for the Huguenots whom he detested their most profitable treaty; he had championed both the Protestants and the anti-Spanish nobles in the Netherlands, and ruined a brilliant opportunity by the insane attack which became known as the Folly of Antwerp; in England he had played with Elizabeth the most ridiculous pantomime of wooing which even that accomplished skirmisher was to know; while his bent for play-acting had transformed even the most ordinary incidents of his life into rich matter for the historical novelist. But nothing that he accomplished, or that Margot accomplished for him, during those thirty years, was so staggering in effect as his death. It created the political situation which led to the Spanish Armada, the execution of Mary Stuart, and the Guise Revolution.

The year of this portentous death marked the beginning of the real power of the Catholic League, with Henry of Guise at its head. Its growth was as systematic as that of a secret society, and it was not long before Paris was with Guise almost to a man. Even more than his father, he had the power of fascinating a mob, and the sweeping changes which were part of the League policy were eminently calculated to appeal to popular feeling. Paris, still alive with fierce memories of St. Bartholomew's Day, was ready to repeat it at the word of command. One faith for France, the Catholic one, was the first plank in the Guise platform. But Henry was also a nationalist. He would have no Papal dictation, and the remarkable idea of a national Catholic church intoxicated opinion in Paris.

Nor was this all. Guise played with electric effect the rôle of the people's hero, and the League aimed directly at the abolition of abuses. From the King Paris had now had almost as much as it was prepared to stand. Riots were frequent and sometimes serious, but Henry refused to listen to unpleasant news and paid no attention to the reports which anxious advisers brought him. His pranks grew more outrageous than ever, and the drain on national and private resources reached fabulous proportions. His *Mignons* quarrelled among themselves, and many met violent deaths, but

## HENRY III
### Painted Terra-cotta Bust, 1574 or later
(Wallace Collection)

even their funerals cost as much as a royal wedding had formerly done.

Catherine could do nothing with him. At times she was nearly desperate with chagrin, and at last she began to feel old. In her younger days she would have flung herself with furious energy into tortuous schemes of rehabilitation, but now when the unhappy fit came upon her she was carried into the fields beyond the city gates and sat there, alone and friendless, brooding on the betrayal of her hopes by the only one of her family whom she had loved. It was coming at last to the old conflict of Guise and Bourbon, and soon there would be none to stand between them. Guise was in alliance with Spain, Navarre with the Protestant Princes of Europe. Everything was as it had been and still the wars went on, while the impotent King made hurried compromises with each side in turn and then sauntered off to amuse himself, as one chronicler ingenuously puts it, "in nunneries and other resorts of pleasure."

Catherine was sixty-nine years old when Guise accomplished his treasonable triumph. In Paris the League had become a democratic revolutionary movement, perfectly organised, waiting only for the signal to take the power into its own hands. Guise and the leaders were at Soissons, and the King had expressly forbidden them to enter the capital. But he overlooked the danger of the Spanish agents, who could come and go freely with generous offers of help to the new party.

On May 9, 1588, Guise defied the ban, evaded the sentinels, and walked into Paris. Standing at the window of Catherine's lodging, her dwarf caught sight of him, and turned to tell his mistress, who gave commands that he should be whipped for lying to her. But then the door opened and M. de Guise was announced. Catherine turned pale and trembled violently as the rash visitor, no more composed than herself, advanced to pay his respects. With a gesture she despatched a messenger to warn the King in the Louvre, while Guise began a hesitant explanation of his action. It was vitally necessary, he said, that she should use her influence with Henry so that he would agree to abide by the programme of the League. Medici was being urged to aid Guise in the final subjection of Valois. It was an odd situation.

Meanwhile, Henry had received his mother's message and was trembling between rage and fear. A courtier was instantly at hand to offer to be Guise's murderer when he should present himself, but the King had not the nerve to accept. While they were still deliberating, Catherine arrived, carried in her chair to the Louvre. She was closely followed by Guise who, as he passed up the stairs between a double row of armed men, had clearly realised the peril into which he had run his head. Henry received him at first brusquely and then angrily. At length he turned his back upon him, and Guise, glancing round at the room of hostile faces, was seized with real terror. He sank down upon a stool, regardless of the breach of etiquette which he was committing in the royal presence. But Catherine saved him. Violent action at this moment would wreck everything more surely than procrastination. Tactfully she led her son aside, and, pointing through the window, showed him the crowd of cheering Parisians who had gathered as if by magic when word had gone round that their adored Guise was in the city. It was the King's turn to be terrified, and in this mood Catherine was able to pacify him. Seizing his opportunity Guise left the room, and was swiftly at work collecting his followers about him and fortifying his lodging.

On May 11 came the Day of Barricades. Paris rose with a unanimity which showed how skilfully the League was organised. There were skirmishes with the royal troops, but there was no massacre, for Guise showed himself capable of an apparently impossible feat, the handling of a Paris mob. With an amused smile upon his handsome face, and armed only with a riding-whip, he rode from point to point and kept his wildly enthusiastic adherents in a state of efficient discipline. The Louvre, with the King inside it, was barricaded, but by the orders of Guise one door was left open. As he expected, the craven Henry took it, and made only one stop on his way to Chartres. As he left his palace he gave way to the theatrical impulse characteristic of the later Valois. "Ah, ungrateful city!" he cried, shedding the tears that came so easily to him, "I have loved you better than my own wife!" —a statement which may possibly have been true.

Guise was King of Paris. As far as Paris was concerned he could have made himself King of France. But once again Spain was an awkward ally, and without Spanish help the hero of the Parisians could not hope to carry the country. Catherine, after all, was to be spared the sight of any but a Valois on the throne, but the days were darkening rapidly. Her son was beyond her reach at Chartres, preparing to concede everything that Guise asked so long as he should be left in peace and safety to enjoy himself. She was alone in Paris, watching the hopes of forty years tumbling like a pack of cards.

## BLOIS

CATHERINE had at last to take to her bed. The Court
was at Blois for the Assembly of the Estates. Guise had
missed his greatest chance of securing the throne, and the
rivalry between the three Henrys, the King, Guise and
Navarre had resulted in a balance of power more precarious
than Catherine, had she been able still to take a hand in
affairs, would have allowed. But while she lay staring helplessly at the lilies embroidered on her canopy the forces which
she had helped to set in motion continued to act, and the
organisation which she had built up was used by others.

For it was Madame de Sauve, the most distinguished siren
of the *Escadron Volant,* who drew Guise to Blois. Perhaps
he would have come in any case, for the leaders of the League
came with him in force, and the Estates were largely composed of his supporters. But her charms doubtless fortified
him against his peril, and he continued to ignore the notes
of warning that were passed to him, at the rate of a dozen
a day, in his serviette, his gloves or his handkerchief. Superb
and gallant, with his mysterious half-smile playing about his
lips, Guise strode freely about the castle of Blois throughout
the closing months of 1588, meeting with elaborate affection
the withered royal dandy against whom he was plotting,
scorning the suggestion that this King who cowered and temporised before the demands of the Estates would dare to lay
a finger on a Guise. But Henry had been exasperated beyond
endurance, and Guise was doomed. Upstairs in her great bed,
watching through leaded windows the sleet and snow of tnis
evil December, the last month of the year of wild weather
that had wrecked the Spanish Armada, lay the Queen-Mother,

the only being who could have saved him. On December 22 Guise spent his last night on earth with Madame de Sauve.

Between eight and nine on the following morning the King burst into his mother's room. "Madame," he asked gaily, "how are you?"

"Not very well, my son," replied the huddled figure in the bed.

"But I am very well," cried Henry, "for I am King of France. I have killed the King of Paris!"

For a moment Catherine could not speak. Her round white face seemed to grow yet paler, and only her dark eyes gave sign of life, staring at her son in horror. Her horror was not for the crime of murder, but for the fatal imprudence of this step which the King had taken without consulting her. Then, speaking quickly and with all her old vigour, she said:

"You must lose no time in making sure of Blois, Orleans, and any other town possible. Paris will be in arms at the news. Above all, let the Vatican know what you have done. Rome may be your only friend after this."

Then she sank back exhausted to her pillows. She could not doubt that the end of the house of Valois was at hand. Guise was dead, and Bourbon would seize the throne. She had spent the whole of her life postponing this day.

Henry had not killed Guise, but he had seen to his killing. He had sent for him to his *vieux cabinet,* and twenty men stationed in and about the dark passage through which the unarmed man must pass had done the deed. The King had come upon the scene in time to gaze down at the mutilated body and exclaim: "How big he is! he is bigger dead than alive! And now I alone am King."

On the next day the Cardinal of Guise was cut to pieces by some French guards. The other prominent members of the League were arrested and kept under close watch. It was now the turn of the Estates to cower before a King who could act so precipitately. The Assembly became meaningless and was shortly dismissed. In Paris, where the news of the murders were received with rage and sorrow, energetic measures were taken. But Guise blood was not to be lightly spilled. The murder of Francis of Guise had found its answer on St. Bartholomew's Day, and the murder of his son was to be revenged within a few months upon the body of the King.

Catherine knew what must happen, but she did not live to see a Bourbon on the throne. The strain of violent emotion was too much for her weakened constitution. She never left her bed again.

The end came on January 9, a solitary end to a long and solitary life. "A few of her servants," says a diarist, "and some of her familiars wept for her. And so did the King—a very little, As for Blois, where she had been worshipped as the Juno of the Court, she had no sooner given up the ghost than she was no more regarded by any than a dead goat would have been." Paris refused to accept her body for interment in the rich tomb which she had previously prepared in St. Denis, and her remains were buried in a common grave at Blois.

If nothing of Catherine de' Medici's character has emerged from this sketch of her life, no generalisations upon her deathbed will serve to reveal her. She herself, absorbed always in the detail of the moment's problem, looked neither back nor forward, and it is better to let her go to her grave without yielding to the temptation of retrospect. To pass a laboured moral judgement upon one who had no moral principles would be absurd. Catherine was not good or bad, she was successful or unsuccessful. Cold, curious, attentive to minutiæ, she could be neither fanatic nor visionary. The epitome of her period, she was intellectually myopic, and her successes, numerous and brilliant, were in small matters; for she could not take the long view. And so her momentary triumphs had their revenge upon her, and the dragon's teeth which she sowed so shrewdly in her earlier years bred armed men to destroy at last the projects of a lifetime.

Nor can we say *"quia multum amavit..."*, and be done with the matter. Love never actuated her, and that makes it so much the easier to regard her as she would wish to be regarded, unsentimentally. She fought a dogged and unscrupulous trench-warfare against more enemies, perhaps, than any other woman in history except Elizabeth of England has successfully faced. Many might have been her friends if she had trusted them, but she would not. Between the death of Francis I in 1547 and her own death in 1589, she had scarcely a single friend, and since her death she has had fewer still. Yet her personality remains as fascinating as the glittering and merciless age that died with her.

# INDEX

Abraham, Heights of, 62
Actæon, 69, 117
Adrian VI, Pope, 20
Æneid, 18
Africa, 150
Agrippa, 114
Aigues-Mortes, 80, 296
Ainay, 116
Alba, Duke of, 41, 168, 242-5, 251, 275, 277, 278, 289
Albany, Duke of, 46, 59
Albertus, Magnus, 78
Alençon, Duke of, 208, 264, 267, 291, 301-3, 307-8
Alexander, 67
Alexiacos, 107
Alcala, 24
Alps, 4, 9, 21, 121
Alsace, 144
Amadis of Gaul, 105
Amaryllis, 137
Amboise, 5-13, 18, 27, 47, 51, 54, 57, 59, 74, 78, 81, 140, 174-90, 193, 218, 224, 231, 243, 246, 249, 274
Amyot, Jacques, 160, 262
Ancy-le-Franc, 65
Anet, 5, 52, 106, 139-48, 172, 191, 214
Angelo, Castle of St., 27, 30, 34, 47
Angouleme, Bastard of, 111, 283, 284
Angouleme, Margaret of. *See* Margaret.
Anjou, 203
Anjou, Henry of, later Henry III. *See* Henry III.
Antæus, 69
Antwerp, 308
Apelles, 236
Apennines, 27
Aphrodite, 69, 121, 125
Aragon, Katharine of, 22, 32
Argona, Tullia d', 126, 147
Arctic Ocean, 125

Aristotle, 103, 125
Armstrong, Edward, 137
Arno, R., 14, 32, 37
Arras, Jean d', 293
Asia, 110
Atahualpa, 63
Ate, 73
Athene, 125
Athens, 70, 115, 126
Augsburg, 6
Aumale, Duke of, 283
Aumale, House of, 165
Aurora, 157
Austria, 150
Azay-le-Rideau, 5, 57, 141

Babylon, 27
Bacci, Andrea, 272
Badius Ascensius, 48
Baif, Jean-Antoine de, 140
Bande Nere, Giovanni delle, 16
Barbary, 43
Bartholomew, St., 63, 228, 240, 245, 257, 265, 271, 282-89, 290, 291, 295, 296, 297, 308
Bartolommeo, Fra, 14
Bastille, 50, 129, 302
Bathsheba, 69
Bavaria, Ludwigs of, 57
Bay de la Paix (a horse), 133
Bayard, Chevalier, 27, 87
Bayeux, 264
Bayonne, 233, 240, 241-46
Beethoven, 10
Bellay, du, brothers, 91
Bellay, Joachim du, 139, 140, 157
Belleau, Remi, 140
Bertoul, Hilaire, 115
Bèze, Theodore de, 134, 202, 207, 209, 212, 220, 252, 289, 296
Biarritz, 241

Birago, 279
Biron, 93
Biscay, Bay of, 233
Blois, 5, 57, 59, 66, 70, 74, 81, 140, 141, 177, 182, 198, 224, 231, 258-70, 301, 305, 306, 312-15
Boccaccio, 125
Bohier, Thomas, 191
Boleyn, Anne, 8, 32
Bonnivet, 7, 22
Bourdeaux, 83, 241
Bothwell, 162
Botticelli, 14, 15, 69, 126
Bourbon, Antoine de. See Navarre
Bourbon, House of, 7, 90, 179, 181, 186, 194, 202, 307, 309, 314
Bourbon, Cardinal de, 47, 164, 259, 297
Bourbon, Charles de, 17, 23-8, 49
Bourbon, Louis de. See Conde
Bourges, Clemence de, 115, 120
Brantôme, 59, 69, 70, 71, 75, 76, 79, 85, 110, 137, 146, 147, 157, 161, 164, 195, 201, 259, 262, 290, 294
Breul, Karl, 245
Brézé, Louis de, 11, 12, 49, 52, 142
Brigella, 264
British Museum Library, 199
Brittany, Anne of, 8
Brozino, 61, 70, 73
Brunelleschi, 15
Brussels, 149, 150, 170, 251
Budé, Guillaume, 86
Burgundy, 23

Caen, 231
Cæsar, 90, 103
Calais, 153, 162, 167, 177, 181, 196, 203, 222
Calisto, 67
Calvin, 60, 115, 182, 197, 202, 210, 212, 246, his Institution Chrétienne, 60
Calydonian Boar, 86, 92
Cambrai, 33
Campaspe, 67
Canada, 62
Canaples, Mme. de, 74
Canterbury, 258

Carbery, 108
Cardan, Jerome, 273
Careggi, 18
Carlisle, 108, 161
Carlos, Don, 195, 243, 267
Cartier, Jacques, 62
Castiglione, 14, 19, 25, 66, 85, 124, 125, 126
Cateau-Cambresis, 153, 167
Catherine de' Medici. See Medici.
Catherine the Great (of Russia), 77
Cellini, Benvenuto, 12, 27, 32, 44, 47, 58, 66, 68, 70, 143
Certon, Pierre, 140
Cervantes, 267
Chabot, House of, 7
Chabot, Guy. See Jarnac.
Chambord, 5, 57-8, 66, 74, 141, 301
Chambre Ardente, 136
Champagne, 214
Chantilly, 57, 179, 218
Charente, R., 234, 252
Charité, La, 299, 300, 303
Charles, Son of Francis I, 81, 85
Charles IX, 109, 139, 200, 208, 209, 215, 222, 224, 249, 253, 256, 258, 267, 276; childhood, 159-60, 232; accession, 193; character, 195, 256, 260-3; aesthetic tastes, 250, 260-3; affection for Mary Stuart, 195-6; admiration for Coligny, 194, 259-60, 274, 277-8, 281; journey to south with Catherine, 232 ff.; marriage, 259; persuaded to Massacre of St. Bartholomew, 280-1; conduct during Massacre, 287; death, 292; Charles V, Emperor and King of Spain, 6, 9, 10, 20, 21, 22, 24, 25, 26, 32, 38, 39, 41, 45, 62, 68, 79-83, 91, 127, 136, 137, 150-54, 224
Chartres, 214, 218, 222, 311
Châtaignerie, La. See Vivonne.
Châteaubriant, Edict of, 136
Chatillon, 274
Chatillon, Cardinal de. See Coligny.
Chaumont, 172
Chenonceaux, 57, 141, 172, 191-200, 239, 300-06
Cher, R., 172, 191, 192, 193, 200
Chevreuse, 86

Chicot the Jester, 288
Childebert, 114
Chinon, 57
Christ, 4, 69
Cibo, Catherine, 43
Cibo, Madalena, 118
Circe, 210
Claude Queene of Francis I, 8, 10, 11, 21, 51, 258
Claude, daughter of Henry II and Catherine, 158, 286
Clement VII, Pope, 16, 17, 19, 21, 23, 24, 27, 29, 31, 33, 34, 37, 38, 39, 42, 43, 44, 45, 46, 47, 54, 59, 63, 65, 75, 87, 157, 186, 198, 208, 272
Clement, St., 122
Clouet, François (Jeannet), 6, 67, 123
Clouet, Jean, 67
Coligny, House of (Chatillon), 107, 181
Coligny, Andelot de, 164, 181, 215, 224, 254
Coligny, Gaspard de Admiral, 181, 198, 291; character, 220; religious inclinations, 108, 112, 178, 183-5, 201-2; conduct of army, 216, 220; regard for constitution, 194, 197; swift advance at Henry II's accession, 108; at Vaucelles, 149-53; captured at St. Quentin, 153, 166, 178; released, 167; letter from Calvin, 182; approached by Catherine, 185-6; at Fontainebleau Conference, 185-6; at Council of Poissy, 201-13; battle of Dreux, 220-3; implicated in murder of Guise, 225-8, 246; Alba demands his death, 244-5; accepts Peace of Longjumeau, 249; complains to Catherine, 250; retires to La Rochelle, 251; defeated at Jarnac, 252; loss of friends, 254; price on his head, 255; his phase of cruelty, 255; turns the tide of defeat, 256; returns to court, 258 ff.; grief at death of Jeanne, 271; official reconciliation with Guise, 274; wounded by assassin, 276 ff.; murdered on St. Bartholomew's Day, 283-4
Coligny, Cardinal Odet de, 107-8, 178, 215, 216, 244, 258, 268

Colonna, Vittoria, 25, 74, 125, 126
Commynes, Philippe de, 5
Compiegne, 100
Conde, Henri de Bourbon, Prince of (the younger), 254, 268, 279, 281, 287, 290, 301, 302, 303
Conde, Eleanore de Roye, Princess of, 179, 187, 189, 193, 206, 207, 212
Conde, Louis de Bourbon, Prince of (the elder), 178, 182, 183, 187-8, 194, 197, 206-7, 212, 213, 215, 222, 226, 227, 231, 232, 245, 249-53, 254, 295
Contarini, 112
Cook, Sir Herbert, 123
Cordière, La Belle. See Labé Louise
Correro, Giovanni, 264-5
Cosseins, 279, 283
Covenanters, 89
Cracow, 291, 293
Credi, Lorenzo di, 14
Cupid, 57, 61, 73
Cyprus, 293
Cytherea, 166

Dampierre, 86
Danville, Marshal de, 268
Dandolo, Matteo, 90
Danès, 160
Danube, 82
Daphnis and Chloe, 116
David, King of, 40, 69
David, Louis, 60
Deianira, 69
Delilah, 205
Despériers, Bonaventure, 68, 87, 115
Diana, 12-13, 69, 78, 140, 219
Dionysos, 3
Dolet, Etienne, 87, 115
Donatello, 14
Doria, Andrea, 43
Dreux, 214-23, 225, 252, 257, 301
Duchartre, P. L., 264
Du Prat, Chancellor, 23

Edinburgh, 38, 155
Edward VI of England, 109
Egmont, 168, 242, 251
Egyptians, 199

*Eidgenossen,* 178
Eleanor, 2nd wife of Francis I, 50, 51, 79, 81
Elizabeth, daughter of Henry II and Catherine, 110, 159, 165, 167, 171, 233, 241-3, 267
Elizabeth of Austria, 259, 260, 286-7
Elizabeth, Queen of England, 47, 90, 113, 127, 146, 160, 161, 168, 195, 202, 216, 222, 231, 233, 237, 241, 243, 267, 275, 301, 308, 315
Elysian Fields, 165
Empire, Eastern, 14
Empire, Holy Roman, 6, 81, 83, 84, 150, 152
Endymion, 12, 118, 139
Enghien, Duke of, 85
England, 4, 6, 10, 38, 63, 83, 109, 116, 150, 161, 163, 204, 216, 237, 238, 243, 274, 275, 289
Epernay, 83
Epinay, 221
Erasmus, 24, 63, 66, 115, 124, 129, 208
Escurial, 127
Este, Cardinal d', 193, 204, 211, 212
Estienne, A., 238
Estienne, Robert, 48
Etampes, Duchess of. *See* Pisseleu, Anne de Europe.
Europe, 19, 23, 38, 41, 46, 48, 53, 66, 90, 91, 114, 121, 125, 141, 182, 266, 309
Evelyn, John, 273

Faenza, 40
Falkirk, 155
Falkland, 108
Ferdinand of Austria, 150
Ferrara, 33, 107, 126
Ferronière, La Belle, 84
Fiesole, 125
Fisher, 63
Flanders, 79
Fleming, Lady, 110, 111
Fleuranges, Sieur de, 7, 20-1
Florence, 4, 9, 11, 13, 14-18, 26, 28, 36, 40-2, 45, 65, 109, 156, 198, 245
Florida, 266

Foix, de, 7, 22
Foix, Françoise de, 8
Folies-Bergère, 70
Fontainebleau, 5, 12, 57-78, 86, 93, 141, 144, 147, 186, 204, 215, 293
Fotheringay, 108, 159
France, Anatole, 236
France, Diane de, 75, 142, 162
Francis I at Amboise, 5-13; at the Field of the Cloth of Gold, 4, 22; at Lyons, 114; at Marseilles, 44-54, 272; capture at Pavia and imprisonment, 23, 80, 91; relations with Anne de Pisseleu, 53, 76, 89, 100, 106, 142, 191; with Catherine de' Medici, 39, 54, 61, 62, 65, 74-5, 83, 87, 156, 198, 315; with Diane de Poitiers, 12, 76, 142; with the Emperor Charles V, 23, 24, 32, 33, 79-83; with Pope Clement VII, 21, 24, 33; with Henry VIII of England, 32, 33, 84; affair of the placards, 60; character, 48-9, 89-93; interest in art and learning, 4, 14, 67-73, 87, 89, 91; in discovery, 62; love of building, 57-8, 66; of hunting, 57, 73, 86; his *Petite Bande,* 74-5, 86, 258; sickness and death, 10, 84-93;
Francis, Dauphin, son of Francis I, 4, 8, 50, 51, 63-4, 79, 171, 193; Francis II, 78, 108, 109, 110, 139, 232; character, 156; ill-health, 156, 184; love of Mary Stuart, 156, 159, 177; marriage to her, 155, 163-6; accession, 172; disgraces Montmorency, 179; at Amboise during the executions, 183-4; urged to kill Navarre, 189-90; death, 190, 219
Fugger News-Letter, 267, 297
Fuggers of Augsburg, 6

Gaillard, Jeanne, 115
Ganessa, Alberto, 238
Ganymede, 69
Gargantua, 129
Geneva, 60, 202
Genoa, 20, 24
George, St., 92

Germany, 19, 150, 216; Protestant Princes of, 91, 136, 291
Ghent, 82
Ghirlandaio, 14
Giorgione, 126
Giotto, 15, 40
Goethe, 242
Goldwyn, Samuel, 72
Gonzague (a horse), 133
Goudimel, 140
Goujon, Jean, 12, 67, 141, 143
Greenland, 293
Gresham, Sir Thomas, 150
Grey, Lady Jane, 160
Gryphius, Sebastian, 48
Guienne, 116
Guienne Herald, 99
Guiffrey, 109
Guillet, Pernatte de, 115
Guise, Cardinals. *See* Lorraine.
Guise, Claude, Duke of, 105
Guise, Francis, Duke of, 105, 153, 163, 183, 189, 190, 204, 215, 216, 220-22, 224-28, 231, 246, 251, 253, 277, 313, 314
Guise, Henry, Duke of, 253, 264, 274, 277, 283-4, 302, 308-11, 312-13
Guise, House of, 57, 76, 83, 85, 91, 103, 104, 105, 106, 107, 108, 112, 138, 152, 153, 157, 158, 162, 165, 166, 178, 179, 180, 181, 183, 184, 185, 187-90, 194, 195, 202, 204, 208, 210, 211, 213, 257, 276, 277, 279, 308, 309, 310
Guise, Mary of, 108, 156-7, 162-3
Guizot, 90

Hamlet, 173
Hapsburgs, 23, 152
Harlequin, 264
Havre, Le, 216
Hawaii, 293
Hecate, 219
Henry II, 8, 81, 84, 85; character, habits and appearance, 130-37, 140, 145; betrothal to Catherine de' Medici, 39, 40, 114; marriage, 47 *ff.*, 61, 62; in Spain, as hostage, 24, 50, 152; love for Diane de Poitiers, 50, 52, 53, 61, 83, 87, 97-8, 110-112, 137-138, 140, 143-48, 149, 167, 191-92; friendship for Montmorency, 76, 83, 89, 98, 107, 111, 112, 116, 166; becomes heir, 64; suspected of death of Enghien, 85; becomes King, 97; relations with Guises, 85, 89, 103, 104-7, 162; at the combat of Jarnac and la Châtaignerie, 98-104; tour in the south-east, 109, 114 *ff.*; affair with Lady Fleming, 110-112; connection with Louise Labé, 119; entry into Paris, 129; sees a Protestant burned, 134-5; treaties with Spain, 149-54; at the wedding of his son with Mary Stuart, 163 *ff.*; death in a tournament, 170-1, 191, 242
Henry III (of France and Poland), 109, 232; childhood, 159; character and appearance, 303-6; elected to Polish throne, 291; return from Poland, 292; accession to French throne, 290, 292, 296; marriage, 304; banquet at Plessis, 299; *Guerre des Amoureux*, 307; interview with Guise, 310; flees Paris, 311; the Blois Estates and murder of Guise, 312-14
Henry IV (Henry of Navarre), 89, 90, 93, 110, 180, 210, 233, 243, 244, 254, 268, 269-270, 281, 287, 290, 291, 301, 303, 307, 309, 310, 312
Henry VIII of England, 5, 6, 8, 10, 22, 23, 32, 54, 59, 63, 109, 127
Hercule, son of Henry II and Catherine. *See* Alençon.
Hercules, 69, 107
Herodias, 74
Hippocrates, 125
Hobère (a horse), 133
Holofernes, 69
Hôpital, Michel de l', 202, 203, 209, 243
Horn, Count of, 251
Huguenots, 177, 180-82, 183, 186, 194, 197, 199, 202, 203, 204, 208, 212, 213, 222, 224, 235, 238, 243, 244,

Huguenots (*Continued*)
245, 246, 249, 250, 251, 252, 254-7, 258, 264, 266, 275, 276, 278-89, 290, 296, 300, 302, 306, 307
Hume, Martin, 163
Hungary, 25
Hymen, 48
Hyperion, 29

Innocents, the Holy, 69
Israelites, 251
Italy, 3, 4, 14-42, 53, 59, 67, 68, 87, 115, 116, 150, 153, 157, 200, 272
Italian League, 20, 24, 25

Jacob, 69, 258
James I of England, 127
James II of England, 201
James V of Scotland, 38, 108
Jannequin, 140
Janovitch (Bême), 284
Jarnac, Battle of, 252, 253
Jarnac, Sieur de, 99-104, 148, 149
Jericho, 233
Jerusalem, 293
Jewel, Bishop, 225
Jezebel, 296
Joan of Arc, 224, 231
Job, 274
John of Austria, Don, 267
Joshua, 231
Julien (a page), 205
Juno, 74, 314
Jupiter, 68, 69

*Kama Sutra*, 70
*King Lear*, 298
Knolles, Sir Francis, 161
Knox, John, 195

La Balue, Cardinal, 5
Labé, Louise, 115, 119, 120, 125, 128, 139
Languedoc, 45, 50
*Laocoön*, 21
Latona, 69, 78
La Tremouille, 7, 22
Lautrec, de, 7
League, the Catholic, 305, 306, 308

Lecky, W. H., 237
Lemaire de Belges, 68
Leo X, Pope, 9, 15, 16, 18, 19
Leonardo da Vinci, 3, 4, 7, 11, 12, 14, 18, 49, 61, 66, 236, 239
Lepanto, 267
Léran, de, 286
Lescot, 57, 155
Leven, Loch, 108
Limaudière, Isabelle de la. *See* Rouet, La Belle Limeuil, Isabelle de, 204-5, 212, 219
Limoges, 67
Limours, 86
Limousin, Leonard, 67, 143
Linlithgow, 108
Lippi, Filippino, 14
Lithuania, 293
Loches, 5, 21, 81
Loire, R., 4, 5, 9, 49, 81, 172, 178, 214, 225, 251, 255, 258
Lombardy, 21, 24
London, Tower of, 273
Longjumeau, 249
Lorraine, House of. *See* Guise, House of.
Lorraine, Charles de Guise, Cardinal of (the younger), 105, 133, 134, 155, 161, 162, 182, 183, 185, 189, 190, 193, 207, 231, 250, 253, 289, 292, 295, 297, 304
Lorraine, Francis of. *See* Guise, Francis Duke of.
Lorraine, Jean, Cardinal of, 63, 92, 104, 107
Louis IX, Saint, 201, 260
Louis XI, 17, 89, 140, 299
Louis XII, 8, 91, 123, 258
Louis XIV, 89, 93
Louis XV, 117
Louis-Philippe, 93
Louvain, 20
Louvre, 57, 66, 141, 239, 271, 276, 278, 279-83, 285-88, 310, 311
Loyola, Ignatius de, 60
Lusignan, 255, 290-98
Lusignan, House of, 293
Lyon, Corneille de, 67, 114
Lyons, 5, 48, 63, 91, 111-28, 129, 178, 275, 288, 292, 297, 305

*Macbeth,* 38, 219
Macchiavelli, 14, 129, 298
Madrid, 23, 24, 38, 80, 245
Madrid, Chateau de, 57, 66
Magny, Olivier de, 119-20, 139
Maillard, Olivier, 122
Maintenon, Mme. de, 93
Maison-Fleur, M. de, 197
Mantua, Duke of, 38
Margaret of Angoulême and Navarre, sister of Francis I, 7, 24, 26, 33, 49, 59, 61, 75, 77, 78, 88, 91, 106, 111, 115, 125, 127, 160, 167, 178, 187-88, 211; her *Heptameron,* 68, 73, 115, 125
"Margot," daughter of Henry II and Catherine. *See* Navarre, Margot of.
Marie Antoinette, 93
Marignano, 3, 79, 86, 91
Marot, Clément, 68, 69, 87, 106, 129, 220, 235
Marseilles, 40, 43-54, 59
Marsyas, 69
Marvell, Andrew, 71
Mary, Queen of Scots. *See* Stuart, Mary.
Mary Tudor, 153, 168
Meaux, 246, 250, 266, 281
Medes, 9
Medici, House of, 4, 9, 15-16, 17, 18, 28, 29-31, 39, 77, 78, 109, 198
Medici, Alessandro de', 16, 29, 30, 31, 33, 34, 35, 37, 38, 40, 41, 45
Medici, Catherine de', her character, 21, 128, 137-38, 147-48, 149, 156-57, 172-73, 184, 198, 206-07, 223, 248, 262-63, 295, 296, 298, 314-15; religious opinions, 138, 185; her attitude to art, 65, 66, 114, 193, 236-240, 263; interest in magic, 77-8, 198-99, 295; her dreams, 168, 253, 295; her use of poison, 224, 271-73; accused of poisoning the Dauphin, 65; Andelot, 254, and Jeanne de Navarre, 271; her birth in Florence, 15-16; taken to Rome, 19; returns to Florence, 19; her childhood there, 21, 28 ff., 109, 128; at Le Murate, 32-37; second visit to Rome, 37; marriage projects, 38-9;

betrothal to Henry of Orleans, 39, 139; return to Florence, 40; leaves for France, 41-2; marriage, 47 ff., 65; relations with Henry, 53, 61, 87, 97-8, 109, 110-11, 147-48, 167, 171, 180; with Francis I, 50, 53, 61, 62, 65, 73-4, 83, 87, 156, 198, 315; with Diane de Poitiers, 53, 75, 97-8, 109, 110-11, 116-17, 127, 137-38, 143, 147-48, 171-73, 179, 191-92; with Montmorency, 49, 50, 76, 83, 107, 179; alliance with the Duchesse d'Etampes, 75, 83; delayed fertility, 75-8, 199, 200; birth of first child, 78; education of her children and ambitions for them, 109-10, 113, 127, 158-60, 198, 232; at Lyons, 115-18, 128; attitude to Mary Stuart, 158-9, 164, 195; her action after St. Quentin wins Henry's favour, 166-7; her treatment of Montgomery, 173; influence over Francis II, 179; allies with Guises, 179 and countenances Amboise executions, 183; approaches Coligny, 185-6; attempts to trap Navarre and Condé at Amboise, 186-190, 218-19; becomes Regent and supports Bourbons, 193-94 but intrigues with Guises, 204-13; her *escadron volant,* 193, 204-6, 219, 288, 302, 304, 312; Council of Poissy, 201-13; attracted by Condé, 206-7, 213, 218, 244-5; attempts to mediate during First War, 216-18, 222-3; attitude at the death of Guise, 225-28, 277; renounces Regency, 232; tour to Bayonne with Charles, 232-40; meets Palissy at Saintes, 235-40; with Alba at Bayonne, 242-6; rejects complaints of Condé and Coligny and plots against them, 251; engineers Peace of St. Germain, 256; marriage-schemes for her children, 290; persuades Jeanne to marriage of Margot and Henry, 268-9; Massacre of St. Bartholomew, 279-89; insulted in Paris, 297; banquet at Chenonceaux, 299-300, 304-6; watches the Princes, 301-3; loses

Medici, Catherine de' (*Continued*)
control over Henry, 309; last illness
and death, 312-15
Medici, Cosimo de', 15, 16, 272
Medici, Ferdinand de', 272
Medici, Giulio de'. *See* Clement VII,
Pope.
Medici, Ippolito de', 29, 30, 37, 38, 39,
45, 59, 63
Medici, Lorenzo de' (the Magnifi-
cent), 9, 16, 17, 28
Medici, Lorenzo de' (of Urbino), 9,
10, 11, 14, 15, 16, 17, 18
Medici, Piero de', 15
Mediterranean, 150
Meissonier, 201
Melusine, 293-8
Melville, Sir James, 147
Merlin, 283
Mervent, 293
Mestays, Robert, 143
Metz, 152, 167, 253
Mexico, 82
Michelangelo, 14, 17, 34, 38, 40, 61,
67-8, 125, 127
Milan, 4, 14, 24, 39, 80, 82, 293
Milton, 10, 298
Minut, Gabriel de, 146
Mirandola, Pico della, 15
Mireau (a horse), 133
Mollison, Mrs. Amy, 199
Monceaux, 301
Moncontour, 256
Montaigne, 247-57
Montaigne, Michel Eyquem, Sieur de,
122, 155-6, 247-9, 253, 256-7
Montaigu, Collège de, 129
Montecuculi, 64-5
Montfaucon, 255
Montgomery, 169, 170, 173, 191, 242
Montmartre, 60
Montmorency, Anne de, Constable of
France, 44, 49, 53, 76, 79-83, 84, 91,
98, 102, 103, 104, 106, 107, 116, 136,
152-3, 157, 162, 166, 167, 179, 181,
190, 203-4, 220, 221, 222, 231, 236,
245, 249, 251, 273
Montpensier, Duke of, 259, 290-95
Montpensier, Mme. de, 304

Montrichard, 192
Morata, Olympia, 150
More, Sir Thomas, 63
Moro, Antonio, 242
Moryson, 303-4
Moses, 215
Muette, La, 57, 66, 86
Murate, Le, 32-37, 40, 43
Muss, Nicholas, 283
Musset, Alfred de, 35
Mussolini, 139

Naboth, 191
Nantes, Revocation of the Edict of,
93
Naples, 21, 24, 40, 41, 107, 152
Napoleon, 93
Nardi, 18
Navarre, 77, 180, 210, 269, 275
Navarre, Antoine de, 155, 164, 166,
178, 180, 187-90, 194, 197, 204, 210-
12, 215, 216-17, 231, 232, 251, 252,
269, 287
Navarre, Henry of. *See* Henry IV.
Navarre, Jeanne de, 166, 178, 179,
187, 204, 210-12, 237, 253, 256, 259,
268-70, 271, 273
Navarre, Margot de, 109, 149, 159,
208, 210, 212, 243, 259, 268, 270,
279, 282, 286, 291, 297, 300-02, 307,
308
Nemours, 279
Nero, 139
Nessus, 69
Netherlands, 41, 150, 153, 242, 243,
246, 251, 266, 267, 274, 277, 289,
291, 303, 307
Nevers, 279
Nevers, Duchess of, 292
New France, 62
Nice, 42, 43, 44
Nicole, Jean, 143
Nimrod, 73
Niobe, 14
Niort, 255
Normandy, 52, 90, 203, 214, 218, 222
Normandy, Herald, 101
Nostradamus, 78, 198, 200

Ockeghem, Jean, 140
Orange, Prince of, 168
Orleans, 59, 81, 177, 215, 222, 224-28, 231, 246, 277, 313
Orleans, Charles of, 81, 258
Orleans, Henry of. *See* Henry II.
Orliac, Jehanne d', 52, 78
Orme, Philibert de l', 67, 98, 106, 114, 142, 192

Pagnini, Sanctes, 114
Palatinate, 291
Palestine, 123
Palestrina, 140
Palissy, Bernard, 235-37, 239, 240, 296
Pan, 107
Pantagruel, 48, 125, 129
Pantaloon, 264
Panurge, 129-30
Pardoe, Julia, 92
Paré, Ambrose, 277, 283
Paris, 5, 57, 58, 59, 60, 66, 74, 79-83, 87, 99, 129-38, 149, 155-173, 199, 201, 203, 211, 214, 215, 216, 218, 221, 222, 224, 226, 228, 235, 246, 248, 249, 255, 256, 265, 266, 270, 271-89, 296, 297, 299, 302, 304, 307-11, 314
Parlement, 82, 132, 136, 166, 255
Parma, Margaret of, 33, 40-1, 245
Parthenay, 255, 293
Pasquino, 19
Passerini, Cardinal, 19, 28, 30, 31
Paul III, Pope, 59, 80, 88
Paul IV, Pope, 127, 153
Paul, St., 121
Pavia, 22, 23, 24, 26, 27, 48, 91, 151
Périgord, 247, 249, 255, 256
Perpignan, 119
Pescara, Marquis of, 24, 25
Peter III of Russia, 260
Peter, St., 25, 233
Pharaoh, 225
Pharisees, 209
Philip II of Spain, 110, 127, 150, 153, 167, 168, 180, 195, 204, 210, 218, 233, 241-3, 258, 264, 289
Phœbus, 78

Photius, 78
Pickering, Sir William, 139
Picrochole, 255
Piedmont, 153
Pilon, Germain, 67
Pisa, 234
Pisseleu, Anne de, Duchesse d'Etampes, 53, 54, 68, 74, 80, 81, 89, 100, 101, 106, 142, 191
Pius V, Pope, 275, 285, 288, 289
Pizarro, 63
Plato, 49, 60, 87, 111, 124, 127, 160
Pléiade, 140-1
Plessis-les-Tours, 298, 304
Plutarch, 125, 160
Poggio a Caiano, 29, 41-2
Poissy, 201-13, 244, 268
Poitiers, 5, 255, 292
Poitiers, Diane de, at Amboise, 11-13; relations with Francis I, 11-12; with Henry II, 12, 13, 50-3, 61, 75-6, 78, 83, 97-8, 105-6, 110-12, 116-18, 130-2, 143-6; with Catherine de' Medici, 78, 109, 110-11; with the Guises, 105-6, 112, 166, 179; with Montmorency, 111-12, 166; with Protestants, 134; character, 13, 51-2, 105-6, 141, 148; loss of power at Henry's death, 172; in Lyons, 116-18, 128; at Anet, 139 *ff*., 214; at Chenonceaux, 191-2
Poitou, 196, 203, 249, 255, 290, 293, 298
Poland, 110, 291-2
Pollaiuoli, 14, 38
Polonius, 149
Poltrot, 225-7
Portugal, Mary of, 168
Pourbus, Frans, 264
Pourzanges, 293
Primaticcio, 65, 67, 70
Provence, 63, 70, 79, 214, 255
Psyche, 69
Puritans, 89
Pyrenees, 81, 233
Pythagoras, 60

Quadragant (a horse), 133

Rabelais, 7, 37, 48, 66, 68, 107, 114, 125, 129-30, 137, 159, 177, 208, 234, 255, 258, 293
Rais, Gilles de, 263
Rambouillet, 84-93
Ramus, 285
Raphael, 61
Read, Master, 161
Red Sea, 251-2
Retz, Gondi de, 279
Rheims, 97, 292, 305
Rheims, Archbishop of. See Lorraine, Cardinal Charles of.
Rhône, R., 114, 116, 214
Richelieu, 91-2
Ripa, Alberto de, 140
Robbia, Girolamo della, 66
Robbia, Luce della, 14, 40
Rochefort, 86
Rochefoucauld, La, 282, 288
Rochelle, La, 251-2, 254, 256, 258, 268, 290
Rohan, de, 7
Romans, 10, 114, 122
Rome, 14, 18, 19-28, 31, 37-39, 59, 129, 141, 275, 289, 313; sack of Rome, 14, 21, 25-28, 33, 49
Ronsard, Pierre de, 140, 157, 160, 177, 193, 233, 261
Roscoff, 108
Rosso, 67-68
Rouen, 59, 162, 214, 216, 217, 231-33
Rouet, La Belle, 204-6, 212, 217
Rucellai, Palla, 43
Ruggieri, 199, 200, 295

St. André, Marshal, 204
St. Cloud, 92
St. Lawrence, R., 62
St. Petersburg, 77
Saint-Denis, 93, 101, 129, 249, 273, 314
Saintes, 234, 235-40, 241, 254
Saint-Gelais, Mellin de, 114, 139, 263
Saint-Germain, 57, 66, 86, 114, 149, 201, 207, 210, 256, 258
Saint-Jean-de-Luz, 241
Saint-Malo, 62
Saint-Quentin, 153, 162, 166, 202

Saint-Vallier, Countess of. See Poitiers, Diane de Salvati, Maria.
Salvati, Maria, 43
Sand, George, 115
Santa Croce, 219
Santa Lucia Convent, 36
Sappho, 125
Sardanapalus, 107
Sarre, R., 144
Sarto, Andrea del, 14, 34, 61
Sauve, Mme de, 299, 304, 312
Savonarola, 15, 17
Savoy, 243
Savoy, Emanuel-Philibert of, 167, 169
Savoy, Louise of, 7, 8, 22, 23, 33, 90, 91
Scève, Claudine, 115
Scève, Maurice, 113
Scève, Sybille, 115
Schiller, 242
Scotland, 108, 109, 140, 156, 157, 161, 162, 163, 165, 195, 204
Seine, R., 201, 213, 226, 284
Senlis, 302
Settignano, 14
Sforza, Lodovico, 5, 21
Shakespeare, 141
Shepard, Odell, 272
Sichel, Edith, 115, 120, 123, 201, 211, 237
Sicily, 151
Simeoni, 139
Simonetta, La Bella, 126
Sixtus, IV, Pope, 30
Smith, Sir Thomas, 222, 225
Soissons, 309
Soliman, 46
Sologne, 57
Sorel, Agnes, 5
Spa, 302
Spain, 20, 24, 50, 51, 110, 127, 150, 151, 180, 218, 233, 243, 245, 254, 266, 267, 280, 309, 311
Stirling, 155
Stratford-on-Avon, 234
Strozzi, Clarice, 18, 29-31
Strozzi Library, 239
Stuart, Jacqueline, 115
Stuart, John. See Albany.

Stuart, Mary, 47, 108-10, 111-13, 114, 140, 155-65, 167, 172, 177, 179, 194-97, 200, 204, 235, 308
Stubbes, 238
Susannah, 69
Swiss, 205, 220, 221, 246, 279, 283

Tasso, Torquato, 193
Terence, 160
Thélème, 7, 68
Themistocles, 252
Thornley, George, 116
Thucidides, 248
Tobbia, 47
Toledo, 24
Touchet, Marie, 260-1
Toul, 152, 167
Toulouse, Counts of, 111
Touraine, 59, 177, 196, 203, 249, 257, 258
Tour d'Auvergne, Madeleine de la, 9, 10, 14, 15
Tour Landry, Chevalier de la, 122
Tournelles, Les, 57, 66, 70, 165, 170
Tournon, Cardinal de, 87, 88, 209
Tours, 22, 59, 74, 177
Trent, 208, 231
Triboulet, 80-81
Troy, 233
Tuileries, 235, 239, 279
Turkey, 40
Turks, 25, 43, 46, 91, 267
Tuscany, 40
Tyard, Pontus de, 140

Urbino, 125
Urbino, Duke of. See Medici, Lorenzo de'.

Vaise, 116
Valentinois, Duchess of. See Poitiers, Diane de.

Valois, House of, 7, 93, 108, 109, 110, 194, 198, 202, 232. 307, 313
Valois, Marguerite de, sister of Francis I. See Margaret.
Valois, Marguerite de, sister of Henry II, 103, 167
Vasari, 41, 43
Vassy, 214, 215, 274
Vatican, 20, 21, 24, 38, 313
Vaucelles, 149-53
Vaudemont, Louise de, 304
Vaudois, 88, 136, 178
Velasquez, 245
Venetian Ambassadors quoted, 58, 60, 84, 90, 93, 112, 130-1, 138, 201, 260, 262, 264-5
Venice, 23, 33, 90, 299
Venus, 3, 57, 61, 69, 73
Verdun, 152, 167
Verroccio, 14
Vésale, André, 170
Victoria and Albert Museum, 92
Victoria, Queen, 201
Vieileville, 104
Villani, Francesco, 17
Villepreux, 86
Villers-Cotterets, 66
Villon, François, 129
Virgin Mary, 3, 69
Vivonne, François de, Seigneur de la Châtaignerie, 99-104, 148, 149
Vovent, 293

Walsingham, 289
West Indies, 266
Whitehead, A. W., 107, 217, 219
Williams, H. N., 160
Wolsey, 6

Yuste, 150, 154

Zanni, 264

(2)